# HOW TO SELL
# YOUR HOUSE
# IN 90 DAYS

**BY MARC STEPHEN GARRISON**

FINANCIALLY FREE

HOW TO BUY YOUR OWN HOME IN 90 DAYS

HOW TO SELL YOUR HOUSE IN 90 DAYS

# How to Sell Your House

## in

# 90

## DAYS

A Ten-Step Plan
for Selling Your House
in Today's Market,
With or Without a Broker

## MARC STEPHEN GARRISON

*Doubleday*
*New York   London   Toronto   Sydney   Auckland*

This publication is intended to provide accurate and authoritative information in regards to the subject matter covered. It is sold with the understanding that neither the publisher nor the author is engaged in rendering legal or accounting service. If legal or other expert assistance is required, the services of a competent professional should be sought.

PUBLISHED BY DOUBLEDAY
a division of Bantam Doubleday Dell
Publishing Group, Inc.,
666 Fifth Avenue, New York, New York 10103

DOUBLEDAY and the portrayal of an anchor with a dolphin are trademarks of Doubleday, a division of Bantam Doubleday Dell Publishing Group, Inc.

Library of Congress Cataloging-in-Publication Data

Garrison, Marc.
    How to sell your house in 90 days : a ten-step plan for selling your house in today's market, with or without a broker / Marc Stephen Garrison.
        p.   cm.
    Includes index.
    1. House selling.   2. Real estate business.   I. Title.
HD1379.G38   1991
333.33'83—dc20                                                    90-20990
                                                                          CIP

ISBN 0-385-41447-1

# DEDICATION

□   □   □

When I was a young, gawky, eight-year-old with a severe case of growing pains, I used to go regularly to Dodger games with a neighbor. He packed us up in his old truck and optimistically risked his sanity by trying to convert us to his love in life—baseball. For a couple of my boyhood friends it worked; today they are certified couch potatoes who glory in the vicarious thrill of watching a baseball game that someone else plays.

For me, baseball's okay, but what I learned at those games was something he never intended. I sat and watched the people selling the shirts, the posters, the pennants, the peanuts, the cotton candy, the drinks, the hot dogs, and the ice-cream bars. During the first week I watched all my friends spend their hard-earned money on stuff that they could have purchased for half as much at the A&P store in our neighborhood.

The very next game saw me loaded down with every kind of candy bar I could afford to buy. As soon as we sat down, I opened up shop. I may not have made much, but it was fun, and I learned a lot.

I am grateful for Thel Fuller, who took me to those games and opened my eyes to my first lesson in investing. I am grateful to my wife DeAnn for the sacrifices that she makes for our children and myself. Most of all I am grateful to those of you who wrote to me, saying that this book needed to be written. It hasn't been easy. But it has been worth it.

# ACKNOWLEDGMENTS

□   □   □

Special thanks to Richard Allen for his use of the Real Estate Contract and its explanation in the For Sale by Owner Section in Step 9. Also special thanks to my agent Russ Galen and Joel Fishman and Wendy Goldman at Doubleday. Your extra help for this book has really meant a lot!

# CONTENTS

□   □   □

# INTRODUCTION

□  □  □

The average real estate commission paid in 1988 was $5,872.63. Some people will look at that figure and say, "That's a lot of money!" Others will look at it and say, "That's not much for all the hassle real estate agents have to put up with!" I have a way to keep the dollars paid for real estate commissions in perspective. Even after making as much money as I have in real estate investing, I put the figure into realistic terms by thinking to myself, "If I were still working as an electrician, how many houses would I have to wire before I could save up and put that much money in the bank?" Looking at the commission that way lets me see that $5,872.63 is a lot of money. It would have taken me years to earn enough to pay for the necessities of life for myself and my family—like indoor plumbing and three square meals a day—and still save that much money in the bank.

In the United States, the average commission paid to real estate agents for the sale of a home or property is 6 percent. (In some areas agents are trying to raise that percentage to as high as 10 percent. But for the examples used in this book we'll stick to the 6 percent figure.) The 6 percent commission is computed on the sales price. Pay attention: sales price includes the amount of mortgage loans, etc., that you have against the property. The 6 percent is not just a percentage of your equity (that is, the amount of cash you have invested), but a percentage of the combined total of equity and loans. If you bought an "average" home in 1984 for $67,500 with an average 10 percent down payment and sold it four years later at a new price of $78,900, you're going to say "Great! I just made $11,400." But let's take a closer look at those figures.

| Purchase Price in 1984 | | Sale Four Years Later | |
|---|---|---|---|
| Purchase Price | $67,500 | Sales Price | $78,900 |
| Down Payment | −6,750 | New Loan Balance | −61,850 |
| | | | |
| Loan Balance | $60,750 | Gross Equity | $17,050 |
| Purchase Closing Costs | | Less Commissions | −4,734 |
| and Points (3%) | 1,822 | Less Closing Costs and | |
| | | Points on Buyer's Loan | −1,578 |
| Actual Loan Balance | $62,572 | | |
| | | Net Equity to Seller | $10,738 |
| | | | |
| | | Less Original Down | |
| | | Payment | −6,750 |
| | | | |
| | | Net Profit | $ 3,988 |

"What? I thought I made $11,400!"

Well, you did, but most of it was given away as closing costs and *real estate commissions.* You might even say that the scenario I just presented doesn't represent the full picture, since you could have left the money you used for the down payment in the bank and earned interest on it during these four years and come out a lot better. Couple that loss—the difference between what you earned on the sale of the home and what you would have earned leaving the money in the bank to earn interest—with the fact that renting could have been a lot cheaper than mortgage payments, and you come close to the true picture. Even adjusting for the tax advantages of home ownership, renting can sometimes be cheaper than owning.

Now don't get me wrong. I am a strong believer in the benefits of home ownership, but what I am asking you to do is look a bit more carefully at the process of selling your own home. Make sure it makes financial sense. Make sure that you know all the costs, and make darn sure that you have exhausted every possible avenue of selling it on your own before you list it. That way *you* could pocket the extra 6 percent of the value of your home. That extra $5,000 or $6,000 could pay for a few blissful weeks on some tropical island for you and your family, be part of the down payment for your dream home, or become the beginning of an education fund for your children.

The purpose of this book is to help you become aware of all the possibilities available to you when it comes time to sell your home or property. Part I discusses the process of selling your home or property and includes sections on how to make sure that you really want to sell and whether you should do it by yourself or with an agent. You'll also learn how to maximize your sales price by employing inexpensive, handy fix-up techniques, learning how to set a realistic sales price, and understanding how to put together a financing package.

From there, in Part II, we explore the process of actually selling your home by yourself. We go step by step through the experience, telling you how to advertise and how to screen buyers on the phone. Then we discuss how to show the home, how to arrange for signing of the contract when you have a valid buyer, and what steps to take in closing the sale yourself.

Part III takes you through every aspect of selling through a real estate agent. We begin by finding the right agent, negotiating the listing contract, and getting a written commitment attached to your contract that requires the agent to perform specific tasks to sell your home—or lose the listing. You won't ever have to be the victim of the agent who lists your home and doesn't come back until the listing is about to expire and he or she wants a renewal. (Remember that the listing agent shares in the commission no matter who sells the home.) We'll talk about how to work with agents before and after the contract is signed and how to make sure they do what they promise. We illustrate what recourse you have and how to light a fire under their tails if they're not doing their job.

The last section addresses the desperate cases. What do you do if you can't sell your home or property on your own and then list through an agent and are still unsuccessful? I show you every alternative method that I feel will work today—ways to creatively market your property quickly at the best possible price.

I conclude with a special section on how to use your home as a key to your financial future. With your own home or property as a base, I show you how to trade up into your dream home or into the position of owning your home free and clear.

Keep a notebook and a pen handy. Use this book as a workbook. Mark key passages. Write down questions. Jot down ideas that come to you as you read it. Make lists. Keep a log.

Why is this so important? Let me list two examples. As you read Step 7 on screening buyers on the phone, a thought suddenly comes to you. A business associate mentioned five weeks ago that his daughter and son-in-law and their three children are moving to town this month. The daughter and son-in-law are flying out for three days to look for a house. You think about giving him a call and offering to show them your place. But it's too late tonight. Write it down so you won't forget. Or suppose you have listed your house with an agent and after three months the agent has yet to bring anyone by or has talked to you only once or twice since signing the listing agreement. You want to terminate the agreement early because he is not living up to the contingencies specified in the agreement. But how do you prove it? He did call you a few times, but when? He explained what he was doing in one of those conversations, but what did he say? If you have documented your dealings with the agent, then you will have an easier time dismissing him.

If you write things down as you go, you will do a more complete job of selling your home and may save time later.

Read the whole book. One chapter may give you an outline, but each succeeding chapter will fill in another area of expertise. Don't sell your home half-informed. If you do, you will lose time and possibly some of the money from your sale.

With all that in mind, let's get started on the process of selling your home or property.

# PREFACE

☐　　☐　　☐

☐ At the end of a long, tiring day you come home hoping for a quiet dinner. What you get is a loud and angry neighbor complaining that your dog has dug up his pansy patch for the third time. "That's it!" you tell your wife when he leaves. "I can't stand this neighborhood anymore. We're putting the house up for sale first thing in the morning!"

☐ The boss has just offered you a tranfer to the city of your choice, at a salary you had only dreamed of in the past, and she wants you to relocate by the middle of next month.

"We'll have to list the house with a real estate agent right away," your husband replies when you call to share the good news.

☐ Looking around the house one quiet afternoon, you realize that there is a lot more space than you need now that the children are out of the nest. When you see your husband that night you say, "Dear, don't you think it is about time we put the house up for sale? We don't really need a place this large anymore and it is a lot of work to keep up."

During the past ten years as an investor I have been personally involved in hundreds of real estate transactions, as a buyer, seller, or outside consultant. I have been amazed at the relative ease with which people make the decision to pull up stakes and move. From an economic viewpoint, their moves are usually financial disasters and the only person who makes any money out of the deal is the real estate agent.

Whatever reason you have for wanting to sell your house, you should give some careful thought to it before you actually commit to making that sale. The biggest mistake you can make is selling your home when you don't really need to. Owning a home is a sound investment but you may be temporarily tempted to sell it when things are getting you down. Before you actually put the house up for sale you need to examine your reasons for wanting to do so as objectively as you can. No matter where you live you can have difficult neighbors. Moving may not be the solution. In the case of our earlier example, maybe you should just confine your dog. The fact that the children are gone doesn't necessarily mean that you should live in a smaller house. If you are comfortable where you are and it is possible financially, you may decide to stay put and just enjoy the roominess. Even if you are transferred to another state you may wish to keep your present home and let it be the first investment property you acquire. Let the renters finish paying for it.

Your decision to sell could be prompted by the need for more room or a desire to have a bay window in the breakfast nook or another bathroom or a family room away from the main living area of the house. Maybe you should remodel your home instead of selling it and moving. If you really like your neighbors and your children are doing well at the local school, it may make more sense to remodel your present home than to sell it and move to an unfamiliar area.

Perhaps you are in a financial bind and think that by selling the house you can get yourself into more comfortable circumstances. Selling the house may be an extreme measure and more than is really called for. Instead, you could look into refinancing the mortgage loan; it may be that you can get a new loan that will get you over your present difficulty and still let you keep the house. Or you may want to get the equity out of the house so you can invest it elsewhere or pay for Junior's college expenses. Again, refinancing may be the answer instead of selling.

*But* after you have examined all the options and still want to sell your house, you then need to make some other decisions. When will you put the house up for sale? What needs to be done to the house to make it more marketable? How quickly must the house be sold? Will you sell it yourself or will you get a professional real estate agent to sell it for you?

These are all questions that only you can answer. I'd like to give you some seasoned advice about each, but the ultimate decision lies in your hands. If you do decide to sell, I'd like to share my expertise with you so that when all's said and done, you can walk away from the closing with the best possible price, the best terms available, and the least amount of hassle. First you must choose either to sell the house on your own, or list it with a real estate agent.

□   □   □

# HOW TO SELL
# YOUR HOUSE
# IN 90 DAYS

# PART ONE

# INITIAL STEPS FOR SELLING YOUR HOME OR PROPERTY, WITH OR WITHOUT AN AGENT

□ □ □

## FOR SALE BY OWNER
## OR LIST WITH A REAL ESTATE AGENT?

☐     ☐     ☐

*Successful people make decisions quickly
(as soon as all the facts are available)
and change them very slowly (if ever).
Unsuccessful people make decisions very
slowly, and change them very often and
quickly.*

—Napoleon Hill

I remember the first time I decided to sell a property. I was in my early twenties and this was our first home. We had done a heck of a lot of work on it and it was gorgeous. A friend of a friend recommended that we contact their second cousin's third nephew who was a real estate agent. Thinking back now I remember how impressed we were when he came over with a tape measure and a pocket calculator, and described all that he was going to do for us.

We signed on the dotted line and that was the last we saw of him for the ninety days we had our house listed for sale through his office. You would expect a competent agent to relay feedback on a regular basis, and to let you know what he is doing to attract buyers to your house (by running ads, for instance). In this case, he wouldn't even return calls. In three months, not one person came to see our house. It was kind of like sending out invitations and decorating for a party, but not having anyone show up. Sure enough, though, just before our listing was to run out, here came our "agent" again. He wanted us to lower the price, since, as he explained, our price discouraged people from coming over to look. Never once did he mention the fact that *he* had set the price. Nor did he give us a reason for his failure to return any of our calls. I sat there seething, planning fifty ways to tell him where he could go, when he made the crowning statement: "If you lower the price by at least $5,000, I might even be willing to take it myself." I smelled a skunk with a three-piece suit sitting in my living room that day, and told him to get out and never come back.

We bounced back from that experience by learning everything we could about what it takes to sell a home. We started our first sale by owner experience with a simple ad that said:

---

Nice Home for Sale
FHA Assumption, XLNT. Loc.
Call Marc or DeAnn

---

In the next few weeks we were flooded with calls. Out of several offers, we picked the best one and had the title company where we closed the transaction write up the contracts. All we did was put a cheap simple ad in the paper, answer the phone a few times, and show the house to several nice couples.

We walked away from that experience shocked. We couldn't believe it. No, we weren't amazed at all the work we did; we couldn't believe how *easy* it was. For the actual time we spent, we made over $300 an hour.

For a young couple with a brand-new child—or anyone for that matter —that's a heck of a lot of money.

As the years went on, I became more and more involved in real estate investing. My wife and I grew adept at buying and selling homes, and I wrote a national best-seller about part-time real estate investing. But nowhere have I ever seen a guide that describes that initial lesson I learned back when we were getting started: your profit on any real estate transaction is made upon sale whether you are a serious investor, or just trying to get the best price out of that home in Temecula that your aunt Sadie left you.

Now that you have made the decision to sell, you need to decide who will sell the house or property for you. Would you like to experience what I did? Some situations make selling your home yourself very attractive; others make listing with an agent the most practical and efficient way to sell your home. Let's look at some examples to see which of these two options is the best for you in your particular circumstances, and which will make the most sense financially. A home is such a big investment that you will want both to protect it while you live in it, and to earn as much as possible from it when you sell.

Every year a large number of home owners sell their properties themselves, without the help of a real estate agent. Many factors prompt them to do so. One that is particularly motivational is the financial saving that can be made when you don't have to pay a real estate agent's commission. The average commission on home sales in 1990 will be over $6,000. You can do a lot of good for yourself and your family with an extra $6,000. You may wish to use the money for a down payment on a more valuable property. You may want to invest it. It could be the beginning of your children's education fund or your retirement package. You may prefer to do some work and sell the house yourself so you can put that money into your own pocket rather than into that of the real estate agent.

Selling your home yourself is especially attractive if your equity is small and the traditional 6 percent commission on the selling price would leave you with little or nothing—or worse yet, having to pay money at the closing to sell your home. I've heard from dozens of people in today's market who have sold properties through real estate agents and who have actually had to come up with cash at the closing to sell their properties to someone else. One couple's experience comes to mind and is typical of those who have had to pay out money to sell their homes. This couple originally purchased their home for $100,000 with a $5,000 down payment. They financed the $95,000 balance with an adjustable rate mortgage that included a negative amortization feature. This negative amortization feature meant that if the index to which their loan rate was tied rose higher than the annual cap (maximum percentage rate that their loan's interest rate could rise each year), the difference, or amount they really should have been paying if the cap wasn't there, would be added to their loan.

After several years of ownership they actually ended up owing more on their mortgage than the original purchase price of their home. When they put it up for sale, they found that they couldn't sell it for much more than they had paid for it. When they closed, they actually had to deliver a check to the closing officer to pay down their loan balance, and to cover the 6 percent realtor's commission and their percentage of the closing fees.

That's not the way it should be. If this couple had sold their home on their own and had a better loan, they wouldn't have had to pay at the closing when the real estate commission wiped out their profit. They would have pocketed money instead. In addition to the financial advantages of selling your home or property yourself, there is the sense of satisfaction in accomplishing something worthwhile: the sense of being in control of your own life. What a high it can be to do a new thing successfully. And selling your own home yourself this time doesn't mean that you will always use that method in the future. You can adapt your approach to selling this and other homes or properties to the circumstances of the moment.

How much work will be required if you decide to be the house agent yourself? You or your spouse will probably have to spend at least one hour a day taking care of the things a real estate agent does, like advertising, screening buyers, and showing the property. You need to ask yourself if you have that much time to put into the project. If the answer is yes, then you will want to think next of how you will advertise for buyers and when and under what circumstances you will open your home to strangers who are interested in buying your house.

Remember, too, that there will be some out-of-pocket expenses if you sell your house yourself. You will have to pay for newspaper advertising and a sign to put on the front lawn. You will also have to pay for an appraisal of the property by a professional so you will have a realistic idea of what the property can sell for in the current market.

One of the biggest surprises owners have when preparing to sell their homes is the difference between what they want for the house and its actual fair market value. I recently made an offer on a home that has been empty for over a year. The owner bought the home as a vacation property by a ski resort. But, as often happens, making the twenty-five-hundred-mile trip from his hometown to the vacation spot was not as easily done as he had thought. He purchased the home for a little over $250,000 and put it up for sale a year later at $425,000. Sounds great: $175,000 in profit in twelve months. But in the time he had owned the home it had been literally torn apart by some people whom he had allowed to use it. The yard was a shambles, the garage full of trash, the fireplace glass broken out, and some walls broken in. I called up the county property records office, found out what he bought it for in a few minutes, and made my offer based on what he paid for it, plus the actual appreciation our area had undergone, minus the fix-up work that needed to be done.

The agent, to say the least, was reluctant even to present the offer, but I reminded him that by law he had to. To make a long story short, the owner promptly countered at $415,000. I countered at exactly what I had offered before plus a little more money down. He then countered at $410,000. I simply finished those negotiations for the time being by telling the agent to call me when the owner got reasonable. Imagine the difference it would have made if the owner had fixed the home up before trying to sell it and if the agent had told him what a realistic market

7

value was before he listed it. I've kept in regular contact with the agent, and to date, no one else has even made an offer. Each month this house sits empty, and a payment is made to the bank.

Other people who put their homes up for sale may experience an opposite situation. They may have bought before property values began to rise and now discover that their home is worth far more than they realized. Sometimes the news isn't so rosy: none of the memories that make your house a home for you will have any value in the marketplace, nor will the prize rosebushes in the backyard. Prospective buyers will look at the permanent value of the house and its location when deciding how much they will pay for it. And that price is often disappointing to the homeowner whose valuation of the house is based on subjective things.

The decision to sell your home or property yourself will also require you to become knowledgeable about real estate contracts; you must know what is legal in your area. You will also need to sharpen your negotiating skills, so you can get the best deal possible. Then you will need to know what professionals will have to be used at various stages of the sale. I have already mentioned getting a professional appraisal to help you set a realistic price for your home. You will also need a title officer to close the sale and perhaps one or two other professionals. These professionals and the sales contract will be discussed at length in steps 9 and 10 (Part II), but for now simply understand that you will need the help of some others when you sell yourself.

If you own your home outright, you are in a good position to sell it yourself. If you have a lot of equity and are in no hurry to sell, you can sell it yourself to good advantage because you are in a good position to set the terms of the sale and reap the rewards of owner financing, greatly increasing your profit. Imagine being on the receiving end of mortgage payments for a change. A typical house selling for $60,000 with a conventional thirty-year loan at 11 percent would yield $185,000 to the lender by the end of the thirty years. Not a bad return on your money if you own the home outright and are financing the sale yourself.

If you are selling a property because you are moving out of state right away, you may consider the real estate agent right off the bat. It is very difficult to negotiate a sale from a thousand miles away and showing the property would obviously be time consuming and expensive.

There are other instances where using an agent makes sense. One is if you have been trying for some time to sell by yourself and haven't been successful. Another is if you or your spouse don't want to be home alone when strangers come to see the property. Agents screen prospective buyers and have a reasonable feel for their reliability before they bring them to your house. And they will be there to show the house, so you or your spouse will not be alone with people you don't know.

If you have an urgent need to sell your home or property quickly, calling in the professionals may again be the wisest choice. Because of cooperative efforts among all real estate firms in your area (known as the Multiple Listing Service, or MLS), many agents will actually be trying to sell your home. The agents also foot the cost of the advertising, pictures, listing in the Multiple Listing Service, luncheons and tours for agents, open houses, and other promotions that may help sell your house.

Selling a home or property is a big financial undertaking and deserves careful consideration on your part. Weigh the options carefully, discuss them with your spouse, and don't make a hasty decision.

While you are choosing between selling on your own and listing with an agent, read Step 2. It contains suggestions for how to get your home into the most marketable condition—and you will need to do that no matter who ends up selling it. The better the appearance and condition of the home, the easier it will be to sell and the better price it should bring.

□   □   □

## APPEARANCE

□   □   □

*All worthwhile men have good thoughts, good ideas, and good intentions—but precious few of them ever translate those into action.*

**N**o matter how you sell your home you are going to have to take a long hard look at it, a realistic look without the rosy glow of pleasant memories and the sense of accomplishment at finally having gotten the last of the crabgrass out of the backyard. One way to do this is to imagine yourself as a potential home buyer. What would you like about the house and the neighborhood if you were seeing it for the first time? What turns you off?

Start with the neighborhood and surrounding area. What makes it a great place to live? Are the neighbors' yards neat and well cared for? Are the shopping areas handy but far enough away not to be seen from the picture window in the living room? Would a prospective buyer be thrilled to know that the freeway entrance is just next door or would he worry about the traffic and noise that may cause? Are the schools close? Too close? Are there churches in the area? What about activities for the kids? Is there a park within walking distance that creates a lot of noise on summer evenings? A golf course, shopping center, grade school, junior high, high school, city park, hospital, church, freeway, and restaurant can all be considered advantages or detriments, depending on proximity and a buyer's needs and desires. If you wonder if the local grade school is considered a plus, think about how you feel about it. Ask your neighbors how they feel.

Decide what you can realistically count as pluses: those conditions that will help you sell at the best price. Decide, too, what the drawbacks are. If you can see them, so can the prospective buyers. You want to be aware of what the negatives are so you can be prepared to discuss them if questions come up. If a buyer objects to a golf course down the road, mention that the golf course has kept property values high. If he doesn't like the grade school across the street, mention that it allows you an unobstructed view of the mountains. Always think positive—and realize that some buyers will find fault with any home. All the positive attitude in the world won't change their minds. Don't worry. There will be others who are less cynical.

Once you have looked at your neighborhood and surrounding area to find its strengths and weaknesses, look at your own home and yard. Start with the outside. Use the checklist at the end of this chapter, following each page in the order given, to do a systematic evaluation of your yard and the outside of the house.

Be objective when you examine the yard. Does the grass need to be fertilized? Are there bare spots where the kids have played ring around the rosy a few too many times? Do the bushes by the front door need to be trimmed so you won't have to use the side entrance all the time? Most of the things that require improvement in a yard can be done by you and your family and will be only a moderate expense. Remember that the yard and outside of the house provide the first impression of your home to the prospective buyer. Make sure it is a good one.

After you have evaluated the yard, turn your attention to the outside of the house itself. Are there any broken windows in the garage? Are there areas where bushes or trees have rubbed paint off the house? Do the screens look as if they have survived a nuclear attack? Is the flashing around the chimney coming loose? Do the downspouts have so much of last fall's leaf harvest in them that no water can get through? Whatever needs to be done, do it. Many of these things you can do yourself for a nominal cost. If the repair is extensive, you may need to call in a professional. If you have termites, you will definitely need to call someone.

After you have looked at your house's exterior, and before you move on to the inside, take a walk and find the three nicest homes in the neighborhood. What makes them look nice? Compare them with your own house.

- ☐ How does the grass look? Are there weeds? Does the grass grow onto the sidewalk or is it neatly trimmed?

- ☐ Are there flowers?

- ☐ Are the shrubs trimmed? Do they look overgrown?

- ☐ Is the driveway clean? Are there large oil spots in the middle of it? Are there cracks? Are weeds growing in the smaller cracks?

- ☐ Is the front yard complete? That is, are both sides landscaped and manicured or does one side of the driveway look like a vacant lot?

- ☐ Are the windows clean?

- ☐ Is the walk clear of bushes and well swept?

- ☐ Does the paint look new or at least in good repair?

- ☐ Are all the brass numbers on the address attached?

□ Is the screen door hanging correctly and in good repair?

□ Are there water marks on the roof where the swamp cooler/air conditioner is installed?

□ In short, does the home radiate *owner pride?*

Consider the top three houses in your neighborhood. Don't they all say: *quality, care, timely maintenance?* Wouldn't you feel safe moving into a home like that? That's the way you want prospective buyers to feel when they get their first glimpse of your home. Believe me, if your home has *owner pride* written all over it, you will be able to sell it quicker and for thousands of dollars more.

Once you have completed the exterior inspection sheet for your house, go inside. Remember to look at it as though you were a prospective buyer. What would you want changed and what would you love as is? Don't let your memories of happy times with your family cloud your judgment. The buyers will not have those same memories to help them gloss over defects. Use the interior inspection sheet to guide you through your evaluation of the house; that way you won't forget anything.

An added advantage to using these sheets is that they can become the basis for advertising data that you will need later when you are ready to offer your house for sale. The sheets are organized and thorough, and they will give you a clear picture of the strengths and weaknesses of your house so you can emphasize its good points when you are selling.

When you have finished with your inspection and have clearly in mind what needs to be done to get your house into marketable shape (and it may not be much if you have been a careful homeowner), continue on in Step 2 where you will find practical and easy hints about improving the appearance of your home. Most can be done by you or by someone in your family at minimal expense.

When I got started in real estate investing with my wife, we were both in our early twenties. We were excited about investing and it seemed as though no home was too dirty for us to buy, fix up, and resell at a profit. The importance of getting your house in shape before you put it up for sale has been repeated hundreds of times for us in the past decade. Consider, for example, a basic three-bedroom, one-bath home that we bought. This home had been for sale for almost six months. The yard in winter looked like a snowbank at a ski resort; not one of the walks had been cleared. The garage and unfinished basement were piled high with old furniture and junk. Inside were broken windows, grimy walls, and several cats, which had taken up residence and were using one of the bedrooms as a latrine.

The seller couldn't understand why his house, which had plenty of potential, hadn't sold. When we made him an offer, he willingly accepted since it was the only one he had received. Two weeks later we had gone through the process of inspection that we talked about earlier in this chapter. Once we had reviewed the home we set about cleaning it. Later, when we showed people the home, it was ready to sell: all the rooms were clean, the snow had been shoveled, the windows fixed, the carpets cleaned. We had spent a couple of afternoons and a Saturday doing the kinds of repairs and improvements that we have been talking about. When we put the house up for sale, three people came the same day we listed it and remarked repeatedly about how nice it was. We sold it, after spending under $200 on repairs, for a little over $20,000 more than we bought it for.

Why didn't the former seller fix it up? Lack of knowledge, laziness, indifference? I'm still not sure, but you shouldn't ever make the same mistake. The following checklists have been put together to make sure that you don't go wrong.

As you prepare to show your home, make several extra copies of these sheets. Gather together copies of any past major repairs done to your home (new heating system, new water heater, etc.) and at least the last twelve months' utility bills. This information will help you answer promptly and accurately the questions prospective buyers are most likely to ask. The majority of the items on these checklists don't require anything other than some elbow grease. If, during your inspections, you notice some repairs that would cost a lot to do, please think twice. Ex-

# OUTSIDE WALK-THROUGH CHART

| Item | Yes | No | When | Comments |
|------|-----|-----|------|----------|
| Curb clearly marked? | | | | |
| Lawn green? | | | | |
| Lawn cut? | | | | |
| Lawn edged? | | | | |
| Shrubs and trees pruned? | | | | |
| Are there spring or summer bedding plants? | | | | |
| Winter sidewalks cleared? | | | | |
| Blacktop driveway sealed? | | | | |
| Exterior bugs sprayed? | | | | |
| Eaves freshly painted? | | | | |
| Gutters clear? | | | | |
| Roof shingles intact? | | | | |
| Chimneys in good repair? | | | | |
| Side yard debris stacked? | | | | |
| All animal droppings cleaned? | | | | |
| Shrubs, trash, and leaves cleared away? | | | | |
| Heating/cooling units cleaned? | | | | |
| Garage cleaned; items stored and stacked neatly? | | | | |
| Area for workbench cleared? | | | | |
| Front door washed and painted? | | | | |
| Outside windows cleaned? | | | | |
| Clapboard, siding, or stucco in good repair? | | | | |
| Doorbell button working and nice looking? | | | | |

| Item | Yes | No | When | Comments |
|------|-----|-----|------|----------|
| New doormat at front door? | | | | |
| Threshold painted? | | | | |
| Screen mended? | | | | |
| Trash can area cleaned? | | | | |
| Garage door closed? | | | | |
| Tools, toys picked up? | | | | |
| | | | | |
| | | | | |
| | | | | |
| | | | | |
| | | | | |
| | | | | |
| | | | | |
| | | | | |
| | | | | |
| | | | | |
| | | | | |
| | | | | |
| | | | | |
| | | | | |
| | | | | |
| | | | | |
| | | | | |

# INSIDE WALK-THROUGH CHART

| Item | Yes | No | When | Comments |
|------|-----|-----|------|----------|
| **Ceilings:** | | | | |
| All cobwebs cleaned? | | | | |
| All light fixtures cleaned? | | | | |
| Ceiling unstained? | | | | |
| Ceiling undamaged? | | | | |
| **Kitchen:** | | | | |
| Oven cleaned? | | | | |
| Drip pans on stove cleaned? | | | | |
| Stove burner reflectors clean or replaced? | | | | |
| Stove control buttons in good condition or replaced? | | | | |
| Sink scrubbed? | | | | |
| Sink organized? | | | | |
| Under the sink organized? | | | | |
| Faucet washers in good condition? | | | | |
| Kitchen curtains clean and pressed? | | | | |
| Refrigerator door and interior cleaned? | | | | |
| Dishwasher door and interior cleaned? | | | | |
| Kitchen plants in good shape? | | | | |
| **Bathroom:** | | | | |
| Faucet washers in good condition? | | | | |
| Hard water deposits removed? | | | | |
| Linoleum in bathroom/toilet in good repair or replaced? | | | | |
| Blue water in toilet bowls? | | | | |
| Air freshener installed behind toilet? | | | | |

| Item | Yes | No | When | Comments |
|---|---|---|---|---|
| All mildew killed? | | | | |
| Shower curtain in good repair? | | | | |
| Medicine cabinet clean/in good repair? | | | | |
| Fixtures spotless and shined? | | | | |
| Grout clear around tub/shower? | | | | |
| Is a plant (or two) needed? | | | | |
| Is the toilet seat in good repair and tightened? | | | | |
| Towels clean without stains or tears? | | | | |
| **Laundry:** | | | | |
| Laundry room area organized? | | | | |
| Washer and dryer clean? | | | | |
| **Closets:** | | | | |
| Coat closet organized? | | | | |
| Linen closet organized? | | | | |
| Hall closets organized? | | | | |
| Bedroom closets organized? | | | | |
| **Front Hall:** | | | | |
| Is there clutter/extra furniture? | | | | |
| All old mail/magazines discarded? | | | | |
| **Living Room:** | | | | |
| Fireplace clean with wood stacked inside? | | | | |
| Wood bin tidy with fresh wood? | | | | |
| Is there extra furniture that could be removed? | | | | |
| | | | | |

| Item | Yes | No | When | Comments |
|------|-----|-----|------|----------|
| **Bedrooms:** | | | | |
| Is there clutter/extra furniture? | | | | |
| Dressers and vanities clear? | | | | |
| Space under beds clean? | | | | |
| Personal items stored away? | | | | |
| Valuables removed? | | | | |
| **Walls:** | | | | |
| Inside windows and mirrors cleaned? | | | | |
| Holes in walls patched? | | | | |
| Wall corner paint chips repainted? | | | | |
| **Attic:** | | | | |
| Stored items straightened? | | | | |
| Floors swept/vacuumed? | | | | |
| **Basement:** | | | | |
| Stored items straightened? | | | | |
| Floors swept/vacuumed? | | | | |
| Is an air freshener needed? | | | | |
| **Garage:** | | | | |
| Stored items straightened and boxed? | | | | |
| Floor swept? | | | | |
| Oil spots degreased? | | | | |
| **Other items:** | | | | |
| | | | | |
| | | | | |
| | | | | |

cept in rare instances, it is not a good investment to spend a lot of money fixing up a home that is going to be sold. Even expensive repairs rarely raise the market value of the house enough for you to recoup the cost of the repairs. If you are going to spend anything, you might consider paint (a light neutral shade to make the rooms and home look larger), professional housecleaning, some potted plants for inside the home (which you can take with you), and perhaps some new curtains if the old ones are totally shot.

## DETERMINING A REALISTIC SALES PRICE

☐    ☐    ☐

*My war stories and a dime will get me a cup of coffee.*
—General George Patton

**N**ow we get down to what selling your home is all about—making money! You can make money on your house only if you sell it, and you will sell it only if you are able to put it on the market at a realistic price. This step can be very traumatic for many homeowners. Your home has so many pleasant family memories that it is sometimes hard to look at it objectively and decide what you think it will be worth in dollars and cents to someone else, someone who doesn't remember that Jimmy took his first steps in this house or that Susan was born here on that snowy January night when you couldn't get to the hospital.

To get you started on determining a realistic price for your home or property, let's consider for a moment the concept of fair market value that comes to us through the field of appraising. Fair market value is the most probable price a property will bring if it has been widely exposed on the market, if sufficient time has been allowed to find an informed buyer, and if neither party is under undue duress. The actual sales price can vary from the fair market value for a number of reasons, including disrepair, poor financing, financial disasters, divorce, foreclosure, etc. Sometimes either the buyer or the seller is in a hurry. A rushed buyer will often pay a little more to get what he needs by the time he needs it and the hurried seller will often take a lower price in order to get a quick sale.

For example, I know a man who was anxious to sell his home because he was going back to school. He knew two important things:

1. He was putting his house up for sale in a soft real estate market.

2. He couldn't afford to make payments on an empty house.

So he set a four-week deadline. At the end of this period he would either have sold the house or have a reasonable expectation (based on the number of buyers and offers) that he would be able to sell it within the next four weeks. If he had no prospects for selling, he would cut the price to the balance on his mortgage. He ended up having to do just that. But he felt lucky to get even that much.

What should you do to find a fair price for your home? First of all, pay attention to what is going on in your neighborhood. Have other homes sold there recently? If so, what kind of money did the sellers get? How long did it take the sellers to find buyers? Did their houses sit on the market for months and then sell for just the amount of the mortgage? Or did they sell within the first week after the FOR SALE signs were put on the front lawn? Then ask yourself how your home compares with the others around you. Is it better than some but not as good as others? Is it larger or smaller than the average house in your part of town? Is the basic construction of the home similar to that of other houses in your area or do you have the only home on the block that isn't brick?

Are you beginning to be able to see your home objectively? Good, because that is the first step toward setting a realistic price so you can sell it in a reasonable amount of time and for a reasonable profit.

What properties are selling for in your area is a good clue to helping you decide what price tag to put on your home. To find out, look around your neighborhoods for FOR SALE and SOLD signs. Ask the owners what they are asking for their home or what it sold for. Also ask them how long their home has been or was on the market and how many offers they had, how many people came to see it, etc. This will give you a feel for the current real estate market in your area.

The next step you should take is to visit your local real estate board office and ask to use the MLS comps (records of what comparable properties have sold for in your area recently). Look at properties that have the same basic structure as yours, are about the same size in terms of square feet, have the same number of bedrooms and bathrooms, and so forth. Also consider the age of your house and whether it is on a corner lot, in the middle of the block, in a cul de sac, or next door to the local supermarket. Find at least three houses that are comparable to yours in as many points as possible and see what they have sold for. That will give you a good idea of what the current market value of your home should be.

Often people try to set the price of their homes or properties more on the basis of what they need or want to get from the sale rather than from a realistic appraisal of what the property is worth in the current market. Times change in real estate as in other things. The 1970s saw an incredible rise in real estate values. The normal profit in home selling grew like Topsy, quite out of all rhyme or reason. Those times of incredible profit and appreciation of real estate values have changed, for the most part depending on where you live. Some areas are still experiencing inflated property values, but most of the country has slowed way down. In some areas market value has even dropped below the mortgage value on many properties. But no matter how bad, no market is dead. Something is selling. Your job is to find out for what price that property is selling.

Now you will want to spend a little money to get a professional appraisal of your home. Real estate agents, bankers, and other professionals can appraise your home but it is probably best to hire the services of a professional appraiser who is trained to be objective. If you can, be there when the appraiser comes to evaluate your home. Pay attention to the items she values and, if she will cooperate, ask how she arrives at her figures. This will help you understand what your home's most marketable features are, which can be useful in preparing advertising later on. You also want to know more than just her final figures. If you know why some areas rate low in the appraisal, then you can at least consider taking steps to improve those areas to try to boost the selling price of your home.

Appraisers are trained in collecting market data and using acceptable analysis methods. There are certain appraisal designations that will tell you something about the appraiser's expertise and compliance with a code of ethics. More than twenty-two designations are awarded by professional organizations, the most common being the American Institute of Real Estate Appraisers (MAI) and the Society of Real Estate Appraisers (SREA). Both require specialized course work, professional experience, and preparation of approved reports. Under the Financial Institutions Recovery and Reform Act of 1989 (FIRREA), appraisers must now meet certain federal requirements. Be sure to check out your appraiser's credentials before hiring her. Also ask for and check her references. A designation indicates the appraiser has qualified at a certain level of competence and integrity but it does not guarantee that her appraisal will be correct.

A good appraisal includes:

☐ a clear and reasonably complete description of the property being appraised

- ☐ An explanation of the appraisal's assumptions and limiting conditions

- ☐ all significant facts on which the appraisal is based

- ☐ a reasonably complete summary of the work done and the appraiser's reasoning

- ☐ the date of the valuation and the date of the report

- ☐ a statement that the appraiser has no direct or indirect personal interest in the property and no personal bias with respect to all parties involved in the appraisal

Two factors other than the current market and the appraisal value of your home or property are involved when you determine the selling price: time and money. Your own circumstances determine how much time you have in which to sell your home or property. If your company is transferring you to another state in two weeks, you can't afford to let the grass grow under your feet. You have to sell the home as quickly as you can and at the best price possible. But time and price work together to accomplish a sale. If you have plenty of time in which to accomplish the sale, you can hold out for a higher price. If you must sell quickly, then you will probably have to drop the price to encourage buyers to make a quick commitment to buy. In hurry-up situations you usually drop the price slightly below market to attract buyers. The amount of money you need to get out of the home, for your next purchase or to meet some other need such as retirement funds, will also affect the sale price you must get. Just getting rid of the mortgage payments is enough for some sellers. Others want the maximum because they need the money.

Recently I heard about a couple who were getting divorced. When their real estate agent met with them to set the price of their home, he had done some extensive research into comparable prices, what other homes had sold for, how long it took for them to sell, and what this couple could expect to sell this home for. The problem was that the couple had something else in mind. They had determined their sales price based on what they needed to sell the home for in order to pay all their bills and to give them money to get on with their lives after the divorce. Fourteen months later their home is still for sale. But some things have changed. They've dropped the price by $50,000 down to where it should have been, but it's almost too late. All the nice furniture that would have made the home look better and helped it sell quickly is gone. The yard has grown wild because the split partners are involved in new relationships and can't effectively divide responsibilities for the house.

If they had started selling the home at the right price, they would have sold it long ago. In fact, a couple who looked at this overpriced home fell in love with it when it was first listed, but they were afraid to make a low offer.

Another couple in the same neighborhood had put up their home for sale, after doing a thorough evaluation, at the right price. The couple who loved the high price home bought the fairly priced home instead and moved right in.

What factors should you ignore when pricing your home or property for sale? For one, strangely enough, your cost in acquiring the property. If your aunt Tillie left you the property in her will, would you expect to give it away instead of selling it because you had no money invested in it? Of course not. The property Aunt Tillie left you has value even though you personally didn't pay a cent for it. The same is true if you made a major goof and paid much more for the property than it was actually worth. You can't expect your buyer to pay for your mistake. Likewise, if you bought your home or property at a bargain or when real estate values were much lower, you can sell it at the current market value and make a handsome profit. So the cost of acquiring the home or property should be ignored in setting the asking price.

Most improvements you have made to your home will not affect its resale value. Upgrading bathrooms and kitchens are about the only improvements that you will recoup in the sales price. Such seemingly attractive items as swimming pools, extensive landscaping, even a new garage are just money down the drain; you will get back only a fraction of their cost or none at all. So, if you are thinking of investing money in remodeling to increase the selling price of the house, think again: you won't get it back when the house sells. It would be foolish to spend $10,000 remodeling your home and have its value only go up $2,000 to $3,000. Cosmetic improvements, on the other hand, do help to sell the home and can usually be recouped. Fresh paint and some basic landscaping, such as putting in bedding plants that bloom at the right moment, are inexpensive ways to improve your property's appearance and help it sell.

The current cost of replacing your home is another item that doesn't matter when you are calculating its sales price, as reasonable as using that as a basis for the home's value would seem to be. That is an approach that counts only when an insurance company is involved either in selling you insurance for the home or in responding to a claim after your house has burned to the ground.

Another evaluation that is of no practical value in establishing the selling price is the assessed value determined by your local taxing agency. As careful as the tax assessor is to arrive at an accurate value for your home, his assessment rarely has any relation to the market value. The market value can change rather dramatically between assessments by the tax office, and in some communities the properties are valued low for tax purposes to keep from overburdening the taxpayers. One property in a neighborhood near me was valued by the tax assessor at $69,500 five years ago, yet it sold for only $56,000. Over the next five years, the tax assessor has given it a value as low as $53,000 and as high as $59,000. Every year the tax valuation changes even though no major changes have been made to the property, which is located in a subdivision where homes sell at a brisk rate.

If none of these things can be taken into account in finding the selling price for your house or property, what can be used to determine the right sales price? How urgent is it for you to make a sale? You can reduce your asking price in proportion to your need for a quick sale. If you have to be in Singapore working for your company's overseas office by the end of the month, you don't want to be worrying about trying to sell your home from that distance. You will do what is necessary to sell quickly. We will discuss what to do in desperate cases in Part IV for those who need that kind of help.

If your home is in a desirable location and there are very few other homes for sale in the area, you can mark up the price for scarcity. If a major employer in your community has just laid off a large number of people, you will probably have to drop your asking price in order to find a buyer. If you are selling with an agent, he or she will be able to help you with decisions of this kind. If you are selling your house yourself, you will need to do your homework so that your sales price is consistent with local conditions. Unemployment figures are a quick guide to the buyers likely to be available to you.

What financing you can offer your buyers will also be an important factor. If you have a low interest rate and an assumable loan (a loan your buyer can simply take over) buyers will be eager to get your home or property. If you will take a second mortgage (hold a note for part of the remaining equity) for most of the down payment, many more buyers can qualify for buying your home. We will talk about financing options in detail in the next step; you should be aware that financing is as much a concern for you as for the buyer. Consider the following example.

**Home A**
$100,000 sales price
$80,000 assumable loan
$20,000 down payment

**Home B**
$100,000 sales price
$80,000 assumable loan
$5,000 down
$15,000 to be taken back in a second mortgage over the next five years (monthly payment at 12 percent annual interest would be $333.67 per month.)

Two identical homes are for sale in your neighborhood. Both have a sales price of $100,000 and a loan balance of $80,000. The only difference between these two homes is that one seller (Home A) wants all his money (equity) in cash. The other seller (Home B) is willing to sell with only a few thousand down to help him move ($5,000) and the rest to be taken back in a second mortgage and paid out over the next five years.

Which do you think would sell more easily? Home A or Home B?

You're right. Home B would be much easier to sell. When you lower the down payment from $20,000 to $5,000, you open up your home to thousands of potential buyers who can't come up with $20,000 but can scrape together $5,000. But you say you don't get all your money at once? Right, but you do sell the home. And in most cases, at 12 percent annual interest, you are getting a higher interest rate on your money than you would be getting by keeping it in a savings account at the bank.

In fact, my experience has shown that if you have two identical homes for sale, one with a large down payment, and the other with a small down payment, the small down payment home will sell first every time and *at a higher price*. You could even easily add $5,000 to the sales price and still sell Home B more quickly than the large down payment home.

Statistics show that the worst mistake a seller can make is to overprice a home. The longer the house is on the market, the lower the percentage of the original asking price is realized when the sale is eventually made. So pricing your house or property in accordance with current market values and taking into consideration the degree of urgency you have in making the sale are the best ways to attract buyers. Base your pricing decision on the current market value of comparable homes that have sold recently, on the unique qualities of your house, on the desirability of the location, and on the value assigned your house by a qualified appraiser. Then you have a very good chance of making the sale you want or need to make.

## FINANCING OPTIONS

☐   ☐   ☐

*Making the house payment has become*
*America's number-one financial worry.*
—The Gallup Poll, citing a
recent nationwide study

**O**ne of the most common obstacles to home and property sales is the seller's inflexibility in offering financing options to the buyer. Every potential buyer who comes to look at your home has a unique financial situation, and the more of these situations you can address with your financing package, the more opportunities you have to sell your home. As a potential seller, you should work out at least three ways that you will be willing to finance the sale of your house, if circumstances permit you to do so.

Sometimes there is only one option, that of having the buyer assume your current financing by making a down payment large enough to pay you the balance between the sales price and the loan (a term referred to as "equity"). For example, if you had $105,000 in loans and a sales price of $120,000, your equity would be $15,000. Your buyer would pay you your equity of $15,000 at closing. If your equity isn't too large, that may be the best way to finance. But if you have a sizable equity, the chances of finding a buyer with enough cash to buy you out is slim. So you want to think through some possible alternatives to financing that will help you sell your house or property and make a reasonable profit as well.

During this step we will look at a number of ways you can tailor your financial package to meet the needs of potential buyers and still look out for your own interests. Other than the traditional buy-out of your equity and assumption of the existing mortgage, what ways are there to finance a home sale?

## THE SECOND MORTGAGE

□   □   □

One way is for you, the seller, to accept a lower down payment and take back a second mortgage on the home. Like any mortgage, the second mortgage allows the buyer to pay off the equity gradually (just what we did with Home B in the example in the last step). In this case he also continues to make interest payments to the bank on the balance of the property's value. The second mortgage allows the sale of the home with a small down payment since the seller is willing to accept less money down than a bank typically allows. The buyer makes a second monthly payment to the holder of the second mortgage, often the seller. This arrangement allows the buyer to move into the house with an affordable down payment, and will net you some money at the closing and then provide you with a monthly income until the second mortgage is paid in full. If you don't absolutely need all the cash out of your home at once,

# SECOND MORTGAGE

$100,000 sale price

$80,000 mortgage

$20,000 equity

$15,000 second

$5,000 down

Equity to be taken back as a second mortgage. Interest to be 12 percent. Payments are to be made monthly over the next five years. Payments are to be $333.67 per month.

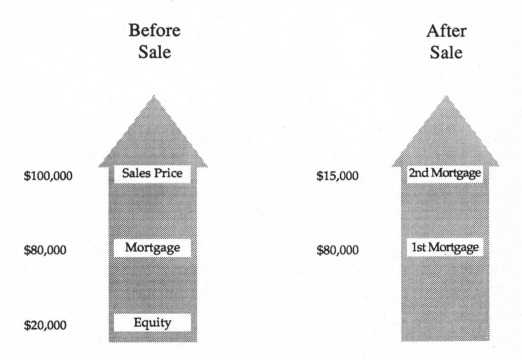

there are some advantages to selling a home with this kind of financing package. First, it opens up the sale to the many people who can come up with a modest down payment more readily than a large one. Second, it delays the tax implications of the sale if you are making a taxable profit. You pay tax on the money as it comes to you gradually instead of in one lump sum. Third, you will be earning a favorable rate of interest on the money involved in the second mortgage.

The second mortgage comes after the first mortgage if repossession or other legal action against the buyer becomes necessary, so you should keep one precaution in mind before accepting a buyer that you will finance with a second mortgage: you need to determine that he or she is a good financial risk. Do an employment check (is the buyer employed where he says he is, how long has he been there, what are his prospects for remaining employed?) and a credit check (does he make timely payments on debts, does he have any tax liens, has he ever filed for bankruptcy?) the same way a bank or other lending institution would. This will help protect you from underqualified buyers.

## THE REFINANCE

☐  ☐  ☐

If you have substantial equity and think most buyers won't be able to meet the down payment, you can refinance your house and regain your equity that way, leaving the buyers to come up with a much smaller down payment. If you have lived in your home for a number of years, you have probably built up a good equity position and have monthly payments and an interest rate that are relatively low. Trading that mortgage for a more current one will still leave you competitive on the market in terms of interest rate and monthly payments while getting your money out even before you sell the home. Most buyers, especially those buying a home for the first time, are more concerned about the

# REFINANCE

**Before:**
$100,000 value
$20,000 loan balance
$80,000 equity

$100,000 — Value

$20,000 — Loan Balance

$80,000 — Equity

**After Refinance Ready to Sell:**
$100,000 value
$95,000 loan balance
$5,000 equity
($75,000 in loan proceeds less
expenses in your money market
account)

$100,000 — Value

$95,000 — Loan Balance

$5,000 — Equity

size of the down payment and the monthly mortgage payments than they are about the interest rate or the number of years left to pay on the mortgage.

You can get the mortgage refinanced in a number of ways. The conventional real estate loan with your bank is one good way. Another option is to refinance with either an FHA loan or a VA loan (if you are eligible). These government loans have the advantage of being assumable by the buyer, which saves a lot in closing costs at the time of the sale and also requires only a modest down payment, opening up a large pool of potential buyers for your home.

## THE LEASE OPTION

□   □   □

**A** good way to ease buyers into committing to buy your home or property is to offer them a lease with an option to buy at the end of a specified period, usually from one to three years. While the lease portion of this agreement is in force, the potential buyers are making the mortgage payments and taking care of the property for you. At the end of their lease, the payments they have been making can apply toward the down payment if they decide to purchase the house or property. This can be a good arrangement if you don't need your equity immediately. It is also a good way to see that your property is taken care of if you have been transferred to another community and haven't been able to sell the home outright before you leave. Another advantage of this arrangement, if it doesn't turn into a sale, is that it makes your property commercial for tax purposes and you can depreciate the home and take advantage of other tax breaks that rental property owners get.

# LEASE OPTION

**Home before the option**
$100,000 Market value today

$80,000 Mortgage at 10 percent
($702 per month principal and interest)

$20,000 equity

$100,000    Mkt. Value

$80,000    Mortgage

$20,000    Equity

**Home during the option period**
$125,000 sale price at the exercise of the option in five years
(5 percent property price appreciation per year).
$1,000 per month lease payment. $250 per month to go toward
down payment if option is exercised. If tenant decides to
exercise his option at the end of the five years, he has $15,000
toward his down payment ($250x12x5). If he decides not to
exercise his option, then he loses the accumulated balance. The
tenant is also responsible for all maintenance during the five-year
period.

$125,000    Sales Price

**Home after the option is exercised**
$125,000 sales price

$70,000 loan balance

$50,000 down payment less $15,000 option balance.

The tenant has had five years to save up or arrange to
borrow the other $35,000.

$125,000    Sales Price

$70,000    Balance

$50,000    Down

# Sample Residential Lease with Option to Purchase

Received from _____

_____, hereinafter referred to as

Tenant, the sum of $_____ (_____dollars),

evidenced by_____as a deposit

which, upon acceptance of this Lease, the Owner of the premises, herein-

after referred to as Owner, shall apply said deposit as follows:

| | Deposit Received | Balance Owing Prior to Occupancy |
|---|---|---|
| Nonrefundable option consideration | $_____ | $_____ |
| Rent for the period from _____ to _____ | $_____ | $_____ |
| Security Deposit | $_____ | $_____ |
| Other | $_____ | $_____ |
| **Total** | $_____ | $_____ |

   In the event that this agreement is not accepted by the Owner or his/her authorized agent within _____ days, the total deposit received shall be re-funded.

   Tenant hereby offers to lease from the Owner the premises situated in the City of _____, State of _____, described

as _____

_____ ,

and consisting of _____

upon the following terms and conditions:

1. **Term:** The term hereof shall commence on _____ 19____, and continue for a period of _____ months thereafter.

2. **Rent:** Rent shall be $_____ per month, payable in advance, upon the _____ day of each calendar month to Owner or his/her author-ized agent, at the following address: _____

_____, or at such other places as may be designated by Owner from time to time. In the event rent is not paid within five (5) days after due date, Tenant agrees to pay a late charge of $_____ plus interest at _____ percent per year on the delin-quent amount. Tenant further agrees to pay $_____ for each dishon-ored bank check.

## Sample Residential Lease with Option to Purchase (continued)

3. **Utilites:** Tenant shall be responsible for the payment of all utilities and services, except _____ , which shall be paid by Owner.

4. **Use:** The premises shall be used as a residence with no more than_____ adults and _____ children, and for no other purpose, without the written prior consent of Owner.

5. **Pets:** No pets shall be brought on the premises without the prior consent of Owner.

6. **Ordinances and Statutes:** Tenant shall comply with all statutes, ordinances and requirements of all municipal, state and federal authorities now in force, or which may hereafter be in force, pertaining to the use of the premises.

7. **Assignment and Subletting:** Tenant shall not assign this agreement or sublet any portion of the premises without prior written consent of the Owner which may not be unreasonably withheld.

8. **Maintenance, Repairs, or Alterations:** Tenant acknowledges that the premises are in good order and repair, unless otherwise indicated herein. Owner may at any time give Tenant a written inventory of furniture and furnishings on the premises and Tenant shall be deemed to have possession of all said furniture and furnishings in good condition and repair, unless he/she objects thereto in writing within five (5) days after receipt of such inventory. Tenant shall, at his/her own expense, and at all times, maintain the premises in a clean and sanitary manner, including all equipment, appliances, furniture and furnishings therein, and shall surrender the same, at termination hereof, in as good condition as received, normal wear and tear excepted. Tenant shall be responsible for damages caused by his/her negligence and that of his/her family or invitees and guests. Tenant shall not paint, paper or otherwise decorate or make alterations to the premises without the prior written consent of Owner. Tenant shall irrigate and maintain any surrounding grounds, including lawns and shrubbery, and keep the same clear of rubbish or weeds, if such grounds are a part of the premises and are exclusively for the use of Tenant.

9. **Entry and Inspection:** Tenant shall permit Owner or Owner's agents to enter the premises at reasonable times and upon reasonable notice for the purpose of making necessary or convenient repairs, or to show the premises to prospective tenants, purchasers, or mortgagees.

10. **Indemnification:** Owner shall not be liable for any damage or injury to Tenant, or any other person, or to any property, occurring on the premises or any part thereof, or in common areas thereof, unless such damage is the proximate result of the negligence or unlawful act of Owner, his/her agents or his/her employees. Tenant agrees to hold Owner harmless from any claims for damages, no matter how caused, except for injury or damages for which Owner is legally responsible.

11. **Physical Possession:** If Owner is unable to deliver possession of the premises at the commencement hereof, Owner shall not be liable for any damage caused thereby, nor shall this agreement be void or voidable, but Tenant shall not be liable for any rent until possession is delivered. Tenant may terminate this agreement if possession is not delivered within _____ days of the commencement of the term hereof.

12. **Default:** If Tenant shall fail to pay rent when due, or perform any term hereof, after not less than three (3) days' written notice of such default given in the manner required by law, Owner, at his/her option, may terminate all rights of Tenant hereunder, unless Tenant, within said time, shall cure such default. If Tenant abandons or vacates the property, while in default of the payment of rent, Owner may consider any property left on the premises to be abandoned and may dispose of the same in any manner allowed by law. In the event Owner reasonably believes that such abandoned property has no value, it may be discarded. All property on the premises is hereby subject to a lien in favor of Owner for the payment of all sums due hereunder, to the maximum extent allowed by law.

In the event of a default by Tenant, Owner may elect to (a) continue the lease in effect and enforce all his/her rights and remedies hereunder, including the right to recover the rent as it becomes due, or (b) at any time, terminate all of Tenant's rights hereunder and recover from Tenant all damages he/she may incur by reason of the breach of the lease, including the cost of recovering the premises, and including the worth at the time of such termination, or at the time of an award if suit be instituted to enforce this provision, of the amount by which the unpaid rent for the balance of the term exceeds the amount of such rental loss which the Tenant proves could be reasonably avoided.

13. **Security:** The security deposit set forth above, if any, shall secure the per-

formance of Tenant's obligations hereunder. Owner may, but shall not be obligated to, apply all portions of said deposit on account of Tenant's obligations hereunder. Any balance remaining upon termination shall be returned to Tenant.

**14. Deposit Refunds:** The balance of all deposits shall be refunded within two weeks from date possession is delivered to Owner or his/her authorized agent, together with a statement showing any charges made against such deposits by Owner.

**15. Attorney's Fees:** In any legal action brought by either party to enforce the terms hereof or relating to the demised premises, the prevailing party shall be entitled to all costs incurred in connection with such action, including a reasonable attorney's fee.

**16. Waivers:** No failure of Owner to enforce any term hereof shall be deemed a waiver, nor shall any acceptance of a partial payment of rent be deemed a waiver of Owner's right to the full amount thereof.

**17. Notices:** Any notice that either party may give or is required to give, may be given by mailing the same, postage prepaid, to Tenant at the premises or to Owner at the address shown below or at such other places as may be designated by the parties from time to time.

**18. Heirs, Assigns, Successors:** This lease is binding upon and inures to the benefit of the heirs, assigns and successors in interest to the parties.

**19. Time:** Time is of the essence of this agreement.

**20. Holding Over:** Any holding-over after expiration hereof, with the consent of Owner, shall be construed as a month-to-month tenancy in accordance with the terms hereof, as applicable. No such holding-over or extension of this lease shall extend the time for the exercise of the option unless agreed upon in writing by Owner.

**21. Pest Control Inspection:** The main building and all attached structures are to be inspected by a licensed structural pest control operator prior to delivery of physical possession, Owner is to pay (1) for elimination of infestation and/or infection of wood-destroying pests or organisms; (2) for repair of damage caused by such infestation and/or infection or by excessive moisture; (3) for correction of conditions which caused said damage; and (4) for repair of plumbing and other leaks affecting wood members, including repair of leaking stall showers , in accordance with said structural pest control operator's report.

Owner shall not be responsible for any work recommended to correct conditions usually deemed likely to lead to infestation or infection of wood-destroying pests or organisms, but where no evidence of active infestation is found with respect to such conditions.

If the inspecting structural pest control operator shall recommend further inspection of inaccessible areas, Tenant may require that said areas be inspected. If any infestation or infection shall be discovered by such inspection, the additional required work shall be paid by Owner. If no such infestation or infection is discovered, the additional cost of inspection of such inaccessible areas shall be paid by Tenant.

As soon as the same are available, copies of the report and any certification or other proof of completion of the work shall be delivered to the agents of Tenant and Owner who are authorized to receive the same on behalf of their principals.

Funds for work to be done at Owner's expense shall be held in escrow and disbursed by escrow holder to a licensed structural pest control operator upon receipt of Notice of Work Completed, certifying that the property is free of infestation or infection.

22. **Option:** So long as Tenant is not in substantial default in the performance of any term of this lease, Tenant shall have the option to purchase the real property described herein for a **Purchase Price** of $_____

(_____ dollars), upon the following

**Terms and Conditions:** _____

_____

_____

_____

_____.

23. **Disclaimer:** The parties acknowledge that speculation of availability of financing, purchase costs and lender's prepayment penalties is impossible. Therefore, the parties agree that these items shall not be conditions of performance of this agreement and the parties agree they have not relied upon any other representations or warranties by brokers, sellers or other parties.

24. **Fixtures:** All improvements, fixtures, attached floor coverings, draperies

including hardware, shades, blinds, window and door screens, storm sashes, combination doors, awnings, outdoor plants, potted or otherwise, trees, and items permanently attached to the real property shall be included, free of liens, unless specifically excluded.

**25. Personal Property:** The following personal property, on the premises when inspected by Tenant, shall be included in the purchase price and shall be transferred by a Warranty Bill of Sale at close of escrow.

**26. Encumbrances:** In addition to any encumbrances referred to above, Tenant shall take title to the property subject to (1) real estate taxes not yet due and (2) covenants, conditions, restrictions, reservations, rights, rights of way and easements of record, if any, that do not materially affect the value or intended use of the property.

The amount of any bond or assessment which is a lien shall be _____ paid, _____ assumed by _____.

**27. Examination of Title:** Fifteen (15) days from date of exercise of this option are allowed the Tenant to examine the title to the property and to report in writing any valid objections thereto. Any exceptions to the title which would be disclosed by examination of the records shall be deemed to have been accepted unless reported in writing within said 15 days. If Tenant objects to any exceptions to the title, Owner shall use all due diligence to remove such exceptions at his own expense within 60 days thereafter. But if such exceptions cannot be removed within 60 days allowed, all rights and obligations hereunder may, at the election of Tenant, terminate and end, unless he/she elects to purchase the property subject to such exceptions.

**28. Evidence of Title:** Evidence of Title shall be in the form of _____ a policy of _____ title insurance, _____ other: _____ _____, be paid for by _____.

**29. Closing Costs:** Escrow fees, if any, and other closing costs shall be paid in accordance with local custom, except as otherwise provided herein.

**30. Close of Escrow:** Within _____ days from exercise of the option, or upon removal of any exceptions to the title by Owner, as provided above, whichever is later, both parties shall deposit with an authorized escrow holder, to be selected by Tenant, all funds and instruments necessary to complete the sale in accordance with the terms and conditions hereof. The representations and warranties herein shall not be terminated by conveyance of the property.

**31. Prorations:** Rent taxes, premiums on insurance acceptable to Tenant, interest and other expenses of the property are to be prorated as of recordation of deed. Security deposits, advance rentals or considerations involving future lease credits shall be credited to Tenant.

**32. Expiration of Option:** This option may be exercised at any time after _____, 19____, and shall expire at midnight, _____,19____, unless exercised prior thereto. Upon expiration Owner shall be released from all obligations hereunder and all of Tenant's rights hereunder, legal or equitable, shall cease.

**33. Exercise of Option:** The option shall be exercised by mailing or delivering written notice to Owner prior to the expiration of this option and by an additional payment, on account of the purchase price, in the amount of $_____ (_____ dollars) for account of Owner to the authorized escrow holder referred to above, prior to the expiration of this option.

Notice, if mailed, shall be by certified mail, postage prepaid, to Owner at the address set forth below, and shall be deemed to have been given upon the day following the day shown on the postmark of the envelope in which such notice is mailed.

In the event the option is exercised, the consideration paid for the option and _____ percent from the rent paid hereunder prior to the exercise of the option shall be credited upon the purchase price.

The undersigned Tenant hereby acknowledges receipt of a copy hereof.

Dated: _____ Time: _____

_____ _____ Tenant's Broker

By: _____ Agent

Broker's Initials _____ Dated: _____

_____ Address and Phone

_____ Name of Tenant

_____ Signature of Tenant

_____ Address and Phone

### Acceptance

The undersigned Owner accepts the foregoing offer.

**Brokerage Fee.** Upon execution hereof the Owner agrees to pay to _____ , the Agent in this transaction, _____ percent of the option consideration for securing said option plus the sum of $_____ (_____ dollars) for securing said option plus the sum of $_____ (_____ dollars) for leasing services rendered and authorizes Agent to deduct said sum from deposit received from Tenant. In the event the option is exercised, the Owner agrees to pay Agent the additional sum of $_____ (_____ dollars). This agreement shall not limit the rights of Agent provided for in any listing or other agreement which may be in effect between Owner and Agent. In the event legal action is instituted to collect this fee, or any portion thereof, the Owner agrees to pay the Agent a reasonable attorney's fee and all costs in connection with such action.

The undersigned Owner hereby acknowledges receipt of a copy hereof.

Dated: _____ Time: _____

_____ Owner's Broker

By: _____ Agent

_____ Name of Owner

_____ Signature of Owner

[Adapted from Professional Publishing Corp. Form 105. Used with permission.]

## EQUITY SHARING

☐   ☐   ☐

**A**nother type of financial arrangement that you can make with the buyer is called a shared equity or participation mortgage. The buyer gives up a portion of the profit (to you or to an investor) when he sells the house in exchange for a lower interest rate during the time he occupies the house as the "owner." This kind of arrangement is complicated and you should have both an accountant and an attorney go over all the papers before you sign them. In *How to Buy Your Own Home in 90 Days* I included a complete copy of a sample equity sharing agreement. It starts on page 197 and goes on to page 219, a little heavy reading, but the basics go like this:

You have a home that you want to sell and someone wants to buy. The buyer can't put up a dime for a down payment, but can produce the monthly payments. With equity sharing you establish a sales price and sign an agreement with your potential buyer; the buyer/tenant moves in and assumes the monthly payments while maintaining the property. After a set period of time (five years is average) the home is put up for sale. The buyer/tenant who lives in the home has the first right to buy the home at your pre–agreed-upon price, or, the home is sold to someone else. At closing, you and the potential buyer who has been living in the home divide the difference evenly between the sales price you established at the beginning of the equity sharing agreement and the actual sales price less expenses of sale.

These types of arrangements are becoming very popular, especially in depressed areas that have a chance of rebounding in a year or two. You can also arrange to sell your house right off the top to an investor who will equity share with one of your potential buyers who doesn't have a down payment.

# EQUITY SHARING

**Today:**

Establish sales price today $100,000
Tenant pays the entire payment,
and maintains the property.

**Five Years from Now:**

$125,000 sales price

$100,000 established sales price

Each equity share partner gets half of the appreciation,
less any expenses.

$125,000

$100,000

Sales Price
Then

Established
Sales Price

## SELLING TO PARTNERSHIPS

☐ ☐ ☐

You can also suggest to prospective buyers, especially young ones who haven't much down payment money, that they have a buying partner. In such a partnership, one partner puts up the money for the down payment and the other occupies the house, takes care of it, and makes the monthly mortgage payments for a specified length of time. At the end of the time agreed upon, the house is sold and the profit from the sale split equally between the partners. The advantage to the partner putting up the money is the return on the investment without having to make mortgage payments or be responsible for property. Meanwhile the live-in partner gets the opportunity to acquire enough money from the profits of the sale to get into a house on his own later. A further advantage for the live-in partner is that he is building his credit rating as he makes the monthly payments on the mortgage, which will also help when he is ready to buy a home of his own. Parents, grandparents, and even unrelated investors can be partners in this kind of purchase.

## SELLING WITH A BALLOON

☐ ☐ ☐

Yet another financing technique is for the seller to take a small down payment and carry a note on the balance, one that will come due in, say, five years. In the interim, the interest on the balance due can be paid to the seller, providing some income along the way. At the agreed-upon date, the balance of the equity is paid to the seller in one lump-sum payment known as a "balloon" payment. In structuring a deal like this you must be very careful that the buyer will be able to meet the balloon payment at the appropriate time or you may end up with a house on

# BALLOON SALE

**At the sale:**

$100,000 sales price

$1,000 down

$19,000 taken back as a balloon at 12 percent interest
due in five years

Assume $80,000 first mortgage

$100,000    Sales Price

$1,000    Down

$19,000    Balloon

$80,000    First

**Five years later:**

$33,484.49 due
($19,000 at 12 percent interest compounded for five years)

$33,484.49    $ Due

your hands that you do not want. You could, however, restructure the note at the time of its due date if the buyer can't pay the whole amount and set up monthly payments until the balance is paid. It is difficult for most people to meet balloon payments, but some are under circumstances that would make such a financing arrangement possible. If the buyers have proceeds from a sale coming due, if they are in a professional situation where their income is likely to increase substantially, or if any number of other fairly reliable circumstances exist (such as bonds maturing), then it would be fine to make such a sale, if you can wait for your money.

These are some time-tested ways to finance the sale of your home. They will increase the number of potential buyers by allowing them flexibility to finance in a way that is most suited to their circumstances. Give some careful thought to your own financial situation and choose at least three ways that are acceptable to you. Be ready to offer these to potential buyers. Then, if you find someone who is really interested in buying your home or property, you can tailor the sale to his needs and stand a much better chance of succeeding with the sale.

Of course, now you are saying that seller financing sounds intimidating and risky. What if the buyer defaults? In such a case you have the same option as any other lender—foreclose and take the house back. If you ever have to foreclose (and the cases of foreclosure with seller financing are rare), then you can sell the house again—often for a higher price than the first time. I always recommend getting the largest down payment possible so that in case you have to foreclose, you've already made some money. It's more complicated than that, and I would hope never to foreclose, but if seller financing is necessary to close a deal then it's a worthwhile risk.

Knowing what financing options you can offer potential buyers coupled with a realistic sales price makes it much more likely that you will be able to sell your home or property in ninety days. If you address the sale of your home or property as a business deal, you will be able to achieve the proper objectivity and the right attitude. Selling your home or property really is a business deal. A house is the largest single invest-ment that most people will make in their lifetimes. You naturally want to protect that investment when it becomes necessary or desirable to make a sale.

# P A R T   T W O

# FOR SALE BY OWNER

☐   ☐   ☐

## SELLING YOUR HOME OR PROPERTY
## ON YOUR OWN

☐    ☐    ☐

*One ship drives east and another west,*
*While the self-same breezes blow,*
*'Tis the set of the sail and not the gale,*
*That bids them where they go.*

This section of the book is for those people who have decided to try to sell their homes or properties by themselves, those who are willing and able to put in some time and effort in order to keep the $3,000 to $30,000 real estate agent's commission in their own pockets. You must understand that saving that sales commission is going to take work, but with this book in your hands you can become an active and well-informed participant in the sale of your home.

Selling your home on your own can be a rewarding and exciting experience. Years ago, when my wife and I purchased our first home, we spent hundreds of hours fixing it up and making everything just right. Our plan was to sell our home and use the profit from the sale to purchase a similar one. Why move into a similar home? We wanted to use the profit from our first home's sale to lower the monthly mortgage payment on our second home. With a lower payment we would be better able to support our family and to finance my dream of going to college at night.

Well, that was our plan. Like thousands of other Americans we didn't know how to sell a home, so we called a real estate agent. He dazzled us with market comparisons and fancy footwork, leaving fifteen minutes later with a signed listing to sell our home. That was the last we saw of him for the entire ninety days of the listing period, during which time no one toured our home, no one made an offer, no one even came by to see it. Like clockwork, on the day the listing expired the agent came by to explain the lack of response on the part of potential buyers—he informed us that we had listed our home at too high a price and that people just weren't buying in that price range. He wanted us to list again with him, but this time for six months at a greatly reduced price. We were a little surprised because we had assumed that an initial listing with a real estate agent was all that was necessary to sell our home. We sat there in silence for a moment thinking about his request. Our dreams for a different home and a smaller mortgage, not to mention our children and the college education, began to fade.

Before we signed the new listing contract I asked him, by chance, to tell us what he had done in the last three months to sell our home. I wanted to know whom he had talked to, how and where he had advertised, and what, if anything, would be different in the next six months. In other words, I wanted him to reassure me that he would really try to sell the home this time. When he wouldn't look into my eyes, I started to get a hint of where he was coming from. When he told me if we went low enough with the price he would consider buying it himself, I became convinced that we didn't need him. It was like a plot from a TV soap. In the years since that day, my wife and I have learned a lot. We've worked with dozens of real estate agents and been personally involved in hundreds of real estate purchases. But we have yet to sell one property through a real estate agent. This isn't to say that we haven't tried, but we keep running into agents who are high on talk and low on action. There are many great real estate agents who would give everything they have to make a customer happy, but I just haven't had a successful selling experience with one yet.

I ended the relationship with my first "agent" by escorting him to the door with his listing form unsigned. My wife and I boldly decided that we were going to sell this home ourselves and save the commission.

But by the next day I wasn't so sure. I didn't know where to start. Motivated by not wanting to be shown up by that agent, who kept calling us back, my wife and I persevered. We went through a self-study crash course on just what it takes to sell a home. Our graduation ceremony came the next month, when we sold our home to a beautiful young family with three children for the full price and the terms that we wanted.

We celebrated that night with a great dinner at our favorite restaurant. We did our best to spend every cent of the commission that we saved, but when we went to bed, we still had an extra $4,000. We invested that saved commission money (along with our normal profit on the sale) by lowering the payment for our next home and buying a piano for the family and some furniture.

At the end of that process of selling our home by ourselves, I was shocked at how easy it had been. We not only made a lot of money (how long does it take you to bank $4,000?—that's bank, not earn) but we also had a great feeling of accomplishment. The objective of this book is to help you have that same feeling, and to increase your profit regardless of whether you decide to sell through a real estate agent or on your own.

As in anything else, success in selling your own real estate comes through action (you're already reading this book), information (that's what I've been gathering for you during the past decade since I sold my first home), and commitment (that's up to you). I know homeowners in some of the nation's worst markets who have sold their homes in three hours. I have a friend in Columbus, Ohio, who, even during the slowest periods of the last decade, has maintained a successful business buying and selling a minimum of three homes a month. How? He uses the tools listed in the next few steps. I also know people in some of the nation's hottest markets who have been trying to sell their homes for the past six months. What's the difference? Not magic or luck; the people who sold their homes used common sense and the expertise that comes from experience—available to you in the steps I have worked out over the years I've spent buying and selling real estate.

The people who are still trying to sell their homes are the ones who are trying to reinvent the wheel themselves. They refuse to use the informed advice of those who have been successful in the real estate market, thinking that it is so easy to sell a home that they can do it without learning from the experience or knowledge of other people.

In Part III we'll talk about how to sell through a real estate professional. But, if you have completed steps 1, 2, 3, and 4 in Part I, I ask you to try your hand at selling your home yourself for at least two months. It's a gamble that may pay off with a $3,000 to $30,000 return for just a few hours of effort on your part. Time is money, and by investing your time to sell your home on your own you will be the one who gets the money in exchange.

Have confidence in yourself as you begin Part II. As you read through these pages, you will be gaining the knowledge you need. Anyone can follow these steps if he or she is willing to make a reasonable effort. The purpose of Step 5 is to strengthen your resolve to sell your home on your own. One of the subscribers to *The Real Estate Advisor* (the nation's leading real estate investment newsletter) recently wrote to me about his own experiences in investing. He was most proud of the fact that in forty years as an investor he has never used a real estate agent once to sell one of his properties. He described a recent transaction in which he had bought a home in a certain neighborhood because a local minister had given him the names of four different people who wanted to buy a home in the area. After he bought the property, he immediately fixed it up, did steps one through four, and invited all four of the couples and individuals over at the same time. Two made offers that day.

A few hours' worth of work on each house he has bought and sold during the past few years has netted him over a quarter of a million dollars in additional profit by saving the real estate commissions.

Even if you decide right away to use a real estate agent, read through Part II so you can have a clear idea of what it takes to market a property. That way you can monitor what the real estate agent is doing, and if he is not taking the necessary steps to sell your home in a reasonable amount of time, you can find a new agent.

□   □   □

## ADVERTISING

☐   ☐   ☐

*Without advertising, a terrible thing happens—nothing.*

If you prepared a small garden patch in your backyard, planted a few seeds from the local nursery in some neat rows, and didn't do one thing more for the next three months, what kind of harvest could you expect? Would you get a bountiful harvest of red, ripe tomatoes, and juicy cucumbers? Or would you have a water-starved weed patch with just a few pathetic vegetables? This law of the harvest applies equally to anything in life in which you expect a return, including selling a home. If you just put a FOR SALE BY OWNER sign out front and leave it to sell your home by itself, your return or harvest may be frustrating and pathetic rather than bountiful. After you have completed Part I of this book, your house should be in good repair, you should have determined a fair sales price, and you should have some specific financing options in mind. You are ready now to learn what else you must do in order to sell your home or property yourself, to get the kind of harvest that those who make the effort and prepare and cultivate a project carefully are entitled to have.

As you'll see, advertising and marketing your home for sale goes far beyond just putting a sign out front. Advertising and marketing can be a really fun part of the home or property selling process. It gives you an opportunity to be creative. It gives you the chance to step back and look at your house with new eyes and decide what its best features are and how you can convey those benefits to your potential buyers.

### Advertising Step 1: Curb Appeal

I have to repeat what we mentioned in Part I, Step 2. The outside appearance of your property is your greatest advertisement. Nice words and eye-catching expressions that give an instantly favorable impression to the readers and potential buyers are worthless if, when they drive by the property, they can see nothing that has even a vague resemblance to the "Cute starter home, needs some fix up" that they read about in the ad. To sell a home you have to get the potential buyers inside. If the property does not have curb appeal, they won't even stop. You'll find yourself sitting around inside waiting for somebody to come to the door when, unfortunately, they drove on by because the curb appeal or outside appearance of your property turned them off. When your ad doesn't match your property, the potential buyers feel cheated.

The best advertising dollars you can spend are for fixing up the curb appeal of your house or property. Put new plants in the flower beds, get rid of the weeds, trim the bushes or hedges, repaint the shutters and the front door, even clean out the gutter in front of your house if it needs it. Don't overlook the little things. The little things tell potential buyers that your home received not only adequate care, but excellent care. What's the difference? A mowed and watered lawn is adequately cared for, but an excellent lawn has also been edged, weeded, and fertilized (all inexpensive chores). An adequate exterior has an even coat of paint, but an excellent exterior sports a foundation that has been hosed off, trim that is nailed securely down, and a gate that doesn't sag. Wouldn't you pay more for a house that has received excellent care? These kinds of repairs usually cost little or nothing and shouldn't take more than an afternoon or two. While you are fixing up your own place you may even want to encourage your neighbors to do a little cleanup in their yards (tactfully, of course). You get only one chance to make a first impression; do everything you can to see that the first impression potential buyers have of your home is a favorable one.

### Advertising Step 2: The Yard Sign

People seem to believe that the majority of prospective buyers find their new homes by purchasing a newspaper, seeing an advertisement that draws their interest, calling the agent, and walking through the home. Wrong! Most people buy their homes by targeting a neighborhood, seeing a FOR SALE sign in the front yard of a home that looks attractive to them, calling for an appointment, and then walking through the home. Whether they are calling an agent who has listed a property for the appointment, or an individual homeowner with a home for sale, the yard sign is the key.

So your second most important investment, once your home and yard are in shape, will be a yard sign. You don't need a fancy, expensive one. But you do need one that is done right. A sign that is professionally painted tells the buyer that you are serious about selling your home.

What should the sign say? Where should it be placed? What color should it be? These are all good questions and you will find the answers by reading through the following list of hints.

*Size.* Your sign should be exactly the size of the largest residential yard sign used by brokers in your area. To find out the exact dimensions, stop and measure a few. Have your sign constructed to match these measurements; this way you won't be violating any local laws and your sign will be as large as the competition's.

*Two-Sided.* Your sign should be painted on both sides and placed in your yard where it will be visible from both ends of the street. Instead of having the sign face directly out to the street, it should face both directions of automobile traffic, like a billboard on a street.

*Color.* The background should be white. The lettering should be bright and stand out. I suggest red lettering because experience has shown me that it is a good color to attract attention, which is what you want it to do.

*Straight and Tall.* Make sure to place your sign firmly in the ground. A leaning sign will not help you sell your property. A tumbledown sign will advertise a tumbledown house, whether or not your house is actually in disrepair. Sloppiness turns people off. A sign that can't be read easily is worse than no sign at all. Check on the sign at regular intervals to make sure it is looking good.

*Wording.* The words **FOR SALE** should be boldly displayed. If you have any special features, these should also be prominent. The sign should give basic information and tell the buyer how many bedrooms, baths, etc., the home has. You may also want to list financing options if they are attractive. Choose your words carefully so that the sign tells the important selling features of the home and the words are still large enough to be readable.

# For Sale
# By Owner

5 bdrm, 2 bth, Dining Room
Pool

# 225-8777

Shown By Appointment

# For Sale

## Assumable Loan
2 bdrm, 1 bth, 2 Car Garage
Dining Room
One Year Home Warranty

# 225-8777

## Shown By Appointment

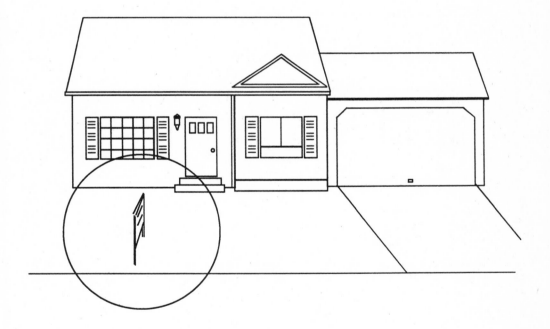

Your sign can be made by any local sign company, or, if you're talented with wood and a budding artist, you could do it yourself. But remember that it must look professional. Think how many fifty-cent FOR SALE BY OWNER signs you have seen stuck up in a window. They probably were soon replaced by real estate brokerage signs out in front of the house. The fact is, most people don't want to deal with sellers who appear cheap, unprofessional, or don't seem to know what they are doing. Your yard sign reflects the seriousness of your desire to sell your home.

### Advertising Step 3: Fliers

Of the thousands of homes that may be for sale in your community why should someone buy yours? Obviously it's because your house has some benefit or appeal for the interested party that puts it ahead of your competition. The reason for advertising a home is to let the maximum number of potential buyers know about the benefits of your property. It is also to save your and the potential buyer's time. A properly prepared flier can help with that.

If you think about it, whenever you go shopping for anything major —from a car stereo system to a washing machine—the salesperson will give you an armful of brochures. The object is to save everyone time, to let the potential buyer know the product's individual benefits, to keep the picture and information about the product in front of him, and to give him a feeling of possession. When putting together a flier about your property for sale, the same points should be kept in mind. Acquaint the prospective buyer with your home; aim at getting the buyer to think of your home as his. Pay attention to the following ideas when putting together a flier:

   a. *Size.* A good, standard size is $8^1/_2 \times 11$ inches: the size of a sheet of typing paper.

b. *Picture.* The picture of your property should be in the upper third of the sheet. As the saying goes, a picture's worth a thousand words. Your picture should be a good quality, high contrast black and white photo, preferably taken during the spring without a car parked in front of the front lawn. If you want a photo that can really reproduce well when copied, you will need what is called a halftone. A halftone takes your picture and breaks it down into little dots. There are more dots where the photo is darker, and fewer where it is lighter. You can turn a black and white photo into a halftone for two dollars; just call any copy shop (the one where you are getting your fliers reproduced should do nicely) and ask how much it costs for one halftone. There are Polaroid cameras that actually produce halftones immediately, but they cost a bundle.

c. *Wording.* The second third of the flier should be a brief description of your property. You should include items such as the number of square feet, bedrooms, baths, kitchen/appliance information, patio, swimming pool, and information about any recent repair or improvement that you've completed. A new roof or a remodeled kitchen are good selling points.

d. *Focus.* The last third of the flier should include the most important information in bold lettering: your name, telephone number, address of the property, and sales price. You might want to put, not only on your yard sign, but also on your flier, the words "shown by appointment." Nothing can be more frustrating than having people knocking on your door at all hours unannounced to tour your home. Appointments to show the home or property should be scheduled reasonably by you and not just happen at someone's whim.

Consider including the words "one-year home warranty." Call one of your local real estate firms and ask them who handles their home owner warranty insurance. Then give that firm a call. The insurance company will have a representative come see your home and give you a quote on insuring it with a one-year home warranty policy for the new buyer.

Home warranties protect buyers from having to bear the costs of repairing breakdowns of built-in appliances and home systems after the closing, which is the final step in the purchase process that transfers legal ownership to the buyer. Warranties can also give you peace of mind. If a major built-in appliance breaks down, you won't have to deal with an angry buyer. This problem can be even more serious if you are providing financing for the buyer (i.e., wraparound mortgage).

After having bought and sold a couple of homes, I had begun to think that I was pretty hot stuff and I knew it all. Thinking back, I wonder what it really was that I knew. There was one particular home that I should have used a home warranty on. My decision to buy this house, an investment with several friends, was based on a combination of excitement and group pressure. What I found out during the next few weeks was the truth of Murphy's law: if it can go wrong, it will. The stove broke. The roof leaked. The refrigerator quit. Need I go on? At each new discovery our profit went down. In fact, so much went wrong that we were lucky to get out of that house without having to sell one of my kids! My lesson was learned. Proper inspection and proper insurance before buying or selling.

Most warranties cover major built-in appliances and structural defects for twelve months. If other appliances, plumbing, and wiring are covered, they are also under warranty for one year. After that, structural defects are about all that's covered.

You may want to look at other warranties in force. For example, are your furnace, water heater, etc., still covered by the manufacturer's warranty? Could you agree with a local contractor to make specified repairs for a lower price than providing insurance? Experts in the housing industry say that for new and newer homes 75 percent of the problems are structural defects, resulting from settling. You may also simply wish to add a little extra to the sale price to cover the cost of a warranty when selling your home.

Is a warranty worth it? According to a 1989 survey of real estate professionals by the National Home Warranty Association (NHWA), homes that offer warranties sell 60 percent faster and for an average $2,200 more than homes that don't offer warranties.

That one year, real estate professionals and consumers purchased 410,000 home warranties. Member companies paid $38 million in claims in 1988, the latest year for which a figure is available, a 5 percent increase over 1987.

The average cost of a home warranty is $325, with some companies also charging a deductible. The warranty covers major housing systems (plumbing, electrical, built-in appliances, heating, etc.) for one year and is renewable.

For more information on how to purchase a home warranty write to:

NATIONAL HOME WARRANTY ASSOCIATION
c/o HOMEOWNERS MARKETING SERVICES, INC.
P.O. Box 9200
HOLLYWOOD, FL 33084

Home owner warranty insurance could be a benefit to the buyer that just might set your property apart from the competition.

Another thing to consider when putting your flier together is that it should be a marketing tool which motivates someone to call, but should never indicate that you are in a panic situation. Words like "Kick me, I'm down" will attract only time wasters or people who would not qualify for a loan. Even if you must sell because of an immediate job change or a family crisis, I wouldn't put that in the ad.

e. *Printing/Color.* Your flier can be inexpensively typeset on a home computer, or through a local quick copy shop. When you reproduce them in quantity, you'll be able to get fliers done for just pennies apiece. The color of the flier should catch the eye, but not make the copy hard to read. I suggest that you stay away from plain white. Not only is it boring, but it just doesn't stand out. It seems that the best responses come from goldenrod, light green, and tan. These colors give a feeling of warmth. For ink I would stick with black.

**f.** *Distribution.* You should first post your fliers on the bulletin boards in local grocery stores, convenience stores, gas stations, community centers, and civic centers. Next, deliver them to bulletin boards and employment offices in local manufacturing and service companies. Lastly, consider delivering your fliers personally to all your neighbors and friends. Quite often homes are sold to friends of neighbors who hear about the property being for sale by word of mouth.

When putting out fliers door to door you want to make sure that you employ someone who is reliable. One friend of mine hired neighborhood kids to distribute his fliers and was surprised when he didn't receive one inquiry. A few days later he got a call from the local police wondering why he had dumped all those fliers in a nearby ditch.

Consider distribution to local churches. A lot of people check with their religious leaders in the area where they want to move. Also try using a brochure box or tube. This is a small mailbox nailed on a metal stake or attached to your yard sign. You could put a supply of your fliers in this brochure box with a sign attached that says, "Free, take one."

In other words, leave no stone unturned and no public contact point unstocked with your brochures. It's true that it takes only one buyer to sell your house, but finding that one buyer is the challenge. Give yourself every possible opportunity to reach him or her by being thorough and inventive in finding ways to get your brochures into the hands of potential buyers.

# For Sale By Owner
## New On The Market

- 1,800 Square Feet
- 3 Bedrooms
- 1 and 1/2 Baths
- Full Landscaping
- Triple Pane Windows
- Air Conditioning

- Fenced Yard
- Levelor Blinds
- Auto Garage Door
- Oak Cabinets
- Sprinkler System
- Fireplace

- Cable
- 2 Car Garage
- Security System
- Garden Area
- Dishwasher
- Dining Room

### ASSUMABLE LOAN
$125,600
Owner Will Carry Second Mortgage
667 Highlander, Placerville
Shown By Appointment
## 225-8777

Marc and DeAnn Garrison

## Advertising Step 4: Newspaper Advertising

As we said earlier, the majority of homes are sold to people who have picked out a specific area of town and have targeted their home buying efforts there. Most major papers divide their sale listings into specific geographic areas, but the advertising rates are very high. Instead of using the major papers, you may want to consider advertising in a low cost local paper that services the area you live in. Potential home buyers will be naturally drawn to these local papers. You can, of course, advertise in the major papers, but don't be shocked when you hear how much running an ad will cost for a basic two-week run. Your budget will help determine where you place your ad, but it shouldn't be the only consideration. Many times the smaller papers yield better results because they are targeted toward people who are interested in the area in which your home is located.

Regardless of where you choose to place your ad, you should pay particular attention to the following tips in ad writing so that someone will read it and respond:

a. *Be brief.* The best ads are short and go right to the point. Grab a copy of the real estate ads from your local paper. You could get eye strain if you tried to read them all. Which ads stand out? Which ads attract you? Most likely not the ones that are two paragraphs long, but the short ones that go right to the point, are full of action words, and start with a strong opening line. Leave them something to call about. An example would be:

---

FOR SALE BY OWNER
3 BDRM, 2BTH, EASTSIDE
$100,000, LOW DOWN
225-8777

---

**b.** *Use action words.* Never mind what grammarians tell you. To my mind, action words are words that produce a reaction and create a desire for action. People buy homes and do things for several basic reasons. They are motivated by love, safety, health, status, and money. The following sample ads and lists of action words correspond to those motivational factors.

## Action Words

**Love Words**
Fresh
Pleasure
Enjoyment
Darling
Cute
Nice
Home sweet home
Your very own
Gratifying

**Safety Words**
Protected
Safe
Secure
Good
Snug

**Health Words**
Clean air
Fresh
Privacy
Gym
Near fitness center
Garden spot
Country air

Near jogging course
Near park

**Status Words**
Luxury
Stately
Opulent
Estate
Mansion
Fashionable
Regal
Lavish
Prestigious
Elegant
Secluded

**Money Words**
Home Owners Warranty
Sale priced
Value
Savings
Benefit
Investment
Advantage
Bargain
Economical
Low down

## Ads That Work

---

By Owner: Like living in the country?
9 1/2% fixed owner financing. $5,000
total move-in. Elegant 3bdrm,
2bth brick home
with fireplace, fenced yard. Low $100s
225-8777

---

Only $105,000 In Country Meadows.
Secluded, cute 2bdrm, 2 bath, 2 story.
By owner.
225-8777 after 5 P.M.

---

First Day of Sale
3bdrm, 2bth, best location
All the extras, $100K, low down
225-8777

---

These ads work because they are clear, to the point, and leave something to the imagination. Let's take a look at the same properties for sale, but advertised in a form that will not work as well.

## Ads That Don't Work

---

House for Sale. Luxury Home.
Darkroom in basement. Wired
for welder in garage. Owner financing
with negotiable down payment
225-8777

---

A little different from the other ads. Notice how narrow the list of features is. As I go through the newspapers, I see this kind of ineffective advertising all the time. People list their "dream features" in ads and disregard the things that most home buyers are really looking for.

---

$105,000 In Country Meadows.
2bdrm, 2 bath, 2 story.
Dishwasher, disposal, air conditioner
Garage door opener, dog house,
new Roof in '71
Not close to any main roads
225-8777

---

Buyers do not get excited about long ads that simply list features. They may even skip over ads like this.

Compare the difference between "secluded" and "not close to any main roads." I've seen that last phrase actually used several times. Do you think it is a sales feature?

Every week there are thousands of examples of real estate ads in your local papers. Your use of action words, a strong opening line that draws attention, and a quick listing of benefits will set your ad apart from the rest.

The real problem with writing ads comes when your property has a negative attribute that you either can't afford to fix or have no control over. You can avoid mentioning such problems in your ads and have the potential buyers drive off in disgust when they see them, or you can prepare the potential buyers with your ad and your telephone conversation to turn such negative things into a positive feature. If you had a property that was run down you could say, "Great savings if you don't mind a little work," or "Fix it up your way and buy at a bargain price." The same idea could apply to neighborhood features. If you lived on an unpaved street, you could call it a "low traffic street."

Two of the previous ads that we used as examples demonstrate this point. One of them described being way out in the country and away from town as being "secluded." The other ad referred to it as being "not close to any main roads." "Secluded" definitely sounds like a benefit, which turns the fact of being "not close to any main roads" into a plus, not a minus.

### Advertising Step 5: For-Sale-by-Owner Magazines

You may want to take a trip down to your local grocery or convenience store to see what type of free magazines they have. In most areas, small advertising tabloids specialize in marketing rentals, student housing, and for-sale-by-owner real estate ads. If you are lucky enough to have one of these magazines in your area, you should consider putting in an ad. Like the local throwaway papers, these magazines target a specific area and a specific type of shopper and the same rules apply for writing the ad. But in this case the magazine may include a picture by a photographer or offer a professional advertisement writer who will help you put your ad together.

In many areas, some of these for-sale-by-owner magazines don't charge you a thing unless you sell your home. How's that for confidence?

In any case, however you choose to advertise, your ads should create an interest, screen potential buyers by providing adequate information, and motivate them to pick up the telephone or drive by so they can find out more.

One final reminder: the most attractive feature of any home is its price. I already warned you that overpricing is the top mistake of any owner attempting to sell a home on his own. It is also a fatal mistake to leave the price (or at least the price range) out of your ads. If you do so, two things will happen:

a. Hurried buyers will skip your ad because they don't know if it is in their price range.

b. Recreational lookers (people who look at homes for fun but are not serious about buying) will call you and waste your time. We will talk about screening them out in the next chapter.

□   □   □

## SCREENING BUYERS ON THE PHONE

☐   ☐   ☐

*Dost thou love life? Then do not squan-*
*der time; for that is the stuff life is made*
*of.*

—Benjamin Franklin

**W**e Americans are much too nice in general to people who call us on the phone. We listen to sales pitches for charities or insurance deals; we listen to our neighbors' problems when we would rather be doing something else. In short, we sometimes allow others to waste our time. Naturally you want to be pleasant to those people who respond to your ads, but you don't want your time taken up by people who are not really potential buyers. As exciting as it can be to have people call in response to your ads, you still must reserve the right to screen them as potential buyers before you invite them to look at your home. One of the keys we put in your yard sign and fliers were the words, "Shown by appointment." *You* call the shots, not your potential buyers.

If the caller wants a four-bedroom rambler home and what you have for sale is a two-story colonial with only three bedrooms, then it is probably a waste of your time to show the house to that particular caller. Likewise, if you need at least $7,500 down and the caller can only come up with $3,000 there is no point in going any further with the discussion. It won't matter how close your home is to the caller's dream house if he can't meet your terms.

In Part I we talked about making your home attractive, establishing a fair market value, and determining realistic financing options. So far in Part II we have talked about the risks and rewards in selling by yourself and how to advertise your home so that you can get some positive response. With all that done, you are 90 percent of the way into the process of selling your home. From now on, it isn't as much *hard* work as *smart* work.

In each of your ads you have prominently displayed your telephone number. Most people will call and make an appointment. You really don't have to worry too much about them knocking on your door unexpectedly, but you need to be prepared for some of the problems that can arise from phone calls.

First, you must decide who is going to answer the phone. If you work during normal office hours and like to sleep at night, there will be a great deal of time when no one is able to answer the phone unless other family members are home during the day. Your spouse can screen the callers using the checklist in this chapter, but you should give your children clear instructions on what to say and how to take phone messages. If they are too young to take messages, you should consider buying or borrowing an answering machine to use while you are selling your property.

**Screening Buyers on the Phone When You're Not There**

Your taped message on the answering machine can tell people more about the home, its benefits, your terms, and when they can see it while you are unable to take the call personally. You could come home to an answering machine with messages and phone numbers from ten people who have heard your recording and would like to set up a time to see the home. If your telephone message is brief, to the point, and specific as to when you will be able to call them back, more callers will leave messages. Here is a sample message:

> *Hello. If you are calling about the house at 318 Oak Lane, here are a few details. The five-bedroom rambler sits on one third of an acre in a quiet, extremely well-kept subdivision. The upstairs features a formal living room, formal dining room, large newly remodeled kitchen, family room, two bedrooms, and three bathrooms. Downstairs is another family room, two bathrooms, and three bedrooms. The large immaculate yard has shade trees that help keep cooling costs low. The home also has an attached, two-car garage and is near, but not too near, golf courses, shopping, and the freeway. It is competitively priced at $135,000. If you would like a personal opportunity to see if this home meets your needs, then please leave your name, telephone number, and date and time of your call. We return all calls promptly.*

It takes about forty-five seconds to listen to this whole message. The size and the price will immediately tell some buyers that this home is too much for them. The phrase "competitively priced" tells callers you are serious about selling.

**Returning and Answering Calls**

One key to using the answering machine successfully in the process of selling your home is to return the calls promptly. Even if you don't use an answering machine and family members take the calls, you should return calls as soon as possible. While you don't wish to appear overeager to sell, you also don't want to appear indifferent. By the way, when you are talking to prospective buyers, never call your home a house. You are not an investor and you shouldn't talk about your property as if you were. Most home buyers calling in response to for-sale-by-owner ads want to feel they are dealing with a homeowner—not a professional real estate person.

### Importance of Screening Out Flakes and Agents

Flakes—those who are just satisfying their curiosity and those who aren't able to buy just now—are a waste of your time and tie up your telephone line when other, genuine potential buyers are trying to call. Find out who they are quickly and don't let them waste your time. Real estate agents who are calling to see if they can list your home are a waste of time for you at this point as well, so don't let them involve you in a lengthy sales pitch or a debate about listing your home with a professional.

To help you spot the time-wasters, use the checklist below to screen all callers. You should fill out a form like this for each person who calls. But never explain the details about your house until the callers give you their names, addresses, and phone numbers. If they object to giving you this information, tell them that you have prepared a flier on the home that you would like to send them. Getting phone numbers will save you from wasting hours talking to real estate agents and people who are not really serious about buying a home. At least 95 percent of all phone calls from people who will not give you that basic information are a waste of time.

You should complete the home sales information section and make several copies to have by each phone. When someone calls with questions about your property for sale, use one of these sheets and fill in the pertinent information about the caller. After you give the information in the sales information area, ask the last two questions and try to set up an appointment for the prospective buyer to come and look at your home. This sounds like Sales 101, doesn't it?

Genuine buyers will usually not waste your time. If it becomes obvious to them as you go down the list that either your home won't fit their needs or your price is out of their league, they will quickly end the conversation. If you sense that the caller is just killing time, you can put an end to the conversation by asking some pertinent questions about his ability to make the right down payment or to qualify for the monthly payments. It is okay for you to end time-waster conversations. They won't help you sell your home, and they may be tying up the line when a genuine potential buyer is trying to call.

By the time you have screened potential buyers on the phone and given them an appointment to come by and see your home, you have come a long way toward finding a buyer. You know that the people who are coming to walk through your home are genuinely interested in the property, and that your home satisfies their basic needs. When they come for their appointments, be ready with fliers that answer the basic questions—with a clean house, kids out of the way, and a smile on your face. Step 8 will give you a more in-depth discussion of how to handle people who come to visit your home with the intent of buying if they like what they see.

Be patient. You are almost through the process of selling your home yourself. You will find the rewards were well worth the time and effort you have put into the project so far. Just keep focusing on the extra thousands of dollars that will end up in your bank account, and the work now won't seem too difficult.

□   □   □

# TELEPHONE QUESTION CHECKLIST

**Potential Buyer Information**

| | |
|---|---|
| Name | |
| Address | |
| City, State, Zip | |
| Phone | |

**Home for Sale Fact Sheet**

| | |
|---|---|
| Price | |
| Bedrooms | |
| Baths | |
| Square Feet | |
| Garage | |
| Storage Space | |
| Interior Features: | |
| Exterior Features: | |
| First Mortgage | |
| **Balance** | % interest rate |
| Second Mortgage | |
| **Balance** | % interest rate |
| Total Monthly Payments | |
| Financing Options | |

**Area Benefits (How many minutes away)**

| | |
|---|---|
| Closest Library | |
| Closest Park | |
| Closest Shopping | |
| Closest Preschools | |
| Closest Elementary | |
| Closest Junior High | |
| Closest High School | |
| Closest College | |

Are there any other questions that I could answer for you?
When would it be convenient for you to come by?

## SHOWING THE HOME

□   □   □

*If it looks good, it is good.*
                    —Old advertising maxim

It's show time! The house is immaculate. Your heart is beating at its maximum aerobic rate and the potential buyers who called for an appointment have just pulled up out front. Now, what do you do?

Here are specific recommendations, a checklist of what to do, where your kids should be, how you should stand, and what you should say when showing someone your home. This step includes the use of the flier that you prepared in Step 6 to give each person who comes to see your home.

1. Make sure that you air the house out at least fifteen minutes prior to showing. Nothing is a quicker turnoff for visitors than bad odors greeting them at the front door. Those doggy odors that have happy associations for you, reassuring you that Homer is safely inside, may affect the potential buyers differently. The lingering odor of pizza or corned beef and cabbage will be a turnoff as well, no matter how satisfying the dinner may actually have been. Cleanliness is the best way to avoid odors. Keep the oven and stove clean, freshen the fridge, keep the laundry pile small. Do whatever you can to enhance the pleasantness of the home for those who come to look at it. A few fresh flowers give the home a pleasant fragrance and a touch of charm that is pleasing to potential buyers. Some other things you can do to freshen up the smell in your house: bake a few loaves of bread—or cookies; boil a pot of potpourri (subtle fragrances such as tangerine or peach), or grind up some orange peels in the disposal. Remember, if it smells good, it is good.

2. Make sure all rooms are warm if it's winter, or cool if it's summer. The period when you are trying to sell your home is not a good time to reduce your heating bill by shutting off the vents in all the bedrooms. You want to give the prospective buyers an impression of comfort inside the home whatever the weather is like outside. Along this same line, be sure that the rooms are well-lit; not necessarily brightly, but effectively to show off the best features. You are demonstrating to the potential buyers that this house is indeed a home, an abode of warmth and graciousness, a desirable place to live.

I remember one house in particular that I had just fixed up. I was debating whether or not it would be worthwhile to go through the hassle of getting the gas turned on to heat the home. Because it was the coldest part of winter, I decided to go down to the gas company to get the gas turned on. That weekend I signed a contract to sell the home. I'm sure that the warmth inside gave the house such a homey feeling compared with the cold outside that it was an important factor in the sale. That next Monday I turned the gas back off. My entire bill was less than $5.00. I can guarantee that selling the home would have taken much longer if it had been cold. The home was clean, neat, warm, and cozy when I let people come and look at it. They could identify with it. They could imagine themselves living there.

3. Just as the potential buyers are pulling up to the curb in front of your house, put a tray of cookie dough (homemade or store-bought) in the oven. Serve the fresh cookies at the kitchen table at the end of the tour. (Make sure to set a timer; you don't want burned cookies.) The odor of baking cookies will be very pleasant, and it will give you the opportunity later to have an informal conversation around the kitchen table, sharing cookies and ideas about your home. This kind of informal conversation is good because it lessens tension and allows for some relaxed give-and-take as you try to agree upon terms for the purchase that both you and the buyer can feel good about. This tip has worked extremely well not only for myself but also for a friend in the Northwest who has bought and sold over thirty-two homes during the past two years. She got started in real estate through my book *Financially Free* and this technique has helped her so that she has never been stuck with a property. Not a bad position to be in.

4. Don't *lead* the prospective buyers through your home, *follow them.* Once the introductions are out of the way, ask what they would like to see first and then point them in the right direction. This should be a lot like welcoming invited guests into your home. Be warm and friendly and avoid the hard

sell. Since you have already done the screening over the telephone, you know that they are probably financially qualified to buy the home. You want to help them feel comfortable and at home so that they will want to buy. Let them go through the house and yard at their own pace. Be prepared to answer their questions fairly as the tour progresses. Don't belabor any faults your home may have but don't try to hide them either. If you have small bedrooms, then admit it. If your fence needs to be fixed, tell them. Let the prospective buyers guide the tour and also the conversation. They will ask about the items that are of interest to them. If they want to see the attic and your termite inspection report, then let them ask.

5. Open the doors to each room or area and then let your visitors step in and look around. Don't breathe down their necks, but stay close enough to answer their questions and point out advantages they may not immediately notice, like the spectacular view of the mountains from your kitchen window. Don't rush them. Let them see that you have nothing to hide and that they are welcome to take a meticulous look at the home before they make a decision. When I sold a home several years ago to a professor at a local college, I just let him look around. As he did, he seemed to be selling himself on the home. When we signed the contract, he commented on how easy it had been to strike a deal and that he had greatly appreciated the fact that I did not pressure him.

6. When sitting at the kitchen table eating cookies after the tour, ask the potential buyers if there are any questions you can answer for them. Listen carefully to what they ask and answer their questions to the best of your knowledge. If they ask how old the home is, who the contracting firm was that built it, what the annual property taxes are, if it is drafty in winter, what the neighbors are like, or what the

crime rate is like in the neighborhood, tell them. Let them ask about schools, spas, supermarkets, and so forth. Much of this information is not in the flier, so patiently answer all their questions.

7. Ask them what they are looking for in a house. Listen to what they say. If they want a family room away from the main level and your house doesn't have one, help them see how easy it would be to convert that unfinished space on the ground floor into the family room of their dreams. One young couple I know had trouble finding the exact house they wanted until they began to think about their wants a little differently. Because of the ages of their children, they were anxious to buy a rambler or similar home that featured three bedrooms on one floor. The husband worked part-time as a writer, so they also wanted an extra room for an office. And finally, they wanted to find a house in a certain price range in a specific area. The problem? All of the houses in their price range in the neighborhood where they wanted to live were split entries—meaning only two bedrooms on one floor. They were beginning to think about abandoning the prospects of living in the neighborhood they had their hearts set on. Then someone suggested that they change their thinking. Why not move the sleeping quarters downstairs in a split entry? Why not turn the family room downstairs into the master bedroom and the master bedroom upstairs into a family room? Then they could have all three bedrooms downstairs and could turn the other upstairs bedroom into an office. The couple began to look at things in a different light and made a bid on a nice split entry that very day. They had been letting the way the houses had been originally designed and used limit their ideas about how they would fit into it. When they began to think of houses as empty shells and imagine how they could

use the space to achieve what they wanted, they were quickly able to find a home that fit their needs.

8. Shut up! Let them do the talking. Don't try to be a brilliant conversationalist or a stand-up comic. Keep quiet and let the prospective buyers talk to you. Buying a home is a serious, if pleasant, business and people who are making the commitment to buy a home want to be taken seriously. They want to ask questions, to know as much as possible about what they are about to buy. Don't get desperate and start making deals. Listen to what they want, what they are concerned about, what they are willing to pay, and how soon they will need to move into the house. This is the toughest part for me still. I don't like silence. Every time I sell a home I have to think twice and bite my tongue when my potential buyers take over the conversation. They're talking about curtains and ruffles; I want to talk about sales price. Selling a home does require patience.

9. Listen intently! Somewhere in all those questions and comments the potential buyers are making while you munch cookies are the terms they will agree to in order to buy your house or property. Pay attention so you know what they are. If they ask about the traffic load on the street because they have preschool-aged children, or a pet dog that has been in the family for years and is now going blind, answer in a way that will calm their fears—unless of course the traffic is horrendous and both their children and the family pet would be in constant danger. If they ask about the neighbors, unless they are drug dealers or really dangerous people, don't air the grievances you have with the Joneses over their barking dog or their teenage son who loves to come home late at night and rev up the motor on his car before shutting it off.

Sometimes the best thing you can do while showing your home is to leave the potential buyers by themselves for a while to discuss the home. Be sure that your valuables are safely put away before the potential buyers arrive; then, when they seem to need some private time, leave them alone. Often they are just trying to be sure they feel the same about the house or they want to be sure they have enough money for the down payment and to repaint the living room to match their new sofa. They may need a few minutes to agree between themselves on the offer they want to make. Don't make them feel too pressured or think you are so desperate to sell that you have to be in there pitching every moment.

Be as tactful and hospitable as you can when you are showing the home. You want the potential buyers to feel at home, too. If at all possible, arrange for the children to be away from home while you are showing it to buyers. No matter how darling your children are, they will probably be a distraction and they may even kill a sale by pointing out some things you would rather not bring up, like the flood that roared down your street last spring when the snow in the mountains melted too fast or the fireplace glass that blew out when you burned the wrapping paper last Christmas.

Several times I've had buyers come over and just rip my properties apart. Room by room they tear up a home verbally. My only answer has been patience, because I know that attacking a property is an arcane tool suggested in some home buying guides. They instruct buyers to knock the owner down so that he will be anxious to sell the property to them. Well, in the real world it doesn't work. Most sellers will throw out such buyers by the time they get done ripping up the first two rooms. I've come to realize that these verbal attacks are just a cheap negotiating technique. Let them complain; if it gets too bad invite them to leave. If they don't like your home, then why are they wasting your time? I would advise you simply to bite your tongue and wait for an offer before deciding whether to throw them out.

You have done your best to get the home ready for showing, you are prepared with different financial arrangements, and your flier covers all the important data. Just relax and enjoy the experience of sharing the pleasantness of your home with the people who come to see if it will be a good home for them, too.

For greatest efficiency when showing your home, keep a fact sheet handy. Include not only the basic information, but also a rough floor plan. And be sure to include your name, telephone number, and address. Not only will people have an easier time remembering your home and the things they like about it, but they may also pass the fact sheet along to family and friends who are also searching for a home.

A last note—be safe. Always have a friend or acquaintance over when prospective buyers tour your home. If possible, let a neighbor know that you're showing your home. Please use caution.

## THE REAL ESTATE CONTRACT

☐    ☐    ☐

*Trust everyone, but cut the cards anyway.*

Don't panic! If you've made it this far, it means that you have someone who's interested in buying your property. It's like having a fish on the line; you've just got to reel it in. Writing offers and arranging contracts scare most people away from selling their home or property themselves, but stay calm and we'll go through how to write an offer with minimum fear and maximum effectiveness. Being able to write the offer is an important step in selling your home or property yourself. As with most things, knowing how makes it easy—or at least possible. Keep reading to see how to handle this very important step in selling your home by yourself.

## WRITING THE OFFER

☐ ☐ ☐

This chapter will describe the hows, whats, and wheres about writing offers, a sample contract form, and all the specific clauses you might need to include when selling a home so your buyer pays as many of the expenses as possible. These clauses include the following: assumption clause, closing cost clause, contract acceptance clause, earnest money clause, escrow clause, financing clause, lease with option to buy clause, property clause, and so on.

Don't be nervous! I know this sounds like a lot to learn and get right, but the fact is that you don't actually have to write the offer yourself. All you need is an escrow officer (in trust deed states) or an abstract company (in mortgage states). If you don't know what type of state your home or property is in, just look in the phone book under escrow companies. Can't find it? Then try abstract companies. That was simple enough, wasn't it?

No matter what state you live in, you don't have to worry about how to complete a real estate contract to write up an offer from a buyer. All you need to do is rough out, at the kitchen table on a scratch pad with your buyer's help and cooperation, these eight basic facts:

1. The address of the property.

2. The purchase price of the property.

3. The down payment amount.

4. How the payments will be made (earnest money and balance of down).

5. The date by which the purchase must be completed.

6. How much money will be held by the escrow company as binder (earnest money).

7. Who pays for what at the closing.
   title insurance/search
   prorated property tax
   closing fees
   fuel in furnace oil tank
   loan fees
   sidewalk assessments
   Etc.

8. The names, addresses, telephone numbers, and signatures of the buyers and sellers.

This information should be taken to your title company or abstract company. The closing officer there will arrange to have the formal purchase agreements drawn up and a closing date established.

Now that you have an idea of the overall process of getting the sales contract written up, let's look at each step in more detail and provide you with some samples of clauses that you may need or want to have included in the final version that everyone signs. First you want to have the legal address of the property as determined by the community in which you live. If your home is situated at 965 Green Street, in Rapid City, South Dakota, that is the address you enter on this rough sales contract. Later, the title (or escrow) company will supply the legal description, which includes the lot number, plot number, etc. All you need for this preliminary step is the ordinary address you give to people who want to mail you something.

The next piece of information to include is the purchase price of the property. This is the amount you and the buyer have agreed on as the total amount you expect to be paid for the home. Use both words and numbers to indicate this amount and be sure they agree with each other.

Write the amount of the purchase price like this: one hundred thousand dollars ($100,000).

The third item to include is how much money the buyer is going to make as a down payment. Again, use both words and numbers to indicate the amount and state exactly how it is to be paid. If the down payment is $15,000, the buyer may agree to pay $10,000 at the time of closing and the other $5,000 in ninety days. Or all of the down payment can be made at the time of closing. How the payment is to be made should be spelled out exactly in terms of both dollar amounts and dates.

You will also want to indicate not only the date but perhaps even the time of day that the purchase must be completed. Time really is money, so you want to be able to get your money out of the sale of your home as quickly as possible. If you have special reasons, such as needing the money for the closing of your next home, then you especially want to be sure the closing date is favorable to you. But don't be too hard-nosed. The buyer has needs also. Perhaps he is waiting for some bonds to mature, or some other predictable source of income to develop. If you can manage it, allow the buyer to leave his bonds to maturity so he will get all of his interest.

Also indicate how much money will be held by the escrow company as a binder (or earnest money). This is the amount of money the buyer puts up to show that he is serious about the deal. The earnest money is applied toward the down payment at the closing.

Let me use an example from my own experience to illustrate an important point about selling a property and having the contract properly written up and the right clauses put in it. Recently I sold a home to a young couple. This was a picture-perfect sale. They put $1,000 down as earnest money to bind the sale. I wrote in an earnest money clause which said that the sale must occur within sixty days: that "time was of the essence" (this phrase makes sixty days legally binding); and that their earnest money was nonrefundable if they defaulted. Sounds great? If everything was so great, why did I specify a time period and write in "time is of the essence"?

Because what I was hoping wouldn't happen actually did. When it came time to close, I was out of state on vacation. I drove with my oldest son about six hundred miles back home to make the closing. When I sat down at the title company to close, the buyers didn't show up. The sale on their home had fallen through and they wanted to wait another two months to close. But who had an empty home, and a monthly payment to make on it? Me, of course. I told them that they could either pay the monthly payment and I'd wait the two months or that I would sell the home to someone else. They didn't want to make the payments and said they wanted their earnest money back. But I had already paid two monthly payments waiting for them to close. The earnest money clause in the contract made it possible for me to keep their deposit to offset my expenses.

The moral of this story is to stay in control. Use the right clauses. I have met people who didn't use the "time is of the essence" clause in their contracts and who've had to wait six months for their sale to go through. Time *is* of the essence; set a specific date by which the closing of escrow must occur. Then add the "time is of the essence" clause. If you just say that the closing will occur by or on December 20, the buyers can take another six months after that if they feel they need to. The "time is of the essence" clause gives you the right to force the closing or keep the earnest money and start selling the home again.

Often the earnest money is forfeited if the buyer fails to adhere to other parts of the deal. One of the clauses the buyer may insist upon is that the sale is contingent on his getting a mortgage or other financing. If he is unable to obtain the financing, the sale is void and the money held as a binder is returned to the unsuccessful buyer. Without such a clause, however, the seller is entitled to keep the binder.

As the seller, you want to get as substantial a binder as you can. The buyer may not think twice about forfeiting $500 to duck out of your deal but will think carefully before giving up $5,000 just because he spots a home that he likes a little better. Once the offer to sell has been agreed upon, you naturally don't keep trying to sell the house. The binder, if forfeited, is your compensation for additional advertising and other expenses you will now incur, as well as any lost opportunities to sell during the period your home was under agreement. You may also want to consider a back-up offer in case their offer falls through.

You also need to decide who will pay which expenses at the closing. A title search will have to be made by a title company; this process ensures that the property is unencumbered by liens or other claims and that the seller owns the property and has the right to sell it. The seller usually pays for this. But practice varies from state to state. Closing costs are the fees that a title officer or closing agent will charge to prepare the documents of transfer and to arrange and file the sale. While the seller typically pays for the title policy and the closing costs are split between buyer and seller, there is no set rule. I have had people I bought properties from pay 100 percent of these expenses. I have also had people to whom I am selling pay 100 percent. Whatever you work out with the buyers needs to be written into the contract.

One of my rules of thumb is that if the sales price is very low, I insist that the buyers agree to pay more of the closing costs. But you must negotiate carefully to avoid killing the deal. It isn't worth losing the sale to save $100 at the time of closing. Other items that may need to be negotiated are the fuel in the furnace oil tank, who will pay pending government fees (a special assessment for sidewalks that are in process of being put in, for example), and any other unusual circumstance that involves money. The buyer usually pays the up-front expense for a new mortgage loan, but none of these costs are controlled by law. Every one of them can become an item to negotiate with your buyer.

The final items to include on the rough draft of the purchase agreement are the names, addresses, and telephone numbers of the buyers and sellers. If a couple is buying your home, you need this information for both spouses. The same is true of you as the seller, so you will need this information for every party to the purchase. Be sure to record the information accurately and legibly so it can be transferred to the final draft correctly.

At the end of this chapter I have included several clauses that I've found quite useful in purchase contracts. These clauses are listed for your convenience. Read through them to see which you would want to include in the contract you will write up for your sale. The buyers will have to agree to any added clauses, so be sure they are aware of the clauses you want to use and don't object to them. With the description of each clause are two examples in which it is being used on a real estate purchase agreement. The exact wording you use will depend on the exact circumstances that you need to have addressed. Just be sure that the clause says what you want it to say. Again, the closing officer and the title company or escrow company can double check the clauses for you before the final draft is made and the final signatures affixed.

Also, before you show the house to prospective buyers, get a sheet ready to act as the rough draft of the purchase offer. You can have the address of the property and the sellers' names, addresses, and telephone numbers already written in if you wish. Those won't change. Leave the rest of the items blank until an actual offer is made.

If you are prepared ahead of time to write up an offer, things will go more smoothly and you won't be so nervous about it when the time comes. If you are armed with three ways you can agree to finance the sale, then you have two methods to fall back on if the buyers can't meet the terms you first suggest.

An explanation of the purchase offer and earnest money form, a list of possible clauses to include in the agreement, and a case example of a sale follow in this chapter. Become familiar with the form and clauses so you can use them with confidence when you are writing the offer.

Prepare your house to be shown, prepare yourself to write up the offer or earnest money receipt, prepare to enjoy the fruits of your labor when you bank the 6 percent sales commission that usually goes to the real estate agent.

*The Earnest Money Receipt and Offer to Purchase.* An earnest money receipt and offer to purchase is just an easy way to remember everything you're supposed to remember when you write up an offer to buy or sell a piece of real estate. The form included in this book is for illustration only. I would not suggest its use, as it is extremely pro-buyer, but it's a good example of what you'll actually see. Check with your local title officer or real estate attorney to get the correct forms used in your state. The twenty-one divisions of this document have been designed to be universal and to represent what you'll find in use just about anywhere. The different parts address the following questions, all of which are vital to the transaction:

1. Date and place the offer is made?

2. Who is involved in the transaction?

3. Which property is involved and exactly what is included in the sale?

4. What is the amount of the deposit and in what form is it given?

5. What is the purchase price?

6. How is the price to be paid?

7. Can the seller deliver clear title to the property?

8. Can the seller attest to the quality of the property?

9. When and how is the closing to take place?

10. Who pays for what at the closing?

11. Is the structure free of termite problems, and if not, what procedure will be followed?

12. What special conditions of the sale are there?

13. Who is liable for the property from the time of acceptance of an offer until the closing?

14. When can the buyer have possession of the property?

15. What happens in case the buyer or the seller fail to comply with the terms of the agreement as promised?

16. How much time does the seller have to accept or reject the offer?

17. What general agreements are binding on the parties to the offer?

18. Is the buyer willing to accept the agreement as written?

19. Does the seller accept the offer?

20. What commission is involved, and how and to whom is it to be paid?

21. Does the buyer acknowledge receipt of the final signed offer?

If the verbiage to answer all those questions had to be written out and negotiated from scratch every time an offer were made, buyers and sellers would be trapped in the paperwork and never get much done. Fortunately, a preprinted form such as the one reproduced here leaves spaces for the optional items constituting the heart of the offer. (If any changes are made to the printed text, both buyer and seller must initial the change to indicate their assent.) Let's examine the earnest money receipt and purchase offer step by step and see how it can be filled out using risk-free entries.

1. *Date and Place of Offer.* Everyone can get this far on his or her own without the slightest tinge of fear or concern.

2. *Principals.* The name of the buyer(s) goes here, with the addition of the vital words "and/or Assigns." If the name "John Doe" appears on this line, then John Doe must follow through with the purchase. But if "John Doe and/or Assigns" appears there, then John Doe may, at his option, assign the agreement to someone else prior to closing and let that person take over the purchase. In most cases John Doe has every intention of following through with the pur-

# Earnest Money Receipt and Offer to Purchase

"This is a legally-binding contract; if not understood, seek competent advice."

**1. Date and Place of Offer** _____ 19____; _____ (city) _____ (state)

**2. Principals:** The undersigned Buyer _____
agrees to buy and Seller agrees to sell, according to the indicated terms and conditions, the property described as follows:

**3. Property:** located at _____
_____ (street address) _____ (city) _____ (state)

with the following legal description:
_____
including any of the following items if at present attached to the premises: plumbing, heating, and cooling equipment, including stoker and oil tanks, burners, water heaters, electric light fixtures, bathroom fixtures, roller shades, curtain rods and fixtures, draperies, venetian blinds, window and door screens, towel racks, linoleum and other attached floor coverings, including carpeting, attached television antennas, mailboxes, all trees and shrubs, and any other fixtures, EXCEPT _____

The following personal property shall also be included as part of the purchase: _____
At the close of the transaction, the Seller, at his expense, shall provide the Buyer with a Bill Of Sale containing a detailed inventory of the personal property included.

**4. Earnest Money Deposit:** Agent (or Seller) acknowledges receipt from Buyer of _____ dollars
$ _____ in the form of ( ) cash; ( ) personal check ( ) cashier's check ( ) promissory note at _____ % interest per annum due _____ 19____;
or other _____
as earnest money deposit to secure and apply on this purchase. Upon acceptance of this agreement in writing and delivery of same to Buyer, the earnest money deposit shall be assigned to and deposited in the listing Realtor's trust account or _____ to apply on the purchase price at the time of closing.

**5. Purchase Price:** The total purchase price of the property shall be _____ dollars $ _____

**6. Payment:** Purchase price is to be paid by Buyer as follows: Aforedescribed earnest money deposit ................................. $ _____
Additional payment due upon acceptance of this offer ................................. $ _____
Additional payment due at closing ................................. $ _____

Balance to be paid as follows:
_____
_____
_____
_____

**7. Title:** Seller agrees to furnish good and marketable title free of all encumbrances and defects, except mortgage liens and encumbrances as set forth in this agreement, and to make conveyance by Warranty
Deed or _____ Seller shall furnish title in due course to the Buyer a title insurance policy insuring
the Buyer of a good and marketable title in keeping with the terms and conditions of this agreement. Prior to the closing of this transaction, the Seller, upon request, will furnish to the Buyer a preliminary title report
made by a title insurance company showing the condition of the title to said property. If the Seller cannot furnish marketable title within thirty days after receipt of the notice to the Buyer containing a written statement of the defects, the earnest money deposit herein receipted shall be refunded to the Buyer and this agreement shall be null and void. The following shall not be deemed encumbrances or defects: building and
use restrictions general to the area, utility easements, other easements not inconsistent with Buyer's intended use; zoning or subdivision laws, covenants, conditions, restrictions, or reservations of record;
tenancies of record. In the event of sale of other than real property relating to this transaction, Seller will provide evidence of title or right to sell or lease such personal property.

**8. Special Representations:** Seller warrants and represents to Buyer (1) that the subject property is connected to ( ) public sewer system; ( ) cesspool or septic tank; ( ) sewer system available but not
connected, ( ) city water system ( ) private water system, and that the following special improvements are included in the sale: ( ) sidewalk, ( ) curb and gutter,( ) special street paving, ( ) special street
lighting; (2) that the Seller knows of no material structural defects; (3) that all electrical wiring, heating, cooling, and plumbing systems are free of material defects and will be in good working order at the time the
Buyer is entitled to possession; (4) that the Seller has no notice from any government agency or knowledge of probable violations of the law relating to the subject property; (5) that the Seller has no
notice or knowledge of planned or commenced public improvements which may result in special assessments or otherwise directly and materially affect the property; and (6) that the Seller has no notice or
knowledge of any liens to be assessed against the property, EXCEPT _____

**9. Escrow Instructions:** This sale shall be closed on or before _____ 19____ by _____
or such other closing agent as mutually agreed upon by Buyer and Seller. Buyer and Seller will, immediately on demand, deposit with closing agent all instruments and monies required to complete the purchase in
accordance with the provisions of this agreement. Contract of Sale or Instrument of Conveyance to be made in the name of _____

10. **Closing Costs and Pro-Ration:** Seller agrees to pay for title insurance policy, preliminary title report (if requested), termite inspection as set forth below, real estate commission, cost of preparing and recording any corrective instruments, and one-half of the escrow fees. Buyer agrees to pay for recording fees for mortgages and deeds of conveyance, all costs or expenses in securing new financing or assuming existing financing, and one-half of the escrow fees. Taxes for the current year, insurance acceptable to the Buyer, rents, interest, mortgage reserves, maintenance fees, and water and other utilities constituting liens, shall be pro-rated as of closing. Renters' security deposits shall accrue to Buyer at closing. Seller to provide Buyer with current rental or lease agreements prior to closing.

11. **Termite Inspection:** Seller agrees, at his expense, to provide written certification by a reputable licenced pest control firm that the property is free of termite infestation. In the event termites are found, the Seller shall have the property treated at his expense and provide acceptable certification that treatment has been rendered. If any structural repairs are required by reason of termite damage as established by acceptable certification, Seller agrees to make necessary repairs not to exceed $500. If repairs exceed $500, Buyer shall first have the right to accept the property "as is" with a credit of $500 to the Buyer at closing, or the Buyer may terminate this agreement with the earnest money deposit being promptly returned to the Buyer. If the Seller does not agree to pay all costs of treatment and repair.

12. **Conditions of Sale:** The following conditions shall also apply, and shall, if conflicting with the printed portions of this agreement, prevail and control:

_____

_____

_____

_____

_ _ _ _ _ _ _ _ _ _ _ _ _ _ _ _ _ _ _ _ _ _ _ _

13. **Liability and Maintenance:** Seller shall maintain subject property, including landscaping, in good condition until the date of transfer of title or possession by Buyer, whichever occurs first. All risk of loss and destruction of property, and all expenses of insurance, shall be borne by the Seller until the date of possession. If the improvements on the property are destroyed or materially damaged prior to closing, then the Buyer shall have the right to declare this agreement null and void, and the earnest money deposit and all other sums paid by Buyer toward the purchase price shall be returned to the Buyer forthwith.

14. **Possession:** The Buyer shall be entitled to possession of property upon closing or _____, 19____.

15. **Default:** In the event the Buyer fails to complete the purchase as herein provided, the earnest money deposit shall be retained by the Seller as the total and entire liquidated damages. In the event the Seller fails to perform any condition of the sale as herein provided, then the Buyer, may, at his option, treat the contract as terminated, and all payments made by the Buyer hereunder shall be returned to the Buyer forthwith, provided the Buyer may, at his option, treat this agreement as being in full force and effect with the right to action for specific performance and damages. In the event that either Buyer, Seller, or Agent shall institute suit to enforce any rights hereunder, the prevailing party shall be entitled to court costs and a reasonable attorney's fee.

16. **Time Limit of Offer:** The Seller shall have until _____ (hour) _____ (date) _____, 19____

to accept this offer by delivering a signed copy hereof to the Buyer. If this offer is not so accepted, it shall lapse and the agent (or Seller) shall refund the earnest money deposit to the Buyer forthwith.

17. **General Agreements:** (1) Both parties to this purchase reserve their rights to assign and hereby otherwise agree to cooperate in effecting an Internal Revenue Code 1031 exchange or similar tax-related arrangement prior to close of escrow, upon either party's written notice of intention to do so. (2) Upon approval of this offer by the Seller, this agreement shall become a contract between Buyer and Seller and shall inure to the benefit of the heirs, administrators, executors, successors, personal representatives, and assigns of said parties. (3) Time is of the essence and an essential part of this agreement. (4) This contract constitutes the sole and entire agreement between the parties hereto and no modification of this contract shall be binding unless attached hereto and signed by all parties to the contract. No representations, promises, or inducements not included in this contract shall be binding upon any party hereto.

18. **Buyer's Statement and Receipt:** "I/we hereby agree to purchase the above property in accordance with the terms and conditions above stated and acknowledge receipt of a completed copy of this agreement, which I/we have fully read and understand." Dated _____, 19____ _____ (hour)

Address _____ Buyer

_____ Buyer

Phone No: Home ( ) _____ Business ( ) _____

19. **Seller's Statement and Response:** "I/we approve and accept the above offer, which I/we have fully read and understand, and agree to the above terms and conditions this day of _____, 19____ _____ (hour)

Address _____ Seller.

_____ Seller

Phone No: Home ( ) _____ Business ( ) _____

20. **Commission Agreement:** Seller agrees to pay a commission of _____% of the gross sales price to _____ for services in this transaction, and agrees that, in the event of forfeiture of the earnest money deposit by the Buyer, said deposit shall be divided between the Seller's broker and the Seller (one half to each party), the Broker's part not to exceed the amount of the commission.

21. **Buyer's Receipt for Signed Offer:** The Buyer hereby acknowledges receipt of a copy of the above agreement bearing the Seller's signature in acceptance of this offer.

Dated _____, 19____ _____ Buyer

_____ Buyer

©1983 The Allen Group, Inc. Form B82GL

chase himself, but those extra words, "and/or Assigns," enlarge his options and add an element of insurance to the undertaking. It is possible, after all, that circumstances may prevent John from following through on his plan to purchase the property. He may be forced to assign his interest and needs the legal right to do so. The buyer's "interest" in the property is the earnest money he puts down and the right it gives him to control the property according to the terms of the agreement. An earnest money agreement is, in fact, a short-term option to purchase. As the seller you are also protected by the "and/or Assigns" phrase; in the event John Doe can't perform, *he* will find someone else to buy your home.

3. *Property.* If the legal description is not available to you at the time you write up the preliminary contract, you may enter the street address and add the words "to be supplied prior to closing" or "escrow agent authorized to add legal description to the agreement." An example of a legal description as recorded in the official records might be: "Lot 23 in Block 16 of Joseph Strator's First Addition to the City of Midvale, as per plat recorded in Volume 7 of Plats, page 78, records of Everett County." As you can see, that is not something you might have access to as you write out an offer at your kitchen table.

The rest of Item Number 3 is boilerplate (standard language included in contracts) identifying as part of the offer anything that might be attached to the property. It is important to list separately any unattached items that you intend to include or the buyer hopes to acquire as part of the purchase: lawn furniture, swing set, storage shed, and so forth. Such personal property might be depreciable for tax purposes at a faster rate than improvements, therefore item Number 3 requires the seller to provide a bill of sale inventorying such items.

4. *Earnest Money Deposit.* The buyer can put up the earnest money deposit in any form acceptable to the seller. The payment is usually in the form of cash (i.e., a check). However, many buyers prefer to use noninterest-bearing promissory notes made out in favor of the seller. If the buyer backs out of his commitments, the seller has recourse through the note, which must be paid according to the previously arranged terms. If the deal goes through as planned, the note is retired in favor of the payment schedule agreed to in item Number 6. Paying the earnest money via a note has two advantages: no cash is tied up during the process of purchasing the property, and the buyer can offer a larger sum. One of the subscribers to *The Real Estate Advisor,* who specializes in buying multi-unit apartment buildings in Los Angeles makes it a practice to use $5,000 earnest money notes when submitting offers. The generous amount of the note impresses the sellers.

If cash is used (currency, checks, etc.), the buyer will want to put down as little as possible and yet stay within the "trust comfort zone" of the seller. Sometimes $100 will suffice; sometimes it will take $500 or more to demonstrate to the seller that there is a sincere desire to follow through with the purchase. As the seller, you want enough money in the deposit to make the sale as secure as possible. The earnest money deposit should be held by a third party—in the trust account of an attorney or escrow officer. If the amount is small and no agent is involved, there is some flexibility on the part of the seller in handling the earnest money. It is also possible to make an earnest money payment in the form of personal property: a car, boat, or stereo or a piece of equipment—anything perceived by the seller as having value.

5. *Purchase Price.* This figure is either the outcome of a process of negotiation already completed or the buyer's opening figure. In general the price is not as important as the terms of repayment. One of the techniques the *Advisor* recommends is called "Raise the Price, Lower the Terms." There is less risk involved for the seller if the terms are "soft," i.e., flexible in the interest rate, size and frequency of the installments, and length of note, than if the terms are quite tough. This also makes the deal more attractive to the buyer. This easing of terms can be offset by a higher sales price, making it a win/win deal for all.

6. *Payment.* This item represents the most important aspect of the negotiation process. Once again, the parties may have agreed orally on the terms and are now providing formal language to prepare for closing. On the other hand, the buyer may be using the earnest money agreement as a tool for negotiation. The terms he is suggesting may be his opening salvo; if you accept the offer too quickly you risk selling at a lower price than you want. The buyer will want terms to minimize risk to himself while avoiding insult to you with too high a degree of one-sidedness. As the seller, you want to minimize risk for yourself. This is the realm where only two rules prevail: "You never know until you ask" and "A lasting and satisfying deal is a win/win deal."

As the seller, you may insist on additional earnest money upon acceptance of the offer. If so, the form provides a place for that figure. The balance of the down payment, if there is to be any, is entered on the line "Additional payment due at closing." The balance of the sales price (after the down payment) is then expressed in terms of the combination of existing loans and new arrangements for paying out your equity.

What are the possibilities? Most transactions are completed using one or more of the following approaches:

**a.** *All cash* (as in a wholesale deal)—this is easy to express.

**b.** *Assumption of an existing encumbrance.* For example: "This Purchase is subject to buyer assuming and paying Seller's current first mortgage and note (first trust deed and note) held by ABC Mortgage Company with monthly payments on the approximate balance of $_____ to be amortized over _____ years and to include interest not in excess of _____ percent per annum, together with monthly allowances for estimated annual property tax and insurance escrows."

In an assumption process, the buyer may have to deal with the original lender, who may want to increase the interest rate prevailing on the existing loan. By using the terms "subject to" and specifying a maximum interest rate ("not in excess of"), the buyer is adding a contingency clause to protect himself in the event the assumption process can also apply to a second mortgage (or second trust deed), an all-inclusive trust deed, a contract, or other existing encumbrance.

**c.** *Purchasing the property subject to an existing encumbrance.* For example: "Buyer to purchase property subject to an existing first mortgage and note (first trust deed and note) of record in the approximate amount of $_____, payable approximately $_____ per month, including interest at _____ percent per annum and allowances for estimated annual property tax and insurance escrows (PITI)."

Purchasing a property "subject to" existing encumbrances means that no formal assumption takes place. The buyer does not go to the lender and pass muster according to the institutional policies for qualifying.

What risk is involved in selling "subject to"? None, really, in the case of an underlying FHA or VA loan, since most such loans are fully assumable. In the case of a commercial loan in which the trust document contains a "due-on sale" clause (acceleration clause), you may be in violation of your agreement with the bank unless you require the buyer to go through a formal assumption process. The recent Supreme Court decision in favor of the lender in such situations must be taken into account. There is still controversy on the subject. There are outspoken advocates on both sides. Friends of the banking industry claim that sellers have the right of "alienation"—the right to sell their property without restraints as long as the loans are not rendered less secure as a result. In this period of tight money, the banks and savings and loan associations are frequently very aggressive about accelerating their loans when sellers sell "subject to" and not through the "assumption" process. The acceleration process means that the full balance on the mortgage must be paid to the lender on sale of the property, causing the buyer to find other financing.

Sellers who are concerned about the legalities of the due-on-sale issue should consult competent legal advice before acting.

The example above had to do with a first mortgage. A "subject to" purchase can also apply to second mortgages (second trust deeds), all-inclusive trust deeds, contracts, or other existing encumbrances.

> **d.** *New loan.* For example: "This purchase is subject to the Buyer obtaining a new loan on the subject property from (name of lender) in the amount of $_____, payable in monthly installments of $_____, including interest of not more than _____ percent per annum, amortized over a period of not less than _____ years, plus monthly allowances for estimated annual property tax and insurance escrows."

The words "subject to" constitute an important element of protection for the buyer. If the new loan is not obtainable according to the terms indicated, then the buyer is not committed to proceed with the purchase. If the seller or the seller's agent is on the ball, he may want to eliminate the specifics from the statement and try to get the buyer to generalize the conditions by saying "at prevailing interest rates." The seller should also insist on a time limit for obtaining the new loan, using wording such as this: "Buyer agrees to make application for the new loan within five (5) business days after acceptance of this offer, and to advise the seller in writing within fifteen (15) business days after acceptance of this offer of his ability or inability to obtain said loan in accordance with the indicated terms and conditions."

    **e.** *Promissory note taken back by seller.* For example: "Buyer to execute promissory note in favor of Seller secured by first mortgage in the amount of $ _____, payable $ _____ per month, including _____ percent interest per annum, amortized over a period of _____ years, balance all due and payable _____ years from the date of execution."

This is the now popular owner financing arrangement so common during tight-money times. Security for the note, depending on the circumstances and local practice, could be in the form of a second mortgage (second trust deed), third mortgage (third trust deed), all-inclusive trust deed, or wrap-around mortgage, which pertains to the situation where the agreement encloses or wraps around an existing encumbrance.

The example used above includes a balloon payment, a lump-sum amount that zeros out the mortgage. Not all do. Transactions often involve owner carry-back arrangements with fully amortized notes. In today's strained real estate market, balloons with terms of less than five years' duration are risky. Seven years or more would be advisable.

    **f.** *Contract.* For example: "Buyer to execute a real estate contract (land sales contract, installment land contract, contract for deed, etc.) in favor of Seller in the amount of

$ _____, payable $ _____ per month, including _____ percent interest per annum, amortized over a period of _____ years, principal and interest all due and payable _____ years from the date of execution."

The word contract (and its variations) implies that the buyer must satisfy the conditions of the agreement before title actually passes. In practice, the buyer should see to it that the escrow agent prepares the deed in favor of the buyer and holds it in escrow. Escrow instructions signed by buyer and seller should provide for release of the deed to the buyer when the contract terms have been satisfied. If the seller is on the ball, he will insist that a quitclaim deed, which immediately transfers ownership from buyer back to seller, be prepared and placed in escrow in case of a default.

By way of summary concerning item Number 6 of the earnest money receipt, payment of the balance of the sales price (after the down payment) occurs through one or more of the following approaches:

**a.** *All cash*
**b.** *Assumption of existing encumbrances*
**c.** *Purchase subject to existing encumbrances*
**d.** *New loan*
**e.** *Promissory note taken back by seller*
**f.** *Contract*

7. *Title.* In some areas of the country, it may be customary for the buyer to share in the costs of title insurance. However, this version of the earnest money receipt presumes that the seller will bear the full burden. This section is an important contingency for the buyer. On occasion a title search will disclose problems with the title—liens or judgments that affect the marketability of the property adversely. The boilerplate of item Number 7 protects the buyer against

such cases and provides an escape from the earnest money receipt if the title defects cannot be resolved.

8. *Special Representations.* Once more, this section contains important protections for the buyer and reduces the risk of the offer. After the section on utilities, there are assurances concerning the structural integrity of the building and its major systems, also a "clean bill of health" in regard to compliance with government agency regulations, freedom from future liens and assessments, etc.

9. *Escrow Instructions.* This item specifies when the closing will take place and which agency will provide third-party (neutral) escrow services. In some states, it is customary for the earnest money offer to specify that complete escrow instructions will be provided by the buyer and seller within a specified number of days following acceptance of the offer.

   The matter of how conveyance will be made (in whose name and precisely how it is to be stated) is a legal question for the buyer to review with competent legal help. For purposes of the earnest money receipt, one might state "To be provided prior to closing."

10. *Closing Costs.* In this section, the responsibility of who pays for what at closing is spelled out. The escrow fees are divided equally between the buyer and seller in this version; however, everything is negotiable. The boilerplate can be changed to fit the circumstances by simply striking out what does not apply or adding different wording.

11. *Termite Inspection.* Once again, an important contingency for the buyer. No one wants to wind up with a property that is going to collapse because of termites.

12. *Conditions of Sale.* Apart from item Number 6 on financing, this may well be the most important risk-reduction section

of all. Here is the place to state whatever contingencies the buyer and seller want to use for their own protection. Some examples of clauses are given later in this step with a guide for when they should be used.

13. *Liability and Maintenance.* An earnest money receipt in force (signed by all parties) is a legally binding contract. Without item Number 13, the buyer may be responsible for all or part of the damages that might occur to a property between the time of acceptance and the time of closing.

14. *Possession.* Not all sellers automatically vacate a property upon closing. This item protects the buyer by stating exactly when he is to have possession. In some cases the buyer may work out a deal with the seller to let him continue occupying the premises for a period of time. There is a clause toward the end of the step that deals specifically with this.

15. *Default.* What happens if the buyer or the seller fails to perform according to the terms and conditions of the earnest money receipt? It is important for the protection of the buyer that his liability in case of default be limited to the earnest money deposit and no more. That is why this particular version of the earnest money receipt and offer to purchase contains this vital sentence: "In the event the Buyer fails to complete the purchase as herein provided, the earnest money deposit shall be retained by the Seller as the total and entire liquidated damages."

In most preprinted earnest money receipts this phrase is not present. Frequently the buyer's liability is expressed as being the amount of the earnest money deposit or a certain percentage of the gross sales price (for example, not more than 3 percent). It might be that the seller will want to retain the right to demand specific performance on the con-

tract: i.e., have recourse to legal means (in addition to re-
taining the deposit) to force the buyer to comply. You and
your buyer can decide how you want to complete the earnest money receipt.

16. *Time Limit of Offer.* This is another important risk-reduction provision to protect the buyer. It is also a wise negotiating tool. The seller cannot have forever to make up his
mind. Sometimes an earnest money receipt will state that
the seller has to give his approval "upon presentation of the
offer." That is *really* putting the pressure on.

In the event of a counteroffer by the seller, the time limit
is then applied to force the buyer to respond quickly.

17. *General Agreements.* This is a collection of legal provisions
placed in virtually every version of the earnest money receipt. Each provision plays a specific part in helping make
the contract accomplish the purpose intended by the buyer
and seller. Of special interest is the provision of mutual
assent and cooperation in effecting an IRS 1031 tax-de-
ferred exchange. If the buyer should find a property during
the negotiations that he could acquire using the subject
property of the offer as an exchange, this provision would
facilitate the process.

18–21. These items constitute formal approval of the offer on
the part of both buyer and seller. Number 20 covers the
real estate commission, which, according to the current
conventions of practice, is paid by the seller. Naturally,
this item is also negotiable, and many transactions involve
situations where the buyer assumes the responsibility to
pay the agent. If this is the case, details should be spelled
out under item Number 6 of the earnest money receipt.

In all cases, you should get competent legal advice before signing the earnest money receipt or any contract.

◻   ◻   ◻   ◻   ◻   ◻   ◻   ◻   ◻   ◻   ◻   ◻

## Case Study:

Let's look at a sample sale to help you get a feel for writing up an offer. Linda Larsen owned a single-level, brick, colonial-style home in a relatively new subdivision. Widowed, she needed to realize as much as possible from the sale for use as additional retirement funds. She decided to put the time and effort necessary into selling the home on her own. She gave herself six months in which to make the sale, after which time she would call in an agent.

To get ready to offer the home for sale, Linda took a good hard look at the condition of her home and yard. She loved the home and had many happy memories of the last few years there with her husband and the younger children. But when she forced herself to step back and look at her home as a house she had never seen before, she realized that some changes were needed to make it more appealing to potential buyers. She didn't want to do any major overhauls, so she spent some time thinking through what would be the most effective improvements she could make to the home and yard.

After completing her worksheets she decided to start with the yard. She called in a landscape firm and listened to their suggestions. The landscaper pruned the trees and bushes, planted some bedding plants, trimmed the lawn edges along the sidewalk, and did other minor improvements to enhance the eye appeal of the house as people drove by to look at it. The total cost was only about $200 and the house and yard looked much nicer.

Next, she decided which rooms needed attention inside the house. The spare bedroom was loaded with old clothing, suitcases, and other articles that weren't really used anymore. Linda got busy and sorted the items into those destined for the trash, those that could be given to family members, and those for donation to the Salvation Army. She noticed how much bigger both the room itself and the closet seemed once the stray articles had been removed. So she spent the rest of that week sorting through closets and cupboards. The result was a much tidier home to show potential buyers—with more spacious-looking rooms and closets.

Linda had her son-in-law come over on the weekend and check the faucets to be sure there were no leaks. He replaced a couple of washers in the downstairs bathroom, but everything else was in good order. Linda used denture tablets in the toilets to remove stains, and soon the whole house was looking good—neat as a pin, roomy, and well cared for. Finally, after investigating and setting a price for the home, Linda had the carpets cleaned and hired a firm to wash all the windows, inside and out.

Then she made up some fliers to distribute in the area, advertised in the local throwaway paper, completed a telephone question checklist, and put a FOR SALE sign in her front yard.

Soon the phone was ringing and Linda scheduled three appointments to show the house on the following Saturday. The Joneses came at ten o'clock. They liked the house a lot, but said they wanted to look at some more homes before making a decision. The Browns came at one-thirty; they loved the house and stayed a long time talking about how the piano would look in the family room, which children would go in which bedrooms, and where they could put the swing set for their two-year-old. They left, and about an hour later, when Linda was showing the house to the Johnsons, the Browns phoned and said they wanted to make an offer on the house. Linda set up an appointment for the next afternoon, and finished showing the house to the Johnsons. They thanked her and said they wanted to think about it for a couple of days.

The next afternoon the Browns came to make their offer. Linda led them into the room off the kitchen where the afternoon sun was streaming in the windows, giving the room a warm and pleasant glow. As they talked about the home, Linda quietly offered the Browns some banana nut bread she had baked that morning. In an atmosphere of pleasantness, not unlike a friendly visit from the neighbors, Linda and the Browns came to terms about the purchase. Linda wrote down the items they agreed on and the next day Linda took the rough draft of the agreement to the title company for finishing.

The terms of the sale were favorable to both Linda and the Browns. They were able to agree on the price of the home easily—$125,000. Linda had $60,000 worth of equity. The Browns were anxious to assume Linda's loan, as it had a very favorable interest rate, but they couldn't come up with the $60,000 immediately to buy out Linda's equity. They discussed various options and then finally settled on the following terms: the Browns would make a down payment of $20,000, and Linda would take a second mortgage at 10.5 percent interest on the balance of $40,000. Mr. Brown was an attorney with a growing practice and his income would make it possible for them to make monthly payments of $500 to Linda. Since Linda wanted to sell the home for retirement income, this arrangement was nice for her, too. With the $20,000 she was able

# SAMPLE OUTSIDE WALK-THROUGH CHART

| Item | Yes | No | When | Comments |
|---|---|---|---|---|
| Curb clearly marked? | ✓ | | | |
| Lawn green? | | ✓ | | |
| Lawn cut? | | ✓ | | |
| Lawn edged? | | ✓ | | *would help a lot* |
| Shrubs and trees pruned? | | ✓ | | *would help a lot* |
| Are there spring or summer bedding plants? | | ✓ | | |
| Winter sidewalks cleared? | ✓ | | | |
| Blacktop driveway sealed? | ✓ | | | |
| Exterior bugs sprayed? | ✓ | | | |
| Eaves freshly painted? | | ✓ | | |
| Gutters clear? | ✓ | | | |
| Roof shingles intact? | ✓ | | | |
| Chimneys in good repair? | ✓ | | | |
| Side yard debris stacked? | ✓ | | | |
| All animal droppings cleaned? | | ✓ | | |
| Shrubs, trash, and leaves cleared away? | ✓ | | | |
| Heating/cooling units cleaned? | ✓ | | | |
| Garage cleaned; items stored and stacked neatly? | ✓ | | | |
| Area for workbench cleared? | ✓ | | | |
| Front door washed and painted? | ✓ | | | |
| Outside windows cleaned? | | ✓ | | |
| Clapboard, siding, or stucco in good repair? | ✓ | | | |
| Doorbell button working and nice looking? | ✓ | | | |

| Item | Yes | No | When | Comments |
|---|---|---|---|---|
| New doormat at front door? | | ✓ | | |
| Threshold painted? | | ✓ | | |
| Screen mended? | | ✓ | | *not necessary* |
| Trash can area cleaned? | ✓ | | | |
| Garage door closed? | ✓ | | | |
| Tools, toys picked up? | ✓ | | | |
| | | | | |
| | | | | |
| | | | | |
| | | | | |
| | | | | |
| | | | | |
| | | | | |
| | | | | |
| | | | | |
| | | | | |
| | | | | |
| | | | | |
| | | | | |
| | | | | |
| | | | | |
| | | | | |

# SAMPLE INSIDE WALK-THROUGH CHART

| Item | Yes | No | When | Comments |
|------|-----|----|----|----------|
| **Ceilings:** | | | | |
| All cobwebs cleaned? | ✓ | | | |
| All light fixtures cleaned? | | ✓ | | |
| Ceiling unstained? | ✓ | | | |
| Ceiling undamaged? | ✓ | | | |
| **Kitchen:** | | | | |
| Oven cleaned? | ✓ | | | |
| Drip pans on stove cleaned? | ✓ | | | |
| Stove burner reflectors clean or replaced? | | ✓ | | |
| Stove control buttons in good condition or replaced? | ✓ | | | |
| Sink scrubbed? | ✓ | | | |
| Sink organized? | ✓ | | | |
| Under the sink organized? | ✓ | | | |
| Faucet washers in good condition? | ✓ | | | |
| Kitchen curtains clean and pressed? | | ✓ | | |
| Refrigerator door and interior cleaned? | ✓ | | | |
| Dishwasher door and interior cleaned? | ✓ | | | |
| Kitchen plants in good shape? | ✓ | | | |
| **Bathroom:** | | | | |
| Faucet washers in good condition? | ✓ | | | |
| Hard water deposits removed? | ✓ | | | |
| Linoleum in bathroom/toilet in good repair or replaced? | | ✓ | | |
| Blue water in toilet bowls? | ✓ | | | |
| Air freshener installed behind toilet? | ✓ | | | |

| Item | Yes | No | When | Comments |
|---|---|---|---|---|
| All mildew killed? | ✓ | | | |
| Shower curtain in good repair? | ✓ | | | |
| Medicine cabinet clean/in good repair? | | ✓ | | |
| Fixtures spotless and shined? | ✓ | | | |
| Grout clear around tub/shower? | | ✓ | | |
| Is a plant (or two) needed? | | ✓ | | |
| Is the toilet seat in good repair and tightened? | ✓ | | | |
| Towels clean without stains or tears? | ✓ | | | |
| **Laundry:** | | | | |
| Laundry room area organized? | | ✓ | | *clean up* |
| Washer and dryer clean? | | ✓ | | *clean up* |
| **Closets:** | | | | |
| Coat closet organized? | | ✓ | | |
| Linen closet organized? | | ✓ | | |
| Hall closets organized? | | ✓ | | |
| Bedroom closets organized? | | ✓ | | |
| **Front Hall:** | | | | |
| Is there clutter/extra furniture? | | ✓ | | |
| All old mail/magazines discarded? | | ✓ | | |
| **Living Room:** | | | | |
| Fireplace clean with wood stacked inside? | ✓ | | | |
| Wood bin tidy with fresh wood? | ✓ | | | |
| Is there extra furniture that could be removed? | | ✓ | | |
| | | | | |

| Item | Yes | No | When | Comments |
|---|---|---|---|---|
| **Bedrooms:** | | | | |
| Is there clutter/extra furniture? | | ✓ | | |
| Dressers and vanities clear? | | ✓ | | |
| Space under beds clean? | | ✓ | | |
| Personal items stored away? | | ✓ | | *clean out clutter* |
| Valuables removed? | ✓ | | | |
| **Walls:** | | | | |
| Inside windows and mirrors cleaned? | | ✓ | | *need to do this* |
| Holes in walls patched? | | ✓ | | *okay* |
| Wall corner paint chips repainted? | | ✓ | | |
| **Attic:** | | | | |
| Stored items straightened? | | ✓ | | |
| Floors swept/vacuumed? | | ✓ | | |
| **Basement:** | | | | |
| Stored items straightened? | | ✓ | | *need to do this* |
| Floors swept/vacuumed? | | ✓ | | |
| Is an air freshener needed? | ✓ | | | |
| **Garage:** | | | | |
| Stored items straightened and boxed? | | ✓ | | *need to do this* |
| Floor swept? | | ✓ | | *"* |
| Oil spots degreased? | | ✓ | | *"* |
| **Other items:** | | | | |
| | | | | |
| | | | | |
| | | | | |
| | | | | |

# For Sale By Owner
## New On The Market

- 2,160 Square Feet
- 4 Bedrooms
- 2 Full Baths
- Full Landscaping
- Triple Pane Windows
- Air Conditioning

- Fenced Yard
- Oak Cabinets
- Automatic Garage Door
- Full Basement
- Sprinkler System
- Fireplace

- Cable
- 2 Car Garage
- Security System
- Garden Area
- Dishwasher
- Dining Room

ASSUMABLE LOW INTEREST LOAN
LOW 100s
1922 Vacaville
Brownsville, CA
Shown By Appointment
## 225-8777

Linda Larsen

## NEW ON THE MARKET

By Owner. Assumable. Your very own beautiful brick colonial, 2,160 Sq. Ft., snug 4 bed 2 bath, close to schools, shopping. Low 100s. By appt. only.
**Ph. 225-8777**
Ask for Linda

# For Sale
# By Owner

4 Bedroom, 2 Bath,
Dining Room,  Low 100's
2,160 Square feet

# 225-8777

Shown By Appointment

# SAMPLE TELEPHONE QUESTION CHECKLIST

**Potential Buyer Information**

| | |
|---|---|
| Name | The Browns |
| Address | 6231 Ournwood |
| City, State, Zip | — |
| Phone | 721-3842 |

**Home for Sale Fact Sheet**

| | |
|---|---|
| Price | 135,000 |
| Bedrooms | 4 |
| Baths | 2 |
| Square Feet | 2,160 |
| Garage | 2 car |
| Storage Space | basement - unfinished |
| Interior Features: | air conditioning / custom decor |
| Exterior Features: | nice colonial finish, brick |
| First Mortgage | assumable |
| Balance | 65,000 @ 9 % interest rate |
| Second Mortgage | — |
| Balance | — % interest rate |
| Total Monthly Payments | 574.98 P & I |
| Financing Options | Assume first, equity on second at 11% |
| **Area Benefits (How many minutes away)** | |
| Closest Library | 5 |
| Closest Park | 5 |
| Closest Shopping | 10 |
| Closest Preschools | 10 |
| Closest Elementary | 5 |
| Closest Junior High | 10 |
| Closest High School | 10 |
| Closest College | 25 |

Are there any other questions that I could answer for you?
When would it be convenient for you to come by? Tonight at 6:30 pm

to buy into a condo with low monthly payments. The Browns would be making payments on the second mortgage for ten years, which would take care of the condo mortgage payments and leave Linda a little extra each month.

The Browns were happy, Linda was happy, and she had saved $7,500 in real estate commissions. In her circumstances, that amount of money was very helpful. During the negotiation of the sale, the Browns had agreed to pay all the closing costs except the title search in order to compensate Linda for working with them so that they could assume the favorable first mortgage. They agreed on a date for the closing, the title company handled all the paperwork, and the closing went along smoothly.

With a reasonable amount of effort and expense, Linda had an extra $7,500 for her retirement. When the Joneses and the Johnsons called back later that week to make an appointment to see the house a second time, Linda was able to tell them that she had already sold the home.

Linda was both smart and lucky in the way she sold her home. You can do the same things she did, such as fixing up the yard and making minor repairs around the house. The luck part isn't so easy to come by, but I have noticed over the years that smart and lucky often go hand in glove in real estate deals.

□　　□　　□　　□　　□　　□　　□　　□　　□　　□　　□　　□

## SAMPLE REAL ESTATE CLAUSES

□　□　□

I hesitate to list some of these clauses since I am not a lawyer and won't even attempt to give you legal advice. But in the last decade plus that I have been investing in real estate, I've come across every imaginable contract situation. I've seen sellers who won't close, buyers who can't come up with the down payment, and closing officers who try to cheat you.

My solution has been to get to know what my rights are, and how I can best protect them when I buy or sell a home.

Each of the following clauses is meant to protect you as a seller. They can be included when appropriate in item Number 12, *Conditions of Sale,*

# Earnest Money Receipt and Offer to Purchase

"This is a legally-binding contract; if not understood, seek competent advice."

1. **Date and Place of Offer:** 9/22 ___ 19___ Brownsville , California
   (city) (state)

2. **Principals:** The undersigned Buyer Jon and Peggy Brown
   agrees to buy and Seller agrees to sell, according to the indicated terms and conditions, the property described as follows:

3. **Property:** located at 1922 Vacaville , Brownsville , California
   (street address) (city) (state)

   with the following legal description: n/a

   including any of the following items if at present attached to the premises: plumbing, heating, and cooling equipment, including stoker and oil tanks, burners, water heaters, electric light fixtures, bathroom fixtures, roller shades, curtain rods and fixtures, draperies, venetian blinds, window and door screens, towel racks, linoleum and other attached floor coverings, including carpeting, attached television antennas, mail-boxes, all trees and shrubs, and any other fixtures, EXCEPT n/a

   The following personal property shall also be included as part of the purchase: n/a
   At the close of the transaction, the Seller, at his expense, shall provide the Buyer with a Bill Of Sale containing a detailed inventory of the personal property included.

4. **Earnest Money Deposit:** Agent (or Seller) acknowledges receipt from Buyer of one thousand and 0/100 dollars
   $ 1,000.00 in the form of ( ) cash ( ✓ ) personal check ( ) cashier's check ( ) promissory note at ___ % interest per annum due. ___ 19___
   or other n/a
   as earnest money deposit to secure and apply on this purchase. Upon acceptance of this agreement in writing and delivery of same to Buyer, the earnest money deposit shall be assigned to and deposited in the
   listing Realtor's trust account or ___ to apply on the purchase price at the time of closing.

5. **Purchase Price:** The total purchase price of the property shall be one hundred twenty-five thousand /100⁻ dollars $ 125,000.00

6. **Payment:** Purchase price is to be paid by Buyer as follows:
   Aforedescribed earnest money deposit. $ 1,000.00
   Additional payment due upon acceptance of this offer. $ _____
   Additional payment due at closing. $ 17,000.00

   Balance to be paid as follows: Buyer to fully assume existing first mortgage with an
   approximate balance of $ 105,000 . Remainder of equity to be taken back
   by Seller as a second mortgage at 10.5%. Payments on the second
   mortgage are to be $ 510.00 per month. The second mortgage is to
   be paid in full within 10 years.

7. **Title:** Seller agrees to furnish good and marketable title free of all encumbrances and defects, except mortgage liens and encumbrances as set forth in this agreement, and to make conveyance by Warranty
   Deed or ___ Seller shall furnish in due course to the Buyer a title insurance policy insuring
   the Buyer of a good and marketable title in keeping with the terms and conditions of this agreement. Prior to the closing of this transaction, the Seller, upon request, will furnish to the Buyer a preliminary title report
   made by a title insurance company showing the condition of the title to said property. If the Seller cannot furnish marketable title within thirty days after receipt of the notice to the Buyer containing a written statement of the defects, the earnest money deposit herein receipted shall be refunded to the Buyer and this agreement shall be null and void. The following shall not be deemed encumbrances or defects: building and
   use restrictions general to the area; utility easements; other easements not inconsistent with Buyer's intended use; zoning or subdivision laws, covenants, conditions, restrictions, or reservations of record;
   tenancies of record. In the event of sale of other than real property relating to this transaction, Seller will provide evidence of title or right to sell or lease such personal property.

8. **Special Representations:** Seller warrants and represents to Buyer (1) that the subject property relating to this transaction, Seller will provide evidence of title or right to sell or lease such personal property.
   connected; (✓) city water system; ( ) private water system; and that the following special improvements are included in the sale: (✓) public sewer system; ( ) cesspool or septic tank; ( ) sewer system available but not
   lighting; (2) that the Seller knows of no material structural defects; (3) that all electrical wiring, heating, cooling, and plumbing systems are free of material defects and will be in good working order at the time the
   Buyer is entitled to possession; (4) that the Seller has no notice from any government agency of any violation or knowledge of probable violations of the law relating to the subject property; (5) that the Seller has no
   knowledge of any liens to be assessed against the property, EXCEPT n/a

9. **Escrow Instructions:** This sale shall be closed on or before Nov. 15 ___ 19___ by Mountainwest Title ___ notice or knowledge of planned or commenced public improvements which may result in special assessments or otherwise directly and materially affect the property.
   or such other closing agent as mutually agreed upon by Buyer and Seller. Buyer and Seller will, immediately on demand, deposit with closing agent all instruments and monies required to complete the purchase in the name of Jon and Peggy Brown

   accordance with the provisions of this agreement. Contract of Sale or Instrument of Conveyance to be made in the name of

130

10. **Closing Costs and Pro-Ration:** Seller agrees to pay for title insurance policy, preliminary title report (if requested), termite inspection as set forth below, real estate commission, cost of preparing and recording any corrective instruments, and one-half of the escrow fees. Buyer agrees to pay for recording fees for mortgages and deeds of conveyance, all costs or expenses in securing new financing or assuming existing financing, and one-half of the escrow fees. Taxes for the current year, insurance acceptable to the Buyer, rents, interest, mortgage reserves, maintenance fees, and water and other utilities constituting liens, shall be pro-rated as of closing. Renters' security deposits shall accrue to Buyer at closing. Seller to provide Buyer with current rental or lease agreements prior to closing.

11. **Termite Inspection:** Seller agrees, at his expense, to provide written certification by a reputable licenced pest control firm that the property is free of termite infestation. In the event termites are found, the Seller shall have the property treated at his expense and provide acceptable certification that treatment has been rendered. If any structural repairs are required by reason of termite damage as established by acceptable certification, Seller agrees to make necessary repairs not to exceed $500. If repairs exceed $500, Buyer shall first have the right to accept the property "as is" with a credit of $500 to the Buyer at closing, or the Buyer may terminate this agreement with the earnest money deposit being promptly returned to the Buyer if the Seller does not agree to pay all costs of treatment and repair.

12. **Conditions of Sale:** The following conditions shall also apply, and shall, if conflicting with the printed portions of this agreement, prevail and control.

n/a

---

13. **Liability and Maintenance:** Seller shall maintain subject property, including landscaping, in good condition until the date of transfer of title or possession by Buyer, whichever occurs first. All risk of loss and destruction of property, and all expenses of insurance, shall be borne by the Seller until the date of possession. If the improvements on the property are destroyed or materially damaged prior to closing, then the Buyer shall have the right to declare this agreement null and void, and the earnest money deposit and all other sums paid by Buyer toward the purchase price shall be returned to the Buyer forthwith.

14. **Possession:** The Buyer shall be entitled to possession of property upon closing or __Nov. 15__ __19__ .

15. **Default:** In the event the Buyer fails to complete the purchase as herein provided, the earnest money deposit shall be retained by the Seller as the total and entire liquidated damages. In the event the Seller fails to perform any condition of the sale as herein provided, then the Buyer, may, at his option, treat the contract as terminated, and all payments made by the Buyer hereunder shall be returned to the Buyer forthwith, provided the Buyer may, at his option, treat this agreement as being in full force and effect with the right to action for specific performance and damages. In the event that either Buyer, Seller, or Agent shall institute suit to enforce any rights hereunder, the prevailing party shall be entitled to court costs and a reasonable attorney's fee.

16. **Time Limit of Offer:** The Seller shall have until __midnight__ (hour) __9/23__ (date) __19__

to accept this offer by delivering a signed copy hereof to the Buyer. If this offer is not so accepted, it shall lapse and the agent (or Seller) shall refund the earnest money deposit to the Buyer forthwith.

17. **General Agreements:** (1) Both parties to this purchase reserve their rights to assign and hereby otherwise agree to cooperate in effecting an Internal Revenue Code 1031 exchange or similar tax-related arrangement prior to close of escrow, upon either party's written notice of intention to do so. (2) Upon approval of this offer by the Seller, this agreement shall become a contract between Buyer and Seller and shall inure to the benefit of the heirs, administrators, executors, successors, personal representatives, and assigns of said parties. (3) Time is of the essence and an essential part of this agreement. (4) This contract constitutes the sole and entire agreement between the parties hereto and no modification of this contract shall be binding unless attached hereto and signed by all parties to the contract. No representations, promises, or inducements not included in this contract shall be binding upon any party hereto.

18. **Buyer's Statement and Receipt:** "I/we hereby agree to purchase the above property in accordance with the terms and conditions above stated and acknowledge receipt of a completed copy of this agreement, which I/we have fully read and understand." Dated __9/22__ __19__ __12:00 noon__ (hour)

Address __6231 Duranwood__ _____ Jon Brown _____ **Buyer**

__Brownsville, California__ _____ Peggy Brown _____ **Buyer**

Phone No: Home ( __721-3842__ ) Business ( )

19. **Seller's Statement and Response:** "I/we approve and accept the above offer, which I/we have fully read and understand, and agree to the above terms and conditions this day of __9/22__ __19__ __1:00 pm__ (hour)

Address __1922 Vacaville__ _____ Linda Larsh _____ **Seller**

__Brownsville, California__ _____ _____ **Seller**

Phone No: Home ( __n/a__ ) Business ( )

20. **Commission Agreement:** Seller agrees to pay a commission of _____ % of the gross sales price to _____ for services in this transaction, and agrees that, in the event of forfeiture of the earnest money deposit by the Buyer, said deposit shall be divided between the Seller's broker and the Seller (one half to each party), the Broker's part not to exceed the amount of the commission.

21. **Buyer's Receipt for Signed Offer:** The Buyer hereby acknowledges receipt of a copy of the above agreement bearing the Seller's signature in acceptance of this offer.

Dated __9/22/__ __19__ _____ Jon Brown _____ **Buyer**

_____ Peggy Brown _____ **Buyer**

©1983 The Allen Group, Inc.   Form B82GL

131

of the earnest money receipt and offer to purchase. If you have any questions about their use, you should consult a professional in your area.

*Assumption Clause*—A clause contained within or added to a purchase agreement that outlines the terms and rights of both the buyer and the seller concerning an assumption of the existing loan or loans. Examples of two assumption clauses are:

> If there is a conflict in assuming the existing loans, purchasers agree to secure financing to pay the above amount.

> Purchaser agrees to assume and pay said mortgage according to its own terms and conditions.

**This clause says that your buyers are to assume your loan or they must find another source of financing on their own.**

*Closing Cost Clause*—A clause contained within or added to a purchase agreement which refers to the payment or terms of a property's closing. Two examples of closing cost clauses are:

> Buyer and Seller to split equally the costs for title insurance, closing fee, and all recording fees.

> Seller shall pay the following costs and expenses of the transaction on close of escrow _____ _____.

> (Here you need to specify charges, such as title insurance, assumption fees, closing fee, transfer tax, legal fees.)

**Earlier, when I mentioned deciding who's to pay for what at the closing, this is the clause I referred to. This must be included or you might find yourself arguing over dimes at the closing table with your buyer.**

*Contract Acceptance Clause*—A clause contained within or added to a purchase agreement which describes terms relating to the acceptance of the contract. Examples of two contract acceptance clauses are:

Said counteroffer expires on _____ (date), _____ A.M./P.M. Time is of the essence.

Seller reserves the right to accept offers from other buyers. All offers must be accepted junior to this offer. If the following conditions are not met

_____

_____

_____ then this offer will be considered null and void and the offer junior to this one will be considered valid. Time is of the essence.

**Remember the problem I had with the couple that never could close? This clause is what I used to end that problem.**

*Earnest Money Clause*—A clause contained within or added to a purchase agreement which refers to the form and terms of a buyer's earnest money. Two examples of earnest money clauses are:

Earnest money and this agreement shall be held by broker or _____ for the benefit of the parties hereto. Said earnest money is non-refundable.

The parties agree to refund earnest money in full in the event financing contemplated by the purchaser is not obtainable.

Earnest money or a binder is the money that someone will pay you to "prove that he is serious" about buying your home. Earnest money is what allows you to quit trying to sell it, and to put your energies into packing up the dishes and getting ready to move. What if he changes his mind, and doesn't want to buy your home? The question of earnest money is addressed in most contracts, but I would advise adding a clause that describes what you want to happen to the earnest money should your buyer decide to back out. Remember this is all negotiable. There are no set rules.

*Escrow Clause*—A clause contained within or added to a purchase agreement that refers to the use of an escrow agent or trustee. Two examples of escrow clauses are:

> Seller agrees to deliver to an escrow agent at closing a warranty deed to be released to Buyer, his assigns, or heirs upon final payment of all obligations at the time and manner described.

> All costs and fees of the escrow agent shall be split equally between both the Buyer and the Seller.

An escrow account can be set up to handle the funds of your closing, or the payment of your second trust deed. In any case, you should specify how this fund will be set up and who will pay for it.

*Financing Clause*—A clause contained within or added to a purchase agreement that refers to the terms and conditions of the financing involved in the transaction. Examples of two financing clauses are:

> Buyer to obtain and qualify for a new _____ year _____ loan in the amount of $_____. Seller's costs in obtaining the loan are not to exceed _____.

Seller is to obtain a new loan against the property for the maximum amount allowable. Buyer is to assume this loan and pay the Seller the balance of the purchase price according to the following terms:

**When you sell your home or property to someone who needs to secure outside financing, you should always include a financing clause such as the first one. You as a seller should specify how much you are going to be willing to pay toward the cost of the buyer's loan. Remember, there are no rules. If you won't pay anything, then spell it out. The second clause refers to the financing technique we mentioned in which you get a new loan, then let your buyer assume it.**

*Lease With Option to Buy Clause*—A lease containing a clause that gives the lessee the right to purchase the property under certain conditions. Usually in a lease with option to buy situation the lessor and the lessee will set a purchase price and terms of sale, a date for execution of the option to buy, and an arrangement wherein a portion of the lease payments made before the option is exercised will be applied toward the down payment upon exercising of the option.

In most lease with option arrangements the amount of the monthly payment to be credited toward the down payment is nonrefundable to the lessee if the option is not exercised.

**Refer to the lease with option to buy form that is included on page 40.**

*Owner Financing Clause*—A clause contained within or added to a purchase agreement that refers to the form and terms of the owner financing involved in the sale. Two examples of owner financing clauses are:

Seller to carry back a second trust deed in the approximate amount of $_____ bearing _____ percent interest per annum on the remaining equity in the property. Payments to be made as follows:

Purchasers agree to pay a $_____ late charge if payment is not received within ten days of due date.

**These two clauses should be used if you are going to be selling your home with some owner carry-back financing such as the second trust deed we talked about. Notice that the second clause notifies the purchaser that this is going to be a serious loan and that he must pay you on time each month.**

*Possession Clause*—A clause contained within or added to a purchase agreement that refers to the condition and terms of possessing a property. Examples of two possession clauses are:

Purchaser agrees to sign a residential lease agreement with Sellers during the period of _____ days before closing. Rent will be paid at $_____ per month.

Seller agrees to sign a residential lease agreement with Buyers during the _____ days after closing. Rent will be paid at $_____ per month.

**What if your buyer wants to move in early? What if you want to stay in the home after it is sold? These two clauses cover both of those circumstances.**

*Price Clause*—A clause contained within or added to a purchase agreement which sets up conditions to the agreement concerning the property's price. Examples of two price clauses are:

Purchase price for the property is _____ dollars ($_____), which shall be paid on delivery of warranty deed and satisfactory evidence of good and marketable title conveyed thereby to the Purchaser.

Price to be established by the average of three independent appraisals.

**Both of these clauses are pro-seller, and they can be very useful if you have a reluctant buyer. These may just be your final negotiating tool to convince him that he wants to buy.**

*Property Clause*—A clause contained within or added to a purchase agreement that refers to the disposition of personal property located on the ground and in the structure being purchased. Examples of two property clauses are:

Buyer accepts the property in its present condition subject only to _____.

Purchaser agrees to pay for remaining oil in fuel tank provided that, prior to closing, Seller obtains a written statement as to the quantity and price thereof from his regular supplier.

**What if you are selling more than just your home? Maybe you want to sweeten the deal with some personal property. You use these types of clauses to include those items. Both clauses are quite simple, and can be adapted to almost any situation.**

*Subordination Clause*—A clause contained within or added to a purchase agreement that refers to the subordination of existing financing. Two examples of subordination clauses are:

Seller agrees to subordinate Seller's equity to Buyer's new mortgage.

Seller hereby agrees to subordinate said note and trust deed to Buyer's new loan; both parties agree that the loan amount of the new deed of trust or mortgage will not be greater than the increase of the value of the property as a result of, but not exclusively from, the new improvements made by Buyer from the proceeds of Buyer's new loan.

**This type of clause is used when you are selling a home that is owned free and clear. If the new buyer is going to get an outside loan and you're going to take back some of your equity in a loan, then ninety-nine times out of a hundred you'll be required to subordinate (shift) your position in title for your equity to a junior position behind the new financing. In other words, the new first mortgage would be in first position.**

*Title Clause*—A clause contained within or added to a purchase agreement that refers to a property's title. Examples of two titles clauses are:

Purchaser and Seller agree that if the title to the above property be defective, ninety (90) days from the date hereof notice shall be given to the Seller, or his agent, to perfect same. If said title cannot be perfected within said time limit, the earnest money receipted for herein shall, upon demand of Purchaser, be returned to Purchaser in full and the contract canceled.

The land contract shall be completed and executed by the parties at the close of escrow. Title to property shall be reserved to Seller, his heirs, personal representatives, and assigns, until full payment of the balance is made, as provided in the land contract.

**These clauses refer to your guarantee as a seller that the property is clear of any liens or encumbrances other than the ones that you have noted to the buyer. The first clause should almost be standard verbiage in every state's real estate contract form.**

Quite often I hear from people who are going to sell their home or property by themselves. One of their main concerns is how to prevent the expense and hassle of foreclosure.

Let me share with you the same advice I give them. In conventional financing situations, a banker ensures the security of a loan by being very sure of the value of the property and the creditworthiness of the applicant. Since you are already fully aware of the first you are left only with the second area. Rather than trusting the buyers to be nice people and leaving it at that, you can make your sales contract with them contingent upon the receipt of their complete credit history. This would include a personal financial balance sheet and a satisfactory credit report from a credit agency.

The following points are the most important to consider:

- ☐ Source of down payment

- ☐ Monthly payment the buyer can carry

- ☐ Employment information for each wage earner
  —Position
  —Name and address of each employer
  —Length of time in that position
  —Length of employment with previous employers
  —Outlook for future employment

—If they are presently a dual-income family, what is the probability of having this continue? (i.e., will the wife quit work soon to have a baby?)

☐ Monthly and annual income figures for the past several years (including any outside income)

If the new buyers are purchasing the property as a personal residence, the total debt service (principal, interest, taxes, and insurance) should not be more than 30 percent of their gross monthly income. If they are buying the property as an investment they should have sufficient assets to handle any balloon payments or negative cash flows from vacancies or unexpected emergency repairs. The buyer's credit history should have no record of delinquency or default against a previous mortgage loan, or bankruptcy.

I am sad to say that most of the above points have been learned through my experiences in selling my own properties. If you take the extra time to prequalify the people you sell your properties to, you may well solve the problem of having to worry about foreclosing on a property you sell.

☐   ☐   ☐

## CLOSING THE SALE

☐   ☐   ☐

**W**ell, you've done it! If you're using this book as a learn-as-you-go guide, you've now got an offer in place and a closing date set. The closing is where and when the sale of your home is completed. If the buyers change their minds and want to back out before closing, they can, but not without penalty—that's what the earnest money deposit was all about. If the buyers default on the purchase of your home, they also give up their earnest money. That is one of the reasons you want a generous earnest money figure as part of the offer to buy. When buyers know

# SAMPLE CLOSING DOCUMENTS

Form Approved
OMB No. 2530-0006

**U. S. DEPARTMENT OF HOUSING AND URBAN DEVELOPMENT**

## SETTLEMENT STATEMENT

A.

**B. TYPE OF LOAN**

1. ☐ FHA   2. ☐ FmHA   3. ☐ CONV. UNINS.
4. ☐ VA   5. ☐ CONV. INS.

6. File Number:       7. Loan Number:

8. Mortgage Insurance Case Number:

C. NOTE: *This form is furnished to give you a statement of actual settlement costs. Amounts paid to and by the settlement agent are shown. Items marked "(p.o.c.)" were paid outside the closing; they are shown here for informational purposes and are not included in the totals.*

D. NAME OF BORROWER:

E. NAME OF SELLER:

F. NAME OF LENDER:

G. PROPERTY LOCATION:

H. SETTLEMENT AGENT:

PLACE OF SETTLEMENT:

I. SETTLEMENT DATE:

| J. SUMMARY OF BORROWER'S TRANSACTION | |
|---|---|
| **100. GROSS AMOUNT DUE FROM BORROWER:** | |
| 101. Contract sales price | |
| 102. Personal property | |
| 103. Settlement charges to borrower (line 1400) | |
| 104. | |
| 105. | |
| *Adjustments for items paid by seller in advance* | |
| 106. City/town taxes        to | |
| 107. County taxes        to | |
| 108. Assessments        to | |

| K. SUMMARY OF SELLER'S TRANSACTION | |
|---|---|
| **400. GROSS AMOUNT DUE TO SELLER:** | |
| 401. Contract sales price | |
| 402. Personal property | |
| 403. | |
| 404. | |
| 405. | |
| *Adjustments for items paid by seller in advance* | |
| 406. City/town taxes        to | |
| 407. County taxes        to | |
| 408. Assessments        to | |

*(Form Continues on Next Page)*

| | |
|---|---|
| 109. | |
| 110. | |
| 111. | |
| 112. | |
| **120. GROSS AMOUNT DUE FROM BORROWER** | |

**200. AMOUNTS PAID BY OR IN BEHALF OF BORROWER:**

| | |
|---|---|
| 201. Deposit or earnest money | |
| 202. Principal amount of new loan(s) | |
| 203. Existing loan(s) taken subject to | |
| 204. | |
| 205. | |
| 206. | |
| 207. | |
| 208. | |
| 209. | |

*Adjustments (or items unpaid by seller)*

| | | |
|---|---|---|
| 210. City/town taxes | to | |
| 211. County taxes | to | |
| 212. Assessments | to | |
| 213. | | |
| 214. | | |
| 215. | | |
| 216. | | |
| 217. | | |
| 218. | | |
| 219. | | |
| **220. TOTAL PAID BY/FOR BORROWER** | | |

**300. CASH AT SETTLEMENT FROM/TO BORROWER**

| | |
|---|---|
| 301. Gross amount due from borrower (line 120) | |
| 302. Less amounts paid by/for borrower (line 220) | ( ) |

**303. CASH ( □ FROM) / ( □ TO) BORROWER**

---

| | |
|---|---|
| 409. | |
| 410. | |
| 411. | |
| 412. | |
| **420. GROSS AMOUNT DUE TO SELLER** | |

**500. REDUCTIONS IN AMOUNT DUE TO SELLER:**

| | |
|---|---|
| 501. Excess deposit (see instructions) | |
| 502. Settlement charges to seller (line 1400) | |
| 503. Existing loan(s) taken subject to | |
| 504. Payoff of first mortgage loan | |
| 505. Payoff of second mortgage loan | |
| 506. | |
| 507. | |
| 508. | |
| 509. | |

*Adjustments (or items unpaid by seller)*

| | | |
|---|---|---|
| 510. City/town taxes | to | |
| 511. County taxes | to | |
| 512. Assessments | to | |
| 513. | | |
| 514. | | |
| 515. | | |
| 516. | | |
| 517. | | |
| 518. | | |
| 519. | | |
| **520. TOTAL REDUCTION AMOUNT DUE SELLER** | | |

**600. CASH AT SETTLEMENT TO/FROM SELLER**

| | |
|---|---|
| 601. Gross amount due to seller (line 420) | |
| 602. Less reductions in amount due seller (line 520) | ( ) |

**603. CASH ( □ TO) / ( □ FROM) SELLER**

Previous Edition is Obsolete

*(Back of Form Continued on Next Page)*

HUD-1 (5-76)

**L. SETTLEMENT CHARGES**

| | PAID FROM BORROWER'S FUNDS AT SETTLEMENT | PAID FROM SELLER'S FUNDS AT SETTLEMENT |
|---|---|---|
| **700. TOTAL SALES/BROKER'S COMMISSION** based on price $ @ % = | | |
| Division of Commission (line 700) as follows: | | |
| 701. $ to | | |
| 702. $ to | | |
| 703. Commission paid at Settlement | | |
| 704. | | |
| **800. ITEMS PAYABLE IN CONNECTION WITH LOAN** | | |
| 801. Loan Origination Fee % | | |
| 802. Loan Discount % | | |
| 803. Appraisal Fee to | | |
| 804. Credit Report to | | |
| 805. Lender's Inspection Fee | | |
| 806. Mortgage Insurance Application Fee to | | |
| 807. Assumption Fee | | |
| 808. | | |
| 809. | | |
| 810. | | |
| 811. | | |
| **900. ITEMS REQUIRED BY LENDER TO BE PAID IN ADVANCE** | | |
| 901. Interest from to @ $ /day | | |
| 902. Mortgage Insurance Premium for months to | | |
| 903. Hazard Insurance Premium for years to | | |
| 904. years to | | |
| 905. | | |
| **1000. RESERVES DEPOSITED WITH LENDER** | | |
| 1001. Hazard Insurance months @ $ per month | | |
| 1002. Mortgage insurance months @ $ per month | | |
| 1003. City property taxes months @ $ per month | | |
| 1004. County property taxes months @ $ per month | | |
| 1005. Annual assessments months @ $ per month | | |
| 1006. months @ $ per month | | |
| 1007. months @ $ per month | | |

*(Form Continues on Next Page)*

1000.

month. @ $          per month

## 1100. TITLE CHARGES

| | |
|---|---|
| 1101. | Settlement or closing fee | to |
| 1102. | Abstract or title search | to |
| 1103. | Title examination | to |
| 1104. | Title insurance binder | to |
| 1105. | Document preparation | to |
| 1106. | Notary fees | to |
| 1107. | Attorney's fees | to |
| | (includes above items number; | ) |
| 1108. | Title insurance | to |
| | (includes above items number; | ) |
| 1109. | Lender's coverage | $ |
| 1110. | Owner's coverage | $ |
| 1111. | | |
| 1112. | | |
| 1113. | | |

## 1200. GOVERNMENT RECORDING AND TRANSFER CHARGES

| | |
|---|---|
| 1201. | Recording fees: Deed $          ; Mortgage $          ; Release $ |
| 1202. | City/county tax/stamps: Deed $          ; Mortgage $ |
| 1203. | State tax/stamps:    Deed $          ; Mortgage $ |
| 1204. | |
| 1205. | |

## 1300. ADDITIONAL SETTLEMENT CHARGES

| | |
|---|---|
| 1301. | Survey | to |
| 1302. | Pest inspection | to |
| 1303. | |
| 1304. | |
| 1305. | |

## 1400. TOTAL SETTLEMENT CHARGES (enter on lines 103, Section J and 502, Section K)

HUD-1 (5-76)

they will lose their money if they don't go through with the purchase, they are more careful about following through.

By the day of the closing, your closing officer (lawyer, escrow, title officer who is handling your closing) will have researched the ownership and title of your property. During the closing these facts will be shown to the buyers, and a title insurance policy should be issued by the title insurance company, which guarantees the buyers that there are no "hidden" liens or debts with which you have encumbered the property. In other words, title insurance guarantees the buyers that they are getting what they are paying for. The buyers then deliver to the closing officer a certified check, or a cashier's check, for the amount required to close the property. If the property is being financed, a loan officer will be involved at closing. The closing officer will then record the deed and other relevant documents at the courthouse. The exciting part about a closing is that there's really nothing for you, the seller, to do but show up and sign a few papers. The buyers haven't much more to do than you, except they have to have come up with the money.

Not all offers to purchase go smoothly through the process and end in a closing. Things can go wrong that you can't prevent. The buyers' credit may not be good enough to assume the loan, and they may not be able to get a new one. One of the buyers may become seriously ill or be notified of an unexpected job transfer. In such cases the only thing you can do is start looking for a new buyer. But there are some other instances you can handle tactfully to get the sale safely through the closing process.

Buyer's remorse is an emotional response that sometimes sets in after someone has committed to buy a property. Sometimes a buyer will regret the commitment he has made. He will feel he is paying too much or that he prefers another part of town or that he has been rushed into the deal. Maybe the wife loves the home but the husband doesn't like its location because it makes a longer commute to work. Once buyer's remorse sets in you could have trouble holding the sale together. But you should do what you can to encourage the buyer to follow through on his commitment. The best way I have found is obtaining a large nonrefundable earnest money deposit. This may sound tough, but after getting a contract signed and preparing to close, it will cost you a lot of money and effort to start the process over again and to make up for your lost time. One couple in particular got cold feet right before the closing; when I told them that they would lose their $5,000 earnest money deposit they warmed up immediately. Today they are living happily in the home. The moral of the story is to get as large an earnest money deposit as possible.

Seller's remorse is not too different from buyer's remorse. Sometimes a seller will regret the deal he has made. He thinks he should have gotten more for the home, or he decides that he likes his neighbors too much to move to a new area, or he just plain doesn't want to make the effort to move. What can you do if the purchase agreement has been signed and you decide you don't want to sell? First ask yourself if you are really ready to back out of the deal. And can you actually do so? Whether you can back out will depend on the sales contract, especially those protective clauses. The buyer may make it easy for you to back out, but don't count on it. I've had sellers who've tried to stop the deal after it has been signed, but I held them to the contract each time. I would suggest that if you think there is a possibility you could have second thoughts, remodel and don't even put your home up for sale. It's almost impossible to change your mind after a contract has been signed.

To deal with either buyer's or seller's remorse you usually need to be firm but patient. Insist on keeping the earnest money if the sale fails. Have dinner with the buyer and calm his fears. If you are experiencing seller's remorse, remind yourself of all the reasons you put the home up for sale in the first place. Then go forward with the sale unless some very extreme occurrence arises to change your mind. Once you are in the right frame of mind, get going immediately with the process of closing your sale.

Check with the closing officer before the closing to make sure that everything is ready. Sometimes a small overlooked item can delay the settlement, and delays can always open up the possibility that the buyer may change his mind. It is up to you to see that delays don't happen.

Using an attorney is a good idea if there are any complications involved with the property or if you are taking back a second mortgage or financing the entire sale yourself. If there is a divorce involved or an inheritance, then of course you will want an attorney to oversee the sales process. Attorney fees for supervising a closing are only about 10 percent of what a real estate agent's commission would be, so you can have expert help without giving up too much of your profit.

The sale isn't final until the legal papers are signed at the closing and the money has changed hands. Don't throw away the names and telephone numbers of other potential buyers who have looked at your home until then. You may have to contact one or more of them if the sale fails. Several times I have seen sales in which an exact closing date was specified. When that date came and went without the buyer fulfilling his part of the contract, the property was sold to the next person in line. I would suggest that if you are worried about a sale going through, take at least one other offer on your home that is junior to your first offer. (These are often known as "back-up offers.")

Keep in touch with the officer handling the closing, make sure everything is moving along on schedule, and you will have done everything in your power to close the sale successfully.

□    □    □

# PART THREE

# SELLING THROUGH A REAL ESTATE PROFESSIONAL

□   □   □

## LISTING WITH AN AGENT

☐    ☐    ☐

*A good real estate agent is worth his weight in gold. A poor one isn't worth anything.*
—Steve Hawkins, Editor, *The Real Estate Advisor*

If you have been unsuccessful selling your home on your own or you're one of the lucky few who has more money than time, this section's for you. I will give you down-to-earth suggestions for employing a real estate agent to sell your home without losing control of the process.

A real estate agent will save you time. Listing with an agency will take the task of showing your home off your shoulders and free you up to look for a new home yourself or to earn more money at the office.

If you have to move on to your next job in another state and leave the family behind until the house is sold, it's good to have a real estate agent accompany people who come to look at your home. The agent is a safe person to have in your home and his presence creates a safety factor for your wife and children. Further, the agency will have screened the buyers before bringing them to your home.

Your realtor will be checking on the property frequently. The coming and going of agents and potential buyers will discourage vandals. The agency can also arrange for lawn care and whatever upkeep each season necessitates.

While the methods for selling your home yourself discussed in the for-sale-by-owner section can be quite effective, selling through an agent allows you the advantage of access to MLS (Multiple Listing Service), which is a program that lists all homes for sale in a given area. Real estate brokers can get copies of the MLS books or be connected to the MLS computer service. As a seller, being listed with MLS is great because it increases the number of potential buyers who are aware of your home. The MLS listing contains a photograph and all the pertinent information about your home that you would have put in a flier. The disadvantage to listing your home with MLS is that your agent may then sit back and let other agents try to sell your home. The listing agent gets part of the commission regardless of who actually sells the home. Pocketing $5,000 or more just for getting the listing is a pretty easy way to make money.

Being able to have your home listed with MLS opens you up to a new world of advertising. Agencies tie their local MLS into a national network through relocation companies and national real estate company networks, giving you broader exposure to qualified potential buyers. Not only are local buyers made aware that your home is for sale, but buyers who are moving into your area will also have knowledge of your home and its availability.

Other ways realtors can help in the sale of your home are:

1. *Screening potential buyers.* Realtors find out if the clients are financially able to buy a house or qualify for financing. They ask questions to see what kind of home and area the

clients are looking for. When a realtor brings potential buyers to your home, he or she is bringing those who are genuinely interested in buying and who are already aware of the asking price of the home and many of its features. Not every buyer who accompanies a real estate agent to your home will buy it, of course, but every one who comes ought to be able to buy it if they choose.

2. *Negotiating with the buyer* to see that your needs are met and you aren't taken advantage of in any way. Because realtors have a lot of experience negotiating deals, they will often be able to suggest compromises that are agreeable to both parties. Also, your realtor is working for you and should protect your interests during the negotiation with his expertise and experience. My good friend Brent is a realtor, and it seems as if half of his time is spent calming down troubled buyers. I've even seen him cut his commission at the last minute just to make a deal go through. There are good real estate agents like him everywhere. But you've got to do some looking.

3. *Arranging for appraisals and financing.* Again, because of their professional experience realtors know who the most reliable appraisers are and which financing options are most suited to the buyer's abilities. Having a loan officer who works with an agent on a regular basis is quite helpful. Even if loan officers won't make the mortgage loan themselves, they will know of private lenders who can help make the sale possible. A good agent will have connections all through town. Right now I am in the process of buying a piece of commercially zoned raw land. The agent I am working with has arranged for me to receive plat maps, copies of zoning regulations, and dozens of other things that would have taken me hours to get by myself. But he has the connections in that town. I don't.

4. *Filling out contracts* to correctly record the items you and the buyer have agreed upon. Precise wording is essential to avoid future misunderstandings. Realtors know the customary language used in contracts and someone in their office will double check each item to ensure that there are no accidental errors. I have a realtor that I work with in buying properties quite regularly. When I make an offer through him, he writes the offer. I simply tell him what I want, and let him go. He certainly makes it a lot easier.

5. *Arranging for the closing.* Closings are handled differently in many states. In some states you'll use a title officer, in other states an escrow agent or real estate attorney. To find out how your state is handled you can contact your local bar association (legal association listed in your phone book), or contact a realtor. Realtors have the expertise to arrange all the details of the closing. They know who the most reliable firms are and because they do business with them frequently they can often arrange for the closing to occur at your convenience. Several weeks ago I went into a closing on a commercial building. It was refreshing to have the agent involved take care of everything. I simply showed up, signed, gave a cashier's check, and left. In fact, the agent even picked me up and dropped me off.

The next step will help you find the right agent to list your home or property. Choosing the right agent is the key to having a pleasant experience selling your home through a realtor.

□   □   □

## FINDING THE RIGHT AGENT

□　　□　　□

*It's not so much making the right deci-
sion, as making the decision right.*

**W**ithout a doubt, there are hundreds of real estate agents in your area who would love to list your home. Which one should you choose? What makes one better than the others?

Every state mandates that anyone who acts as an agent in the sale of real estate be licensed. The licensing process usually requires formal schooling to familiarize the would-be sales agent with the rules, regulations, and laws governing real estate sales and exchanges. A real estate broker's license is more difficult to obtain than that of the sales agent. Brokers typically manage offices; sales agents list and show properties.

## CHOOSING AN AGENT

☐ ☐ ☐

With an abundance of agents and brokers available to you, how do you know which to choose? One easy way is to find several agents with a lot of FOR SALE signs around your area (or, better yet, SOLD signs). This is a sure indication of an active agent. The agent's name on the FOR SALE sign means that he or she is the listing agent for the home or property. Once you have a list of agents with numerous FOR SALE signs to their credit, contact several of the sellers who are listing with them and ask if they are satisfied with the job the agent is doing for them. Or get a list from a local real estate agent of all properties that have recently sold in your neighborhood, and ask the sellers which agent they listed with and if they would recommend that agent to you.

Other factors to consider when choosing a real estate firm are the company's reputation, office location, and nationwide contacts (relocation companies, etc.). You list with a particular agent but the rest of the real estate firm is important to the sale of your home as well. If the agent seems good but the firm he works for has a shady reputation, you would do well to keep on looking. If, when you call to talk to the agent, the secretary is rude and uncooperative, try someone else. If the secretary is rude to you, chances are that she isn't any more polite to anyone else. Imagine how a prospective buyer would react to such rudeness. It might be a discouragement to the prospective buyer if this rude secretary is the first (and perhaps only) person he encounters in that particular real estate firm.

When you have narrowed the list of possible agents, have at least three different agents give you marketing proposals (complete written proposals listing the specifics of what they are going to do to sell your home). This should include a written advertising campaign, the amount they will spend on advertising and where and when the ads will appear, how many times they will hold an open house, if your home will be listed with the Multiple Listing Service, and if there will be a special open house, tour, or promotion directed to real estate agents to help market your home. Automatically eliminate any agent who refuses to give you a marketing proposal. You are going to be paying thousands of dollars for the services of this agent. She should earn that commission.

Other questions to ask the candidates for your listing:

1. "Are you a full-time real estate agent?" You want someone who's selling real estate as a profession, not a hobby. The weekend realtors may occasionally sell a property but they generally lack the expertise to do a really professional job. Occasional dabbling doesn't give them the opportunity to establish lasting relationships with mortgage loan officers and title company closing officers. When I tried to sell my first home, I didn't ask this question. I simply listed it with someone.

2. "Have you sold any homes in the immediate area in the last year? Would you mind if I contacted the seller?" If they hem and haw, watch out. Good real estate agents know the importance of their reputations. They will be happy for you to contact people whose homes they have sold in the recent past. Every time I ask this I either get a nod of understanding and a list of referrals or a bunch of excuses. Go for the referrals, let the new agents practice on someone else.

3. "Did you get the asking price for this property?" Verify this with the seller. Again, protect yourself against the real estate agent who tries to get you to lower your asking price to accommodate a buyer he has waiting in the wings. You have taken time and made the effort to arrive at a fair market price for your home; there is no reason why you shouldn't be able to get it. It is always good to talk with the people the agents refer you to. You'll find as I have, that there is no

middle ground. Either people are pleased with an agent's services, or they are furious.

4. "Is your commission negotiable?" It is against federal laws to have a mandatory "set" real estate commission. Watch out if the agent says that a set 6 percent commission is a state or local requirement. The agent is not being truthful and is hardly someone you should trust with the sale of your home. Don't negotiate too hard on the commission, though. If the agent agrees to a very low commission, she probably won't expend much effort in trying to sell your home when she can sell others at the customary 6 percent. You may have some special circumstances that make taking a smaller commission agreeable to the agent. Your home may be located in a hot area of town and sell very quickly, for example. Don't be afraid to ask for a reduced commission. You never get anything if you don't ask.

5. "Do you have any mortgage brokers or financing sources that you work with on a regular basis?" Good agents, or their brokers, always have at least one financial institution to use in selling properties. Remember, they're going to need that connection with financing sources to help the buyer in most cases. Further, the agent may know some private investors who specialize in financing second mortgages. That could mean getting all your equity out and letting the financier hold the paper while you hold the money.

6. "Could we make your marketing proposal part of our listing agreement?" You should make your listing contingent upon performance. Asking this question will give you a clear idea how serious the agent is about selling your home. If she won't commit to the marketing strategy in writing, it's usually because she has no real intention of carrying it out. You want the marketing proposal included in the listing agree-

ment because, in the event the agent doesn't perform within the first three months of the listing, you have legal grounds for dismissing her and signing with another agent who will actually try to sell your home. If I had had the marketing proposal as part of my first agent's listing, he wouldn't have lasted a month. Instead I had to wait until his listing expired.

After you've looked over marketing proposals from at least three real estate agents and asked them the above questions, you need to make your decision. Be careful. Once you sign up an agent you are stuck with her for the listing period. Don't forget that your agent should accommodate your needs and work within your schedule. Once you've made your choice, organize the data pertinent to the sale that you gathered in Step 8 of For Sale by Owner, and set up a meeting to negotiate and sign the listing contract. The next step in this section, Step 7, will guide you through the listing process. Read it before calling the agent of your choice.

There is one very important thing I should tell you about real estate agents. They are your fiduciary agent. This means they have a legal obligation to represent your best interests. An agent is bound *by law* to do her very best to get you the most money as quickly as possible on the sale of your home. She is bound *by law* to carry out every jot and tittle of your listing contract. So put all your expectations in writing and then make sure the agent sticks to the listing contract. She works for you, not for the buyer.

Step 5, "Listing with an Agent," started with a quote from Steve Hawkins, one of the editors at *The Real Estate Advisor:* "A good real estate agent is worth his weight in gold. A poor one isn't worth anything." If you are buying a car, don't trust a handshake, get those new mag wheels in writing. If you're going to get your house painted, get in writing that it will be done to your satisfaction by a week from Tuesday. If you're going to sell a home, set down on paper exactly what the agent is going to do for you. Every time I use this principle I take many potential problems and arguments out of a situation. Every time I forget to "get it in writing" I end up kicking myself.

## NEGOTIATING THE LISTING CONTRACT

☐    ☐    ☐

*If someone is honest, what objection will*
*he have to putting it in writing?*

**N**egotiating the listing contract with the agent is an important step in selling your home. Too often we get the impression (usually from the agent) that he is in charge of the listing agreement and nothing about it is negotiable. Never lose sight of the fact that the agent stands to earn thousands of dollars from the sale of your home. He is working for you, and you are paying a handsome commission for his efforts. The listing agent gets a portion of the sales commission even if he isn't the one who actually sells the house, so let him earn his reward.

Let's look at some of the ways you can control the listing contract.

The traditional 6 percent commission is not fixed by law, only by custom. Neither is the time of listing commitments fixed—it doesn't have to be for six months nor does it have to be an exclusive listing. Agents try to give you the impression that there are firm laws governing both the commission and the length of the listing. If the agent you have chosen won't negotiate on either of these points, say good-bye and look for a new one. You are in an especially good position to negotiate if your property is in a prime selling area or has other qualities that make it likely to sell quickly. No matter what, though, you should stay in control of the listing contract.

These are some of your options in negotiating a listing contract:

1. *Negotiate the commission.* The traditional commission is 6 percent; some agencies request up to 10 percent. If the commission is cut to 2 or 3 percent, the agent may not work very hard on your property. But you could try to negotiate for, say, 5 percent, or ask that the percentage of the commission be lowered if the home is not sold by a given date. Also renegotiate the commission if the broker or agent can't get your full asking price. You might agree to accept a lower selling price if the realtor agrees to accept a smaller percentage on his commission.

2. *Choose the listing contract that best fits your circumstances.* Review the different listing agreements discussed below and decide which one best suits you.

   a. The listing known as *Exclusive Right to Sell* is the most common. If you sign a contract for this type of listing, you'll have to pay a commission to the agent even if you end up selling the home to your parents. The exclusive listing allows the broker/agent to list your property through the MLS. Other agents can advertise and show your property, but all offers to you must be made through your listing broker/agent. With this type of listing, the agent is 100 percent motivated to sell your property. The drawback is that you are bound to pay a commission even in exceptional circumstances. Some listing agreements require you to pay a commission if the home is sold after the listing period to someone who looked at it while it was listed. If at all in doubt, have legal counsel explain exactly what your agency's listing agreement means. To avoid the down side, you should add the performance stipulation that we talked about.

b. *Exclusive agency.* Most real estate agents don't want you to know about this one. This listing grants one broker/agent the exclusive right to sell the property but you reserve the right to sell the property on your own without paying any commission to the broker/agent. You can see why this is a well-kept secret. If you were an agent you would want a commission whether or not you were the one who sold the home, too. But as the seller you hardly want to pay a commission to an agent if you sell the property yourself through your own contacts. With this listing you have the best of both worlds. You can work on selling your property on your own when you have time, and the agent can do his job. On the other hand, the agent may not put you on the MLS—giving you only limited exposure—and he may put you on the back burner in terms of efforts to sell your home. I've heard of sellers turning this option into a contest. They make a personal bet with the agent to see who can sell the home first. If the homeowner loses, he has to treat the agent to dinner. If the homeowner wins, the agent has to treat. Either way, of course, the homeowner wins.

c. *Open listing.* In addition to giving a broker/agent the right to sell your property, this option allows you to sell the property through another agent as well as on your own. You may think you have good reasons for wanting this listing, but few agents will work very hard to sell your property under an open listing. There are too many risks for them to want to invest a lot of time and expense in showing and advertising your property when you or someone else can sell it too. On the pro side, you keep your options open, but the down side is that you don't have an agent who is 100 percent committed to your home. But if you are in an extremely active sales area, this tool can work to your advantage. I've seen agents actually bid for a home until it finally sold for $55,000 over its original listed price. How would you like to be that seller?

□    □    □    □    □    □    □    □    □    □    □    □

| Type of Listing | Pro | Con |
| --- | --- | --- |
| Exclusive Right to Sell | Agent is fully motivated to sell your property. | You must pay a commission no matter who sells your house. |
| Exclusive Agency | You and the agent can simultaneously work on selling your property. | Agent may put less effort into the listing. |
| Open Listing | You can list with multiple brokers, and also sell your property yourself. Works well in active sales areas. | Agents consider this type of listing risky, and few will make a full commitment. |

□    □    □    □    □    □    □    □    □    □    □    □

In any case your listing contract should contain the following items and a provision that the real estate agent's failure to fulfill his marketing proposal will void your listing contract and allow you to list with someone who is willing to do his job.

1. *The date.* This is a key point because the time covered by the listing begins on the date of the listing contract. Double

check the date to make sure the month, day, and year are all correctly written in.

2. *Street Address* and block and lot number for your property (get it from your title policy). You can only agree to sell property that is yours. Don't inadvertently list your neighbor's home for sale.

3. *The price of the property.* Spell the amount out in words and use numbers in parentheses for clarity. Make sure they agree with each other before you sign.

4. *Any special conditions regarding financing* (all cash, etc.), possession (when you can move out, when the buyer moves in), special terms of sale, (performance of marketing proposal), list of items included in sale (be specific). If the kitchen includes the range and refrigerator but not the microwave, it should be clear in the listing agreement.

5. *Amount of commission,* stated as a percentage of the sale price. This is an item that must be clearly agreed upon between you and the agent and stated precisely in the contract. Don't let the agent fill in an amount and tell you the percentage can change later if you choose. The listing contract is a legal document and you will be held to its terms.

6. *A statement that the commission is to be paid only upon closing* should be included (protection for you if the buyer backs out of a contract). Some agents will feel they have earned their commission when a purchase contract is signed. But any number of things can prevent the sale from being completed. You don't want to pay a commission for an almost-sale.

7. *An expiration date* to spell out clearly what deadline the agent is working against (a specific date for not more than three months from the signing of the listing agreement if possi-

# LISTING AGREEMENT

FORM A

## SALES AGENCY CONTRACT
(Exclusive Right to Sell)

This is intended to be a legally binding agreement. Read it carefully.
If not understood, seek other advice.

...........................................................................................................
Member of Multiple Listing Service of _____ Board of REALTORS°

1. In consideration of your agreement to list the property described on Form B and to use reasonable efforts to find a purchaser or tenant therefore, I hereby grant you for the period stated herein, from the date hereof, the Exclusive right to sell, lease or exchange said property or any part thereof, at the price and terms stated herein or at such other price and terms to which I may agree in writing.

2. During the life of this contract, if you find a party who is ready, able and willing to buy, lease or exchange said property or any part thereof, at said price or terms to which I may agree in writing, I agree to pay the Principal Broker listed below a commission of $_____ or _____% of such sale, lease or exchange price which commission unless otherwise agreed in writing, shall be due and payable on the date of closing the sale, lease or exchange.

3. Should said property be sold, leased or exchanged within _____ months after expiration of this contract to any party to whom the property was offered or shown by me or you or any other party during the term of this listing or extension period, I agree to pay you the commission above stated if I am not obligated to pay a commission on such sale, lease or exchange to another Principal Broker pursuant to another valid sales agency contract entered into after the expiration date of this contract.

4. You are hereby authorized to accept a deposit as earnest money from any potential buyer on the property as described on the property description and informational form (Form B). Said deposit to be held in a trust account.

5. I hereby warrant the information contained on the property description and informational form (Form B) to be correct and that I have marketable title or an otherwise established right to sell, lease or exchange said property, except as stated herein. I agree to execute the necessary documents of conveyance or lease and to prorate general taxes, insurance, rents, interest and other expenses affecting said property to agreed date of possession and to furnish a good and marketable title with a policy of title insurance in the amount of the purchase price and in the name of the purchaser. In the event of sale or lease of other than real property, I agree to provide proper conveyance and acceptable evidence of title or right to sell, lease or exchange.

6. In case of the employment of an attorney to enforce any of the terms of this agreement, I agree to pay a reasonable attorney's fee and all costs of collection.

7. You are hereby authorized to obtain financial information from any mortgagee or any other party holding a lien or interest on this property.

8. You are hereby authorized and instructed to offer this property through the Multiple Listing Service of the _____ Board(s) of REALTORS°.

9. You are hereby authorized to share the commission listed above (paragraph 2) with another (cooperating) Principal Broker, whether that Principal Broker represents the buyer(s) or the seller(s).

10. You are hereby authorized to place an appropriate sign on said property.

11. In the event of a forfeiture of earnest money deposits or payments made by prospective purchaser and/or lessee, the sums received shall be divided between the broker and the owner(s), one-half to the broker (not to exceed the commission agreed upon herein) and the balance to the owner(s).

12. Mansell and Associates advises and recommends that the owner(s) retain legal and tax counsel to advise owner(s) in connection with the contemplated sale, lease, or exchange of the property.

13. This Sales Agency Contract may not be changed, modified or altered, except by prior written consent executed by the Principal Broker and the owner(s) shown below, except that the listing price shall be changed by written request received from the owner(s).

14. _____

_____

┌─────────────────────────────────────────────────────────────────────────┐
│ The parties hereto agree not to discriminate against any person or persons based on race, color, sex or national origin in connection with the sale, lease, or exchange of │
│ properties under this agreement. │
└─────────────────────────────────────────────────────────────────────────┘

LISTED PROPERTY _____
                                    (Address)

_____                    _____
         (City)                                       (State)

LISTED PRICE _____

This contract is entered into this _____ day of _____, 19___ This contract expires on the _____ day of _____, 19___

_____                    _____
      (Listing Company)                          Owner (Signature)

_____                    _____
      (Principal Broker)                         Owner (Signature)

BY _____
      Authorized Agent (Signature)

1. OWNER'S AUTHORIZATION AND INSTRUCTIONS
The undersigned owner(s) hereby authorize and instruct the above named persons and or firms as follows, with respect to my unoccupied or occupied listed property.
(Designate the scope of your desired authorization and instructions with owner's initials in the space provided below.)

OPEN HOUSES
(_____) You are hereby authorized and instructed to show the above referred to listed property properties for the purpose of exposing the property/properties to prospective purchasers.

KEY AUTHORIZATION
(_____) a. You are hereby authorized to have possession of key/keys permitting access to the above-referred property/properties for the purposes of showing the property/properties to prospective purchasers.
(_____) b. You are hereby authorized to have possession of a key/keys permitting access to the above-referred property/properties by you or others authorized by you for the purpose of showing the referred property/properties to prospective purchasers and/or purposes to facilitate the sale of the referenced property/properties, i.e. associate inspections.

KEY BOX AUTHORIZATION
(_____) You are hereby authorized and instructed to have a key box system installed at the above-referred to listed property/properties at the address/addresses indicated.

2. OWNER'S INDEMNIFICATION AGREEMENT
The undersigned owner(s) recognize the possible risk of loss of personal property, property damage and even bodily injury through the misconduct of others, but notwithstanding said risks, the undersigned owner or owners unconditionally accept full responsibility and risk for any loss, theft, or damage arising out of or resulting from the showing of my property/properties (either privately or in open houses) in accordance with the above-designated Broker and Agent, the _____ Board of REALTORS°, its employees, Multiple Listing Service and committee members, harmless from any and all claims, demands, loss, damage, expense and liability arising out of or resulting from the use of my key, in showing the property, the misconduct, negligence of others resulting from my key being lost, stolen or otherwise unaccounted for.

3. OWNER'S RELEASE AGREEMENT
The undersigned owner(s) further hereby unconditionally release(s) and completely discharge(s) the above listed Broker, Company and Agent, the _____ Board of REALTORS°, its employees, Multiple Listing Service and committee members from any liability, claims, demands, losses, costs or expenses, including attorney fees, arising out of, relating to, resulting from, or by reason of the showing of my property by the above listed persons or firms, caused by the intentionally and/or negligent misconduct of others or by reason of my key being lost, stolen or otherwise unaccounted for.

Signed and agreed to this _____ day of _____, 19___

_____                    _____
      Owner                                        Owner

I hereby acknowledge receipt of completed copies of this document (Form A) and the property description and information form (Form B).

_____
      Owner

Complete both Form A and Form B

White — Listing Office    Yellow — Owner    Pink — Listing Agent

# REALTOR SALES INFORMATION SHEET

*I.O.C. _____

## RES  RESIDENTIAL

MLS # (For Board Use Only) _____  RELIST Y ☐ Yes  N ☐ No

PREVIOUS MLS # _____

**PROPERTY TYPE** (X only 1)
RS ☐ Residential
MH ☐ Mobile Home
CT ☐ Condo/Towne House

**AREA** (X only 1)
☐ 1   ☐ 6   ☐ 13   ☐ 19
☐ 2   ☐ 7   ☐ 13A  ☐ 20
☐ 2A  ☐ 8   ☐ 15   ☐ 21
☐ 3   ☐ 9   ☐ 16   ☐ 22
☐ 4   ☐ 10  ☐ 17   ☐ 23
☐ 4A  ☐ 11  ☐ 18
☐ 5   ☐ 12

**LIST PRICE**
$ _____
**LIST DATE** (01-JAN-87) _____
**EXP. DATE** (01-JAN-87) _____

**HOUSE #** ___   **HS DIR** ___   **STREET NAME/NUMBER** (Do Not Abbreviate) ___   **CROSS ST. #** (Apx.) ___   **QUADRANT**

*SUBDIVISION ___   CITY ___   ZONING ___   *UNIT # ___

(X only 1)
N ☐ NORTH   E ☐ EAST
S ☐ SOUTH   W ☐ WEST

**ELEM NAME** ___   **JRHS NAME** ___   **SRHS NAME** ___

**ELEM TRANS** (X only 1)   **JRHS TRANS** (X only 1)   **SRHS TRANS** (X only 1)
B ☐ Bus  W ☐ Walk        B ☐ Bus  W ☐ Walk         B ☐ Bus  W ☐ Walk

N/S RANGE ___   E/W RANGE ___

## OWNERSHIP

OWNER NAME ___   OWNER PHONE ___

OCCUPANT/APPOINTMENT ___   OCC/APT PHONE ___

**POSSESSION** (X only 1)
IM ☐ Immediate
30 ☐ 30 Days
NG ☐ Call LO/Negotiate
UC ☐ Upon Closing

**OCCUPANCY** (X up to 2)
ON ☐ Owner
RN ☐ Renter
VA ☐ Vacant
MG ☐ Management Co (Mgmt. Co)

**APPOINTMENT** (X up to 4)
ON ☐ Call Owner
LO ☐ Call LO
OC ☐ Call Occupant
KL ☐ Key at LO
KB ☐ Use Keybox
NA ☐ No Appt Necessary
MG ☐ Management Co

## FINANCIAL

TAX ID# ___   TAXES $ ___

*1 BAL (Enter Dollar Amount) ___   *2 BAL (Enter Dollar Amount) ___

$ *1 INTEREST ___   $ *2 INTEREST ___

% *1 PAYMENT (Enter Dollar Amount) ___   % *2 PAYMENT (Enter Dollar Amount) ___

*PMT INC (Circle As Applies) P I T I M (MMI)

*MORTGAGEE(S) ___

**ADDITIONAL ENCUMBRANCES** $ ___

**ADDITIONAL PMT** $ ___

**LOAN TYPE** (X 1st and 2nd)
VA ☐ VA
FH ☐ FHA
F2 ☐ FHA-245
UH ☐ Utah Housing
CV ☐ Conventional
CT ☐ Contract
WR ☐ Wrap
OT ☐ Other
☐ None

**PMT TYPE** (X only 1)
F ☐ Fixed
A ☐ Adjustable

**ASSUME EXISTING LOAN** (X up to 2)
C ☐ Yes, at current rate
RK ☐ Yes, with int increase
Q ☐ Yes, buyer to qualify
N ☐ No
L ☐ Call L A

**DOWNPAYMENT** (Enter $ Amount Other Than Refinances)
$ ___

**ASSESSMENTS** (X only 1)
P ☐ Paid
N ☐ Not Paid
☐ None

**TERMS** (X up to 5)
CV ☐ Conventional
FH ☐ FHA
AS ☐ Assume
UH ☐ Utah Housing
VA ☐ VA
WR ☐ Wrap-Around
CS ☐ Cash
EX ☐ Exchange
LO ☐ Lease Option
SF ☐ Seller Finance
RT ☐ Will Rent
OT ☐ Other

*ASSOC. DUES ___

## DESCRIPTION

**SQUARE FEET** (Approx)
(Enter exterior Square Feet for each level)

*SQ FT UPPER (All upper levels) ___
*SQ FT MAIN ___
*SQ FT LOWER (All lower levels) ___
SQ FT TOTAL ___

**BEDROOMS** (Enter # for each level)
*BDRM UPPER (All upper levels) ___
*BDRM MAIN ___
*BDRM LOWER (All lower levels) ___
BDRM TOTAL ___

**BATHS** (F = Full 1, ¾ = ¾, ½ = ½, 2Fm = 2 Full 1 ¾ ½)
*BTHS UPPER (All upper levels) ___
*BTHS MAIN ___
*BTHS LOWER (All lower levels) ___
BTHS TOTAL ___

**UTILITIES** (X up to 5)
CC ☐ Culinary Wtr-City
CW ☐ Culinary Wtr-Well
SW ☐ Sewer
ST ☐ Septic Tank
NG ☐ Natural Gas
EL ☐ Electricity
PP ☐ Propane
IR ☐ Irrigation
OL ☐ Oil
OT ☐ Other

**FIREPLACES** (Enter # for each fn)
*FIREPLACE FIN ___
*FIREPLACE UNFIN ___
*FIREPLACE TOTAL ___

**STYLE** (X up to 3)
4L ☐ 4 Level Split
SE ☐ Split Entry
SL ☐ Split Level
RM ☐ Rambler
2S ☐ Two Story
3S ☐ Three Story
PD ☐ Pind Unit Dvlpmnt
TW ☐ Twin Home
AT ☐ Attached
DT ☐ Detached
OT ☐ Other

**CONSTRUCTION**
FR ☐ Frame
ST ☐ Stucco
BR ☐ Brick
MA ☐ Masonite
CD ☐ Cedar
RK ☐ Rock
AL ☐ Aluminum
CB ☐ Cinder Block
AB ☐ Asbestos
LG ☐ Log
CC ☐ Concrete
SS ☐ Steel Siding
VY ☐ Vinyl Siding
OT ☐ Other

**ROOF** (X up to 3)
AS ☐ Asphalt
BA ☐ Bartile
SH ☐ Shingle
TG ☐ Tar & Gravel
AL ☐ Aluminum
SK ☐ Shakes
MT ☐ Metal
WD ☐ Wood
AB ☐ Asbestos
OT ☐ Other

**CARPORT** (X up to 3)
1 ☐ 1 Car
2 ☐ 2 Car
3 ☐ 3 Car
4 ☐ 4 Car
A ☐ Attached
D ☐ Detached
B ☐ Built in Bsmt

**GARAGE** (X up to 3)
1 ☐ 1 Car
2 ☐ 2 Car
3 ☐ 3 Car
4 ☐ 4 Car
A ☐ Attached
D ☐ Detached
B ☐ Built in Bsmt

**HEAT** (X up to 2)
GS ☐ Gas
EL ☐ Electric
OL ☐ Oil
HW ☐ Hot Water
SO ☐ Solar
PP ☐ Propane
FA ☐ Forced Air
BB ☐ Baseboard
HP ☐ Heat Pump
SH ☐ Space Heat
☐ Other

**INSIDE INCLUSIONS**
HA ☐ Handicap Access
FE ☐ Formal Entry
FD ☐ Formal Dining Room
WC ☐ Window Coverings
WS ☐ Water Softener Owned
SP ☐ Sump Pump
WB ☐ Wet Bar
DO ☐ Garage Door Opener
HT ☐ Hot Tub
WP ☐ Whirlpool
PO ☐ Pool
SA ☐ Sauna
EF ☐ Central Air Filter
HM ☐ Humidifier
WO ☐ Walk-out Basement

**OUTSIDE INCLUSIONS** (X up to 7)
CG ☐ Curb & Gutter
SW ☐ Sidewalk
SS ☐ Storage Shed
BA ☐ Barn
CR ☐ Corrals
TV ☐ TV Antenna
SD ☐ Satelite Dish
CB ☐ Cable TV
RV ☐ RV Parking
WS ☐ Work Shop
AR ☐ Animal Rights
PO ☐ Pool

**APPLIANCES** (X up to 5)
DW ☐ Dishwasher
GD ☐ Garbage Disposal
RF ☐ Refrigerator
CG ☐ Counter Top Grill
CR ☐ Complete RNG
RH ☐ Range Hood
CO ☐ Compactor
WS ☐ Washer
DR ☐ Dryer
MW ☐ Microwave
WO ☐ Wall Oven
OT ☐ Other

**WATER HEATER** (X only 1)
GS ☐ Gas
EL ☐ Electric
SO ☐ Solar

**LANDSCAPING** (X up to 3)
FF ☐ Fenced - Full
FP ☐ Fenced - Part
LF ☐ Landscaped - Full
LP ☐ Landscaped - Part
SF ☐ Sprinkler - Full
SP ☐ Sprinkler - Part
SA ☐ Sprinkler - Auto

**FLOOR COVERINGS** (X up to 3)
TL ☐ Tile
LN ☐ Linoleum
WW ☐ Wall-Wall Carpet
HW ☐ Hardwood
OT ☐ Other

**PATIO/DECK** (X up to 2)
P ☐ Patio
PC ☐ Patio Covered
D ☐ Deck
DC ☐ Deck Covered

**ENERGY CONSERV**
1P ☐ Single Pane
2P ☐ Double Pane
3P ☐ Triple Pane
SW ☐ Storm Windows
SD ☐ Storm Doors
WS ☐ Wood Stove
AF ☐ Attic Fan
CF ☐ Ceiling Fan
☐ Other

**AIR COND.** (X up to 2)
GS ☐ Gas
EL ☐ Electric
EV ☐ Evaporative
HP ☐ Heat Pump
CA ☐ Central Air
WW ☐ Window Unit

**LAUNDRY** (X up to 2)
U ☐ Upper
M ☐ Main
L ☐ Lower
☐ None

**FAMILY RM** (X up to 2)
U ☐ Upper
M ☐ Main
L ☐ Lower

**BASEMENT** (X only 1)
F ☐ Full
P ☐ Partial
N ☐ No
FINISHED % (Basement) ___

**LOT SIZE** (Dimensions, Description or Square Feet, etc) ___

*ACRES (# only) ___

*YEAR BUILT ___

*NEW CONSTRUCTION (X only 1)
U ☐ Under Construction
T ☐ To Be Built

## *REMARKS (For New Construction Or Conversion, List Type, Thickness, And R-Value Of Insulation In All Areas Of The Property)

___

Compensate Buyers Broker  yes ☐  no ☐   Amount (if yes) $ ___ %

FIRM NAME ___   FIRM PH ___   CODE FIRM ___

Dual-variable rate commission  Yes ☐  No ☐   **LISTING TYPE** (X only 1)  EAL ☐  ERS ☐

LIST AGENT NAME ___   LIST AGENT PH ___   LIST AGENT CODE ___   SUB AGT COMM # = D/V Commission ___

*REASN/NO PHOTO
The photographer will take a photo unless otherwise indicated below:
P ☐ Photo Not Available
U ☐ Under Construction
O ☐ Outside Photo Taking Boundaries
L ☐ Photo Submitted by Listor

RECEIVED (Date Form Was Received) ___

I hereby authorize and instruct the listing broker to submit the above data to the MLS along with timely changes to this listing, including selling information. The MLS may disseminate this information to its participants. I acknowledge receiving a copy of this agreement, and warrant the information contained hereon to be correct

Sellers Signature ___   Date ___

Revised 3/90

# REALTOR DISCLOSURE SHEET

## SELLER'S PROPERTY DISCLOSURE
### THIS DISCLOSURE SHOULD BE COMPLETED BY THE SELLER

PROPERTY ADDRESS:_____     DATE _____

Seller states that the information contained in this Disclosure is correct to the best of Seller's CURRENT ACTUAL KNOWLEDGE as of the above date. Broker may deliver a copy of this Disclosure to prospective purchasers.

### 1. THE FOLLOWING ARE IN THE CONDITIONS INDICATED:

| a. APPLIANCES | None/Not Included | Working | Not Working | Do Not Know |
|---|---|---|---|---|
| Built-in Vacuum System | | | | |
| Clothes Dryer | | | | |
| Clothes Washer | | | | |
| Dishwasher | | | | |
| Disposal | | | | |
| Freezer | | | | |
| Gas Grill | | | | |
| Hood/Fan | | | | |
| Microwave Oven | | | | |
| Oven | | | | |
| Range | | | | |
| Refrigerator | | | | |
| Room Air Conditioner | | | | |
| T.V. Antenna/Dish | | | | |
| Trash Compactor | | | | |

| b. ELECTRICAL SYSTEM | | | | |
|---|---|---|---|---|
| Air Purifier | | | | |
| Burglar Alarm | | | | |
| Ceiling Fan | | | | |
| Garage Door Opener/Control(s) | | | | |
| Inside Telephone Wiring and Blocks/Jacks | | | | |
| Intercom | | | | |
| Light Fixtures | | | | |
| Sauna | | | | |
| Smoke/Fire Detector | | | | |
| Switches & Outlets | | | | |
| Telephone Instruments | | | | |
| Vent Fan(s) | | | | |
| 220 Volt Service | | | | |

| c. HEATING AND COOLING SYSTEM | | | | |
|---|---|---|---|---|
| Attic Fan | | | | |
| Central Air Conditioning | | | | |
| Evaporative Cooler | | | | |
| Fireplace(s) | | | | |
| Fireplace Insert(s) | | | | |
| Furnace/Heat-Electric | | | | |
| Furnace Heat/Gas | | | | |
| Heat Pump | | | | |
| Hot Water Heat System | | | | |
| Humidifier | | | | |
| Propane Tank | | | | |
| Solar House Heating | | | | |
| Woodburning Stove | | | | |

| d. WATER SYSTEMS | | | | |
|---|---|---|---|---|
| Hot Tub | | | | |
| Plumbing | | | | |
| Pool | | | | |
| Septic/Leaching Field | | | | |
| Sump Pump | | | | |
| Sprinkling System | | | | |
| Underground Sprinkler | | | | |
| Water Heater/Electric | | | | |
| Water Heater/Gas | | | | |
| Water Heater/Solar | | | | |
| Water Purifier | | | | |
| Water Softener Owned/rented | | | | |
| Well/Water Rights | | | | |

### 2. ROOF:

| Age (if known): ___ Years | Yes | No | Do Not Know |
|---|---|---|---|
| a. Does the roof leak? | | | |
| b. Is there present damage to the roof? | | | |
| c. Is the roof under warranty? | | | |
| d. Is the warranty transferable? | | | |
| e. Expiration date of warranty: | | | |
| f. Have you ever had any leaks repaired? | | | |

### 3. HAZARDOUS CONDITIONS:

| Are there any existing hazardous conditions on the property: | | | |
|---|---|---|---|
| methane gas | | | |
| lead paint | | | |
| radon gas in house or well | | | |
| radioactive material | | | |
| mineshaft | | | |
| toxic materials | | | |
| ureaformaldehyde foam insulation | | | |
| asbestos insulation or materials | | | |
| Explain under additional comments. | | | |

### 4. OTHER DISCLOSURES:

| | | | |
|---|---|---|---|
| a. Are the improvements connected to public water system? | | | |
| b. Are the improvements connected to public sewer system? | | | |
| c. Are the improvements connected to private/community water system? | | | |
| d. Are the improvements connected to private/community sewer system? | | | |
| e. Are there any encroachments? | | | |
| f. Are there any violations of zoning, building code, or restricted covenants. | | | |
| g. Is the present use a non-conforming use? | | | |
| h. Have you received any notices by any governmental or quasi-governmental agency affecting property? | | | |
| i. Are there any structural problems with the improvements? | | | |
| j. Have any substantial additions or alterations been made without a required building permit? | | | |
| k. Are there any moisture and/or water problems in basement/crawl space? | | | |
| l. Is there any damage due to wind, fire, flood, termites or rodents. | | | |
| m. When was fireplace/wood stove, chimney/flue last cleaned? Date: | | | |
| n. Are there any geological hazards (ie. unstable land, land fill, settling or fault lines, expansive soil? | | | |
| o. Is property located within flood plain | | | |

Any representation as to square footage of subject property is approximate only. It is the responsibility of the Purchaser to verify accuracy of said approximate square footage to Purchaser's satisfaction.

### 5. ADDITIONAL COMMENTS AND/OR EXPLANATIONS:

Additional Information Attached     Yes _____     No _____

This statement is a disclosure of owner's knowledge of the condition of the property as of the date signed by owner and is not a substitute for any inspections or warranties the purchaser may wish to obtain. IT IS NOT A WARRANTY OF ANY KIND BY OWNER OR WARRANTY OR REPRESENTATION OF THE LISTING AGENT, ANY COOPERATING BROKER AND THEIR AGENTS, THE BOARD OF REALTORS®, THE BOARD'S MULTIPLE LISTING SERVICE OR THE UTAH ASSOCIATION OF REALTORS®. Any changes to the above will be disclosed by Seller to Purchaser prior to closing. Seller/Purchaser hereby acknowledges receipt of a copy of this Disclosure.
Seller and Purchaser understand that_____(Brokers' Firm Name) in no way warrants or guarantees the above information on the property. Property reports and/or home protection plans may be purchased.

| Seller | Date | Purchaser | Date |
|---|---|---|---|
| | | | |
| Seller | Date | Purchaser | Date |

ble). Agents like to have six months on the listing agreements because they do have up-front expenses in advertising and showing your home and they want ample opportunity to sell the home and recoup their expenses through their commission.

8. *Signatures.* You and your spouse and the agent must all sign the listing contract. If someone other than a spouse is a co-owner of the property, then that person must be a party to the listing contract. Again, the listing contract is a legal document and only those with a legal interest in the property can agree to sell it.

9. Your contract should also specify *how long after the listing period you are liable for a commission* from the sale of the home to someone who viewed it during the listing period. It sometimes happens that someone who saw your house when it was listed with an agent comes back in a few months and makes an offer on the home. Decide until what point the agent should get the commission from such a sale, and when he no longer deserves the reward.

Make sure you get a copy of the contract. Don't let the agent leave your home, or don't leave his office unless you have a copy in your hands.

□   □   □

## WORKING WITH THE AGENT

□    □    □

*Many receive advice, only the wise profit from it.*

—Syrus

You need to start off on the right foot with your real estate agent. Once you have negotiated the listing contract, since you'll be paying her to sell your house you should trust her enough to do as she suggests. You need to cooperate with her efforts to sell your home during the listing period. She is the professional, after all, and has a lot more experience selling homes than you do. That's why you signed a listing contract in the first place.

Read through the suggestions below to help you work with the agent after she has listed your property. Also, take a look again at Step 2,

"Appearance," which gives you tips on improving the first-impression value of your house.

1. *Keeping your house clean.* No potential buyers like to see obvious dirt and disorder, even if he or she is a messy housekeeper. Potential buyers expect the houses they tour to be neat and clean. The appearance of your home while you are trying to sell it is an indication of how well you have maintained it while you lived there. Give those who come to look at your home the best possible impression by taking extra time and effort to keep it sparkling.

2. *Let the agent show your home.* Don't hover. Trust the agent to do a good job of playing up your home's selling points. She doesn't get paid for her time unless it sells, so she is as interested in selling the home as you are. If there is information the agent needs from you, she will let you know. Unless asked to participate, stay busy in another part of the house while the agent earns her commission.

3. *Keep the yard up.* What the potential buyers see as they drive up to your front yard makes an important impression. Keep the yard tidy, well watered, and generally spruced up. Just a short time working in the yard every day should be enough to keep it ready for inspection. Try to enlist the help of your neighbors in keeping their yards up as well. If the whole neighborhood is attractive, buyers are more likely to feel as though they'd like to become a part of that community. Tact should be used in asking neighbors for their cooperation, though.

4. *Be prepared to show your home at a moment's notice.* This is the hard part. After all, you have to live in the home while you are waiting to sell it. However, until it is sold, it is very important that the home be available for showing whenever

the agent has an interested buyer. This may require some very strict household rules for a while, and it may not be as restful as you would like home to be, but it is necessary. Remember that the agent has already qualified the potential buyer, so everyone who comes to the home could be someone who ends up buying it. There are usually enough houses on the market in most areas so that the agent can simply take the buyer to another available house, very similar to yours, if you can't or won't let your home be shown.

5. *Plan to have your children away from the home for all open houses.* Your job is to be a gracious host on those days without a million distractions. The open houses are on prearranged days and times, so it should be relatively easy to arrange for child care elsewhere during these open houses. If you can't work out any baby-sitting arrangements, let your spouse stay in the home and you take the children to the park or the zoo or a movie.

6. *Dress nicely when someone comes to look at your home.* Again, first impressions are important ones. You want the potential buyers to think they are important enough for you to want to look good for their visit. The way you present yourself suggests something about how you take care of your property as well. Make the effort to look nice when someone comes to see your home; it could be the final point that results in a sale. Everything—the way you look, the way you talk, the tidiness of your home—contributes positively or negatively to the buyer's frame of mind.

When selling your home through a real estate agent, you need to know how to cooperate with the agent's efforts to sell your home without losing control of the situation. Read through the suggestions below to help you stay in the driver's seat.

1. *Establish from the start when you can be available to show your home and when you absolutely can't.* You naturally want your home to be available to potential buyers as often as possible (showing the home is how you will sell it) but there will be times when your family needs privacy. You don't want people touring the home in the early morning hours when you are trying to get ready for work and send the kids off to school. Nor do you want strangers passing through the dining room while you are having your evening meal. Decide what showing schedule is workable and then request that the agent sticks to those hours.

2. *Ask the agent to keep you posted on a regular basis as to what she's doing to sell your home.* You should know about newspaper ads, being listed in the MLS book, and any fliers that are distributed to advertise your home. Often the MLS realtors will take other agencies on a tour of your home to acquaint them with it so they will be able to encourage buyers to look at it as well. You should hear from your agent at least two or three times a week with progress reports on advertising and how often the home has been shown and what the results of those tours have been. If there is one feature of the home or financing package that is turning buyers away, you need to know what it is so you can make the necessary adjustments.

3. *Ask the agent to send you a copy of all advertisements she runs for your home.* This will keep you up to date on what the agent is doing in your behalf and let you make suggestions about what features you think will help sell the home.

Some agents are more energetic than others. Since the listing agent gets part of the commission no matter who sells the home, some listing agents are content to sit back, let someone else sell your home, and then pocket their share of the commission. The reason that you had the agent prepare a marketing plan for selling your home before listing the home with her is that you wanted some assurance that an honest effort would be made to sell the home. If you were careful, you also got the agent to include the marketing plan in the listing contract. If the agent fails to do what she promised to sell your property (see Step 9), you can cancel the contract and look for an agent with more on the ball.

You should also make sure all your personal items and valuables are locked away when people are looking at your home. It isn't fair to the agent or the people viewing your home if you leave valuables lying around. If something is missing, it could create a lot of tension between you and the agent. Do the smart thing and put away any item of value that is small enough to be taken during a tour of your home.

What about a lockbox? A lockbox is a device that looks like a large padlock locked onto your front door knob. The agent will keep a key to your house inside the lockbox, and then other agents in the area get a special key that can open the lockbox. This way, any licensed real estate agent can show your house when you're not at home. In many areas a lot of people have had trouble with lockboxes. If you are in an area where you are worried about crime, you should consider showing your home only by appointment and controlling your own house key instead of allowing an agent to install a lockbox.

You may be willing to take the risk and allow multiple listing system agents to have access to your home when you are not there. I strongly suggest that if you really aren't home much you give your listing agent a copy of your key to keep under her control at all times, with the understanding that she must be present for all showings when you are not home. This allows some of the flexibility of the lockbox without any of the risk.

When showing your property to potential buyers, one of your most important tasks is making visitors feel at ease in your home. You will want to treat them with the same courtesy you extend to invited guests and family members who visit. Make them feel that their presence is a pleasure and that you want them to be comfortable.

Greet your visitors at the door. Introduce yourself to the first person to walk in. Let them introduce you to the rest of their party. Pay attention during these introductions so you can call the potential buyers by name as you talk with them about the house. We all like to hear our own names, and this is one way to let them know you think they are important and you are taking them seriously.

If the real estate agent or the potential buyers ask, point out any items of interest. Tell them you installed a new water softener last year, and that the den really has been a gathering place for the family because it's so warm and cozy with the fireplace. Don't hover though. Let the agent direct how much you participate in showing the home. Trust her judgment; she knows these potential buyers much better than you do. Recently I went with an agent to look at several properties. One homeowner was so excited to have someone touring the house that she wouldn't shut up. It was as though she thought that if she could get in over ten thousand words in five minutes we would magically buy. Instead, her endless chatter drove me out of the home with a headache.

Allow the agent to do the showing unless you are asked to help. The agent is a professional; she knows what the buyer is looking for and is able to point out the features the buyers are most interested in. Too often sellers display an anxiousness to sell that puts buyers off. When a seller is too anxious, the buyers can't help wondering why—and the conclusions they arrive at may keep them from buying the home.

My wife and I recently purchased an office complex through a real estate agent. One of the things I enjoyed most about buying it was the friendly attitude the seller displayed. He answered our questions quickly and thoroughly, and provided us with a warm introduction to the property. He wasn't pushy, anxious, or offensive. I knew he was hurting for money since he was behind on his taxes, but he never mentioned it and neither did I. If he had come on too strong, or lied and said he didn't need to sell at all, I probably would have walked out without buying.

Keep large pets outside and under control. You may even consider leaving them with a relative or in a kennel while you are showing the home. No matter how much you and your family love Rover, he may have an entirely different effect on prospective buyers. Being intimidated by a large dog while trying to look at a home is not pleasant and will probably kill your sale. Also, some people are allergic to pets and seeing one in the home could make them uncomfortable or ill.

My wife and I recently went with an agent to look at several properties. At one beautiful home, located in the country on ten acres of land, we were greeted outside by a gigantic snarling German shepherd. We sat in the agent's van for a few minutes trying to get the courage to step out. Finally, protected by her Multiple Listing Book, the agent ventured out to scare off the dog. Then, after we all got into the house, we forgot that we had to get out again. The dog was even less agreeable to that. In essence, the dog did nothing to help us want to buy the home. If I asked my wife today about the home, she would say, "Oh, the home with the big German shepherd!" That's what she remembers.

Let the potential buyers know that other people are going to be looking at the home. Nothing makes an offer come more quickly than knowing that someone else is looking at the house that could be yours. Don't overdo it, however. Unless you are in an area where there are more homes than buyers or you really do have a list of people scheduled to see your home, it is better not to stress the competitive aspect too much. Most people want buying a home to be a pleasant and smooth experience. If you put too much stress on them or suggest that buying the home may not be possible for them much longer, they can and will look at another home.

Remember from the for-sale-by-owner section to bake those cookies while the potential buyers are being shown through your home by the real estate agent. Then try to end up sitting at your kitchen table as they finish the tour, so you can answer any questions the buyers or the agent may have.

If a buyer asks for a repeat showing, you should consider not being home. Let the agent handle this second tour by herself. Asking for a second look usually means that a buyer is very interested and may want to check everything out over the course of a long showing. The buyer will feel less comfortable about doing that if you are there since it can be discomforting to a seller to hear his home analyzed and criticized by an outsider—even if the outsider is a possible buyer. Most of us have some emotional attachment to our homes and we have chosen to decorate in a manner that pleases us. We are better off not being around when potential buyers begin to draw flaws out into the open. Often they are trying to see if they can mold the home to their needs and expectations, but they will feel uncomfortable about suggesting changes when the owner is present. It is important for the buyers to be able to see your home in light of their own lives if they are to buy it; so stay away and let the real estate agent earn his commission.

To sum up, be as cooperative as you can with the realtor who is trying to sell your home. She has up-front costs in marketing your home that she will recoup only if the house is sold; in other words, she is as interested as you are in selling the home. In your efforts to be cooperative, though, you needn't become a slave to the agent. Keep control by setting definite hours when your home will be available for showing, keep yourself and the home and yard neat and presentable for all showings, and avoid the use of a lockbox if at all possible. Be cooperative with reasonable changes the realtor may suggest in pricing or financing your home, but don't agree to any changes that you are not truly comfortable with.

Once you have signed a listing contract with an agent, see that she does her part, do your part, and the home should sell in a reasonable amount of time. If it doesn't, read Part IV, "Desperate Cases," to see what further action you can take to sell your house.

□   □   □

## IF THE AGENT ISN'T DOING HIS JOB

☐      ☐      ☐

*Show me a good loser and I will show you a loser.*

—Vince Lombardi

**Y**ou buy a gallon of milk, take it home, sit down at the table for breakfast, pour a bowl of cornflakes, and twist the blue cap off the milk jug. Before you pour the milk, you smell an awful odor. Spoiled milk. What do you do? Take it back.

It's Christmas and you open up your aunt Sarah's present. A bright orange knit sweater that's two sizes too small. What do you do? Exchange it.

Sign a listing contract with an agent, and as was the case with my first property, you don't see him once during the entire listing period. What now? Most people in this situation don't know what to do. This step is designed to help you set a course of action if the agent you sign a listing contract with isn't doing his job.

If you've negotiated your listing contract with a real estate agent as detailed in Step 7, it will be *contingent* upon the performance of the agent. If the agent doesn't comply with the marketing proposal and advertisement schedule he committed to, then you need to notify him in writing of the breach, contact his broker and express your displeasure, and then contact another agent to sign a new listing contract. You've got to document your original agent's failure to perform, though (remember that notebook I suggested keeping at the beginning of this book?). This is why you need to keep in close contact with the agent. Record the content of your conversations, especially if you start to feel dissatisfaction with his performance. Most of the time the agent will be aware of his failure to live up to the contract and when you complain, one of two things will probably happen.

First, the agent may get his act together, buckle down, and really start conforming to the specifications of the contract. It's always better to get the full story from the agent before canceling the contract. There may have been a death in his family or other extenuating circumstances that you can overlook on a one-time-only basis if he agrees to enter into full compliance right away. You chose the agent with care and you should be careful about dismissing him as well. If there is any way to work things out to your satisfaction, do so unless you have learned more about the agent and it is not favorable.

Second, the agent will agree to cancel the contract to avoid any more trouble. After all, it is very important for the full-time real estate agent to protect his reputation. Many people choose a real estate agent by word of mouth and a poor performance can keep the agent from getting more listings.

However, if the agent tries to keep you from canceling the contract and looking for a new agent, simply call your local state government offices and ask for the State Real Estate Commission Office. Your state government has a watchdog agency that oversees the real estate industry in your area. If you are having a problem, call and file a complaint against the agent. Experience has shown that there isn't a better way of turning off a problem agent since all complaints must be investigated.

My hope is that any problem you may encounter with a real estate agent would never go this far. Most agents are professionals who want to protect their reputations and satisfy their clients. I would rather you spent a little more time from the beginning to choose the right agent and to write up a contract that requires an agreed-upon level of performance. Keep open lines of communication to talk out problems rather than force yourself to put your energy into arguing with your agent.

However, if you don't feel the agent is keeping his commitments and nothing changes after a straightforward discussion, then get out of the situation by implementing the clauses in the listing contract that protect your position and enable you to find a new agent if necessary.

Don't feel bad if you have to cancel a contract with an agent. If he isn't doing his job, you shouldn't allow him to waste your time. Look at it this way. What if you asked the agent to list your house, show buyers through it, work on offers, and then—if you think he has done a good job—receive some sort of commission, the amount to be determined by you? What do you think he would say? That's right—good-bye. He won't work for free or for a chance to make an unspecified amount of money. He wants to be fairly sure he is going to receive a substantial sum of money for his work. That's a reasonable expectation. And your expectations are also reasonable. You expect to sell your house as quickly as possible for as much money as possible and you'd rather not have Bozo the Clown in charge of the process.

□   □   □

## FINALIZING THE DEAL

☐     ☐     ☐

*It's not over till it's over . . .*
                    —Yogi Berra

***When an Offer Comes In.*** Your agent's responsibility by law is to act in your behalf to get you the very best price and terms for your house. That's what you are paying for. If a potential buyer is interested in your home, his agent and your agent will work out a deal. You can expect your agent to call you and let you know he has an offer that the Jones family would like to have presented. Your agent will set up a time to meet with you. By law the agent is required to present all offers, no matter how ridiculous or absurd. You might want to have the agent explain the offer over the phone to see if you are even interested in getting together. If it sounds good, then set a time and go over the proposed offer.

You should evaluate each offer in terms of:

1. *Price.* Is it what you want? Research has shown that only one property in ten actually sells for the listed price.

2. *Terms.* Are the terms that you are being offered acceptable? Are you getting your down payment? If taking back a note, is your money left in the property secure? Is the payment schedule reasonable?

3. *Clauses.* In the for-sale-by-owner section we talked about all the different clauses that can be used in writing up offers. Many of them are for your protection. It is assumed that your real estate agent will take care of these, but you should be aware of the possibilities. If you are worried about anything in the offer, have a lawyer review it and explain the implications before you sign anything.

4. *Personal Property.* What about TV antennas, mirrors, chandeliers, lawn chairs? The contract being presented should include those items. Make sure there are no "gray areas" of potential misunderstanding. You should specify what is not included as well as what is.

5. *Earnest Money.* Who keeps it? What happens if your buyer backs out? The earnest money is usually kept in a broker's escrow account. You should insist that the deposit is nonrefundable and large enough ($5,000 would be my target) to make it difficult for the buyer to walk away. The earnest money sales agreement, also called the realtor's offer to purchase, comes in a variety of forms. One sample appears at the end of this chapter.

If you like the offer and don't want to make any changes, then sign. If you're not quite sure and want to have your attorney look it over, sign your name and write over your signature "subject to the approval of my attorney." This way the buyer will know you are serious, but want to have a few questions answered.

If you don't like the offer, reject it. You don't have to sell unless you want to. Or, you may want to make a counteroffer, which represents a compromise. Your agent is the person who is kept busy in this process. His job is to represent you, to screen all offers, render advice, be your confidant, and help you get the very best price that you can.

***Before You Take Your Home off the Market.*** Before you pull up the sign and start packing, you should have some assurance that the transaction is really going to go through. The amount of earnest money is a reflection of how serious your buyer is. If he wouldn't put up more than $100, then he isn't serious. If he put down a nonrefundable deposit of $5,000 then you can probably start packing. If you aren't sure that your buyer really will end up closing, I suggest you instruct your agent to keep showing the property and to take back-up offers. There are several ways to do this. One is that the back-up offer is subject to the nonperformance of the existing contract with the Joneses. The other way is to have your original contract with the buyer allow you to continue showing your home. If you receive another offer that you want to accept, your first buyer must meet the terms of the second offer, increase the earnest money deposit, and specify a final date of sale. Or your first buyer can void his contract and allow you to sell to your new buyer. The wording for this proceeding varies by state. Talk to your agent about back-up offers.

***The Closing.*** After you've signed the sales contract, the realtor will do everything necessary to get the property ready to close. After all, you're giving the agent a good chunk of the sales price of your property. All you will be required to do is to show up at a closing, sign a ton of papers, and get a check. This process is regulated by law in all fifty

# EARNEST MONEY SALES AGREEMENT
## EARNEST MONEY RECEIPT

Legend   Yes(X)   No(O)

DATE: _____

The undersigned Buyer _____ hereby deposits with Brokerage

as EARNEST MONEY, the amount of _____ Dollars ($ _____ ),

in the form of _____

which shall be deposited in accordance with applicable State Law.

_____    Received by _____

Brokerage                    Phone Number

## OFFER TO PURCHASE

**1. PROPERTY DESCRIPTION** The above stated EARNEST MONEY is given to secure and apply on the purchase of the property situated at _____

_____ in the City of _____ County of _____ , Utah,

subject to any restrictive covenants, zoning regulations, utility or other easements or rights of way, government patents or state deeds of record approved by Buyer in

accordance with Section G. Said property is owned by _____ as sellers, and is more particularly described

as: _____

CHECK APPLICABLE BOXES:

☐ **UNIMPROVED REAL PROPERTY**   ☐ Vacant Lot   ☐ Vacant Acreage   ☐ Other _____

☐ **IMPROVED REAL PROPERTY**   ☐ Commercial   ☐ Residential   ☐ Condo   ☐ Other _____

(a) **Included items.** Unless excluded below, this sale shall *include* all fixtures and any of the items shown in Section A if presently attached to the property. The following personal property shall also be included in this sale and conveyed under separate Bill of Sale with warranties as to title: _____

_____

(b) **Excluded items.** The following items are specifically *excluded* from this sale: _____

(c) **CONNECTIONS, UTILITIES AND OTHER RIGHTS.** Seller represents that the property includes the following improvements in the purchase price:

| | | |
|---|---|---|
| ☐ public sewer ☐ connected | ☐ well ☐ connected ☐ other | ☐ electricity ☐ connected |
| ☐ septic tank ☐ connected | ☐ irrigation water / secondary system | ☐ ingress & egress by private easement |
| ☐ other sanitary system _____ | # of shares _____ Company _____ | ☐ dedicated road ☐ paved |
| ☐ public water ☐ connected | ☐ TV antenna ☐ master antenna ☐ prewired | ☐ curb and gutter |
| ☐ private water ☐ connected | ☐ natural gas ☐ connected | ☐ other rights _____ |

(d) **Survey.** A certified survey ☐ shall be furnished at the expense of _____ prior to closing, ☐ shall not be furnished.

(e) **Buyer Inspection.** Buyer has made a visual inspection of the property and subject to Section 1 (c) above and 6 below, accepts it in its present physical condition, except: _____

**2. PURCHASE PRICE AND FINANCING.** The total purchase price for the property is _____

_____ Dollars ($ _____ ) which shall be paid as follows:

$ _____  which represents the aforedescribed EARNEST MONEY DEPOSIT:

$ _____  representing the approximate balance of CASH DOWN PAYMENT at closing.

$ _____  representing the approximate balance of an existing mortgage, trust deed note, real estate contract or other encumbrance to be assumed by buyer,

which obligation bears interest at _____ % per annum with monthly payments of $ _____

which include: ☐ principal; ☐ interest; ☐ taxes; ☐ insurance; ☐ condo fees; ☐ other _____ .

$ _____  representing the approximate balance of an additional existing mortgage, trust deed note, real estate contract or other encumbrances to be

assumed by Buyer, which obligation bears interest at _____ % per annum with monthly payments of $ _____

which include: ☐ principal; ☐ interest; ☐ taxes; ☐ insurance; ☐ condo fees; ☐ other _____ .

$ _____  representing balance, if any, including proceeds from a new mortgage loan, or seller financing, to be paid as follows: _____

_____

_____

$ _____  Other _____

| $ | TOTAL PURCHASE PRICE |
|---|---|

If Buyer is required to assume an underlying obligation (in which case Section F shall also apply) and/or obtain outside financing, Buyer agrees to use best efforts to assume and/or procure same and this offer is made subject to Buyer qualifying for and lending institution granting said assumption and/or financing. Buyer agrees to make application within _____ days after Seller's acceptance of this Agreement to assume the underlying obligation and/or obtain the new financing at an interest rate not to exceed _____ %. If Buyer does not qualify for the assumption and/or financing within _____ days after Seller's acceptance of this Agreement, this Agreement shall be voidable at the option of the Seller upon written notice. Seller agrees to pay up to _____ mortgage loan discount points, not to exceed $ _____ . In addition, seller agrees to pay $ _____ to be used for Buyer's other loan costs.

Page two of a four page form    Seller's Initials ( ) ( )    Date _____    Buyer's Initials ( ) ( )    Date _____

3. **CONDITION AND CONVEYANCE OF TITLE.** Seller represents that Seller ☐ holds title to the property in fee simple ☐ is purchasing the property under a real estate contract. Transfer of Seller's ownership interest shall be made as set forth in Section S. Seller agrees to furnish good and marketable title to the property, subject to encumbrances and exceptions noted herein, evidenced by ☐ a current policy of title insurance in the amount of purchase price ☐ an abstract of title brought current, with an attorney's opinion (See Section H).

4. **INSPECTION OF TITLE.** In accordance with Section G, Buyer shall have the opportunity to inspect the title to the subject property prior to closing. Buyer shall take title subject to any existing restrictive covenants, including condominium restrictions (CC & R's). Buyer ☐ has ☐ has not reviewed any condominium CC & R's prior to signing this Agreement.

5. **VESTING OF TITLE.** Title shall vest in Buyer as follows: _____
_____

6. **SELLERS WARRANTIES.** In addition to warranties contained in Section C, the following items are also warranted: _____
_____

Exceptions to the above and Section C shall be limited to the following: _____
_____

7. **SPECIAL CONSIDERATIONS AND CONTINGENCIES.** This offer is made subject to the following special conditions and/or contingencies which must be satisfied prior to closing: _____
_____
_____
_____
_____

8. **CLOSING OF SALE.** This Agreement shall be closed on or before _____ , 19 ____ at a reasonable location to be designated by Seller, subject to Section Q. Upon demand, Buyer shall deposit with the escrow closing office all documents necessary to complete the purchase in accordance with this Agreement. Prorations set forth in Section R shall be made as of ☐ date of possession ☐ date of closing ☐ other _____

9. **POSSESSION.** Seller shall deliver possession to Buyer on _____ unless extended by written agreement of parties.

10. **AGENCY DISCLOSURE.** At the signing of this Agreement the listing agent _____ represents ( ) Seller ( ) Buyer, and the selling agent _____ represents ( ) Seller ( ) Buyer. Buyer and Seller confirm that prior to signing this Agreement written disclosure of the agency relationship(s) was provided to him/her. ( ) ( ) Buyer's initials ( ) ( ) Seller's initials.

11. **GENERAL PROVISIONS.** UNLESS OTHERWISE INDICATED ABOVE, THE GENERAL PROVISION SECTIONS ON THE REVERSE SIDE HEREOF HAVE BEEN ACCEPTED BY THE BUYER AND SELLER AND ARE INCORPORATED INTO THIS AGREEMENT BY REFERENCE.

12. **AGREEMENT TO PURCHASE AND TIME LIMIT FOR ACCEPTANCE.** Buyer offers to purchase the property on the above terms and conditions. Seller shall have until _____ (AM/PM) _____ , 19 ____, to accept this offer. Unless accepted, this offer shall lapse and the Agent shall return the EARNEST MONEY to the Buyer.

| (Buyer's Signature) | (Date) | (Address) | (Phone) | (SSN/TAX ID) |
|---|---|---|---|---|
| (Buyer's Signature) | (Date) | (Address) | (Phone) | (SSN/TAX ID) |

CHECK ONE:
☐ ACCEPTANCE OF OFFER TO PURCHASE: Seller hereby ACCEPTS the foregoing offer on the terms and conditions specified above.
☐ REJECTION. Seller hereby REJECTS the foregoing offer. _____ (Seller's initials)
☐ COUNTER OFFER. Seller hereby ACCEPTS the foregoing offer SUBJECT TO the exceptions or modifications as specified below or in the attached Addendum, and presents said COUNTER OFFER for Buyer's acceptance. Buyer shall have until _____ (AM/PM) _____ , 19 ____ to accept the terms specified below.
_____
_____
_____
_____

| (Seller's Signature) | (Date) | (Time) | (Address) | (Phone) | (SSN/TAX ID) |
|---|---|---|---|---|---|
| (Seller's Signature) | (Date) | (Time) | (Address) | (Phone) | (SSN/TAX ID) |

CHECK ONE:
☐ ACCEPTANCE OF COUNTER OFFER. Buyer hereby ACCEPTS the COUNTER OFFER
☐ REJECTION. Buyer hereby REJECTS the COUNTER OFFER. _____ (Buyer's Initials)
☐ COUNTER OFFER. Buyer hereby ACCEPTS the COUNTER OFFER with modifications on attached Addendum.

| (Buyer's Signature) | (Date) | (Time) | (Buyer's Signature) | (Date) | (Time) |
|---|---|---|---|---|---|

## DOCUMENT RECEIPT

State Law requires Broker to furnish Buyer and Seller with copies of this Agreement bearing all signatures. (One of the following alternatives must therefore be completed).

A. ☐ I acknowledge receipt of a final copy of the foregoing Agreement bearing all signatures:

SIGNATURE OF SELLER                                          SIGNATURE OF BUYER

_____    Date _____    _____    Date _____

_____    Date _____    _____    Date _____

B. ☐ I personally caused a final copy of the foregoing Agreement bearing all signatures to be mailed on _____ , 19 ____ by Certified Mail and return receipt attached hereto to the ☐ Seller ☐ Buyer. Sent by _____

**Page three of a four page form**

states. As long as you are using a reputable title company, loan officer, or real estate attorney to close, you shouldn't have to worry about a thing.

If you'd like to be more than a paper signer, read "Closing the Sale" (Step 10) in the for-sale-by-owner section. The closing is usually rather anticlimactic after all the sweat and work in getting a home ready for sale and working with your agent. The closing is just a few minutes' worth of pen work.

What happens if you're all ready to close but you don't feel good about everything? Don't worry, you still have rights. Many states require that all real estate sales be reviewed by an attorney, and fully explained to the seller and buyer before they close. If your state does not require a lawyer to close, you might consider hiring one anyway. Call your local bar association and get a referral to a local real estate attorney. You might want to hire a professional to review everything and make sure that you understand everything that you are signing. It's always worth it if you have any doubts.

In conclusion, take the necessary steps to get your home in order for showing, select a real estate agent with care, and then step back and let the agent sell the home for you. When you are needed, the agent will let you know. He or she can't sell the home without your approval, so just relax, help when asked to, and wait for the sale to happen.

# P A R T   F O U R

# DESPERATE CASES

□   □   □

# DESPERATE CASES

□　□　□

*Desperate times call for desperate measures.*
> —Winston Churchill

If it's been three months or so and you still haven't had a serious offer, you are probably beginning to wonder why. A variety of circumstances could keep your home from selling. Maybe your reasons for selling don't seem so important anymore and you are only making a half-hearted attempt to sell the home. Often you will be financially ahead if you stay in your present home. The interest rate on the existing mortgage may be much better than the current market rate, your kids may be almost grown, and buying a new, larger home now could mean that you and your spouse are rattling around in a barn in a few years when the kids are gone.

---

If you really are committed to selling, then you should sit down with your spouse to go over the facts as objectively as possible. Look for the item or items that seem to be impeding the sale of your home. Have you priced your home too high to attract buyers? Discuss this with your agent if you have been using one, or consider having a realtor do an analysis of your home's marketability if you have been trying to sell on your own. Sometimes using the advice of an expert to adjust price will solve the problem. If you are using a realtor, are you satisfied with the efforts she's been making to sell your house?

If this doesn't help, then review the appropriate chapters in this book to see what changes you can make to ensure a sale. Once you have eliminated price as the source of the problem, start at square one by going outside to see how the "curb appeal" of your home measures up. If you are comfortable with the curb appeal, go back through the other steps that prepared you to put your house up for sale. Then, when you're sure the home is in excellent shape, look at the neighborhood anew. Often even in the tidiest communities there will be one yard and home that isn't up to par. If that home is close or next to yours, it could be the problem. Based on your knowledge of the neighbor's temperament and past experiences with him, you may consider talking to him tactfully and politely about external improvements to his yard and home so that you can sell your house. You might even offer to pay the gardener and/or the painter to encourage the neighbor to do the needed improvements. I know that is drastic, but remember we are talking about desperate cases and your neighbor will be doing *you* a favor. The gardening and paint should cost less than a thousand dollars. How many payments on your home is that? Probably two, on the average. Wouldn't it be worth the cost to remove the problem and be able to sell your house?

If you really need to move tomorrow and no buyers are in sight, you might consider changing your home from a personal residence to an income property. Move to your new home and rent your previous residence to another family. Usually, the rent will more than cover the mortgage payment. Let the renters finish paying off the mortgage while you enjoy your new home. Later, when the market changes you can put the house up for sale again. In the meantime, there are tax advantages to having rental property. If you decide to rent, consult an accountant or a tax attorney about depreciation, expenses, the interest on the mortgage —all can be deducted from your taxable income.

If you're going to be living locally, you could consider managing the rental home yourself. This entails checking on the property from time to time to ensure the renters are taking reasonable care of it, collecting the rent, and finding new renters when the old ones move. If you are going to move out of state, you will have to hire a professional manager. Contact your local board of realtors or apartment owners' association for a recommendation. Make sure to check the references of the person you consider hiring, and talk to people who own properties that he or she manages. Even hiring a professional property manager can be a less than ideal situation, but it is better than trying to be a long-distance landlord.

A variation on the usual rental arrangement of month-to-month or yearly leases is to rent your home to people who have a temporary need for housing. Your renters could be a family who are new in town and waiting for their new home to close escrow, or who have sold their home and must vacate before their next residence is available. Another possible source of temporary renters, especially if your home is near tourist attractions like ski resorts, amusement parks, athletic arenas, and so forth, is people who are coming to the area for a vacation. Renting to these families for a week or two would yield more rent than the usual longer-term situations. Utilizing your home would be cheaper and pleasanter for the families than renting by the day at a local hotel or motel. I know of a lady who moves out of her home for several months each year. She lives near a ski resort, and each winter she packs up her personal items and moves in with some friends. The income she receives from renting out her home to vacationers more than pays her mortgage payments for the entire year. You might consider making up a flier and sending it to local travel agents and to organizations like the American Association of Retired Persons that sponsor group tours. Offer free concert tickets or tickets to sporting events as an added incentive to the renters. A house with three or four bedrooms can accommodate several couples on vacation. Have a bare minimum of furniture in the house, and let the renters use the garage for temporary storage. You could also prepare fliers for local rental agencies and real estate agencies to let them know your house is available for short-term rental. This would help you rent the home more regularly and might also get the attention of realtors and others who might develop an interest in buying the property. The local newspapers are another good way to advertise your temporary rental service, too.

If you have already bought your next home and making two house payments each month is killing you, it is time to think of some unusual ways to sell your home. To begin with, you could hold an open house for everyone living in the immediate neighborhood—say, an area six to eight blocks square, or your subdivision if it is clearly defined and reasonably small. Prepare one-page fliers that have a picture of your home, a rough floor plan of the house and yard, and all the pertinent information about sales price, assumable mortgage, interest rate, and so forth (see Step 6 in the for-sale-by-owner section). On the reverse side have an invitation for families to come get acquainted with your home in case they have co-workers, friends, or relatives who might be interested in buying in the area.

Prepare some attractive refreshments that complement the season: hot chocolate and doughnuts or popcorn in the winter, lemonade, homemade ice cream, or melon slices in warmer weather. Indicate on the flier that refreshments will be served. Organize the refreshments so they are convenient for the visitors and so there is a quick way to dispose of paper cups and paper plates once they are done eating.

One of the most active subdivisions I know of is also one where realtors seldom participate in home sales. The people who live in the subdivision always seem to have friends or family members interested in buying a home in the area, and most sales are made directly through such contacts.

If your situation seems really desperate and time is of the essence to you, contact a real estate broker and offer a higher than usual commission, say 15 percent, if he sells the home by a certain date for at least a predetermined minimum price. You may have to give up your profit, or even take a loss, but that is better than making payments on two home mortgages every month or having your home repossessed. How long before two house payments a month would eat up your profit on the sale anyway? Probably not long. If you are paying $750 a month in mortgage payments on your original home and your equity is less than $10,000, in ten months you will have lost $7,500 in mortgage payments. In three more months the entire equity will be consumed by mortgage payments. Why not just bite the bullet and take the loss up front, get rid of the stress, and get on with your life?

Put modern technology to work for you in selling your home. You could list the pertinent information (see Step 6 in the for-sale-by-owner section on writing ads for the newspaper) in a computer bulletin board. Include your telephone number and whether they can ask you questions through a computer modem. Be prompt in responding to such questions to keep the prospective buyers interested.

You can also send your flier over a FAX machine to local real estate firms and other large companies that you think have newly hired and/or relocated employees. Your telephone directory may list their FAX numbers, or simply call them and ask for it. Limit your transmission to one page; include a rough floor plan and the financial information. Use some discretion in choosing where to send the flier, though. Some companies are annoyed by this kind of unsolicited mail.

In some states it is legal to hold an auction to sell your house. In your advertising, indicate the minimum acceptable bid and the terms: Is your mortgage assumable? What kind of cash is necessary to close escrow? Which closing costs are you willing to pay? How would a prospective buyer qualify? A realtor may be a good person to act as the auctioneer, receiving the bids and conducting the formal part of the auction. In many states there are major companies that specialize in real estate auctions. You might want to call your local board of realtors and ask for the name and number of a local real estate auction firm.

And finally, think about offering some unusual incentives for the buyers. For example, young couples starting out have very limited capital. Offer the buyers their choice of *new* appliances, a color TV, drapes for the living room, or some landscaping of their choice. These extras could make the difference between selling and not selling your home. They will cost you money, but you need to weigh the cost of the incentives against the cost and stress of not selling your home. Decide what you can afford to offer as incentives, and then *advertise*.

Good selling takes time, effort, know-how—and a little luck. If at first you don't succeed, decide if you really want to sell or if you could be content staying and making a few changes to your home. If you definitely want to sell, then leave no stone unturned, no gimmick or incentive untried. Be creative in marketing your home; then, if you can't sell it, rent it out for a while.

# HOME OWNERSHIP AS AN INVESTMENT

□  □  □

# HOME OWNERSHIP AS AN INVESTMENT

□　　□　　□

*Home ownership is America's wealth.*
—Salim Abu Daoud, business-
man, commenting on the
difference between the
wealth of his country
and ours

Today more than ever, your home is the key to your financial future. Surveys through the National Association of Realtors and *The Real Estate Advisor* show that rents are rising faster than the cost of housing. With that in mind, it is more important than ever to own your own home. The 1986 Tax Reform Act did not affect the tax deduction taken on interest paid on mortgages, so owning a home can shelter several thousand dollars a year from taxes. If you rent, you don't have that same kind of tax break. A long-time acquaintance of mine bought a modest home five years ago. Her monthly payments are $600 a month, totaling

$7,200 per year. The interest portion of that payment totals about $6,000 a year. If you multiply $6,000 by 28 percent (her federal tax bracket), you will see that she saves $1,680 in taxes every year on the interest alone. She receives an additional tax shelter from the property taxes that are included in her $600 monthly payment. She is also building a modest equity. As the years pass, less of her payment will be interest and more will go toward equity.

Renting a comparable home in the area where she lives would cost $750 a month. The difference, $150 a month for twelve months, means a cost of $1,800 more per year to rent than buy, and she would lose the tax shelter. The difference in buying a home vs. renting one would be close to $2,000 a year in tax savings plus the $1,800 additional rental costs. My friend saves nearly $4,000 a year by buying instead of renting. With a larger mortgage, or in a state where property taxes are higher, the savings of buying over renting could be substantial.

In most cases the first home your parents bought wasn't their last. They moved up to their dream home by degrees. Buying and selling, stepping up, playing Monopoly, or living in your investment, whatever you call it, it is one of the smartest strategies a person can use.

With today's high prices you've got to move into that dream home one residence at a time. You need to be willing to buy and sell, buy again a little larger, sell again, buy again larger still until you have the home you want, in the neighborhood you like. Many couples use this strategy not only to move up but to pay off their homes in full. Each time they sell, they take their profit and apply it to the down payment on another home. Each time they sell and then buy again, they have more money for the down payment and less of the purchase price to finance through a mortgage. The lower mortgage means more equity is accumulating and less of the monthly payment is going to interest. So with each sale and subsequent purchase you not only get a better house but grow closer to owning that home outright.

Starting with a modest home is a good way to begin using your home as a live-in investment. As you are making the mortgage payments, you are building equity and a good credit rating which will help you move up gradually to the home you really want. Fixing up your first home in ways that will pay off when you sell it is the first step toward realizing your financial goals through investing in real estate. Get the yard in shape until it is the most attractive in the neighborhood. Later on, the outside appeal of your home will attract buyers. Paint the portions of the exterior of the house that need it; this will not only improve the value of your home but will prevent more costly maintenance later on. Paint protects as well as improves the eye appeal of your home. Take care of needed household repairs on the inside as well; replace the washers in those leaking faucets, put new linoleum in the kitchen, revarnish the kitchen cabinets. If possible, avoid making major repairs to the home. Most of the money spent in major repairs will not be recovered when you sell the home.

The second step, after you have whipped the property into shape, is letting it appreciate. This takes patience. In some areas prices right now may be soft. But don't worry too much. Real estate has cycles. It goes up and comes down. Think back ten years to the prices homes were selling for in your area. They have changed a great deal and I guarantee that in the years to come, they'll change again. History shows that real estate values will go up. No one can add more land, but the population grows every minute. It's only common sense.

This might mean living in your first house for a couple of years and keeping it up while the value of the home rises. Your patience will be rewarded by an extra few thousand dollars when you do decide to sell.

If you're willing to pay the price and do the work that this old-fashioned but not outdated strategy requires, you can do more for your financial future than almost anything but winning the lotto. If you keep up this process, you can own the home of your dreams outright. It may take up to ten years, but eventually you will have the security of living in a home that is fully paid for.

That is where the importance of this book comes in. If you are going to sell your home, you must do it for the maximum price in the minimum time. Each time you're ready to sell and move up a notch toward that dream home, review the steps in this book to sharpen your sales ability. Then involve yourself in the next move to improve your financial situation. Having your home paid for is one of the nicest feelings in the world. Imagine what it would be like never to make a mortgage payment again!

You are ready now to succeed with real estate selling. Go for it!

# APPENDIX

□   □   □

# AMORTIZATION SCHEDULE

# 9.00%

# MONTHLY
## PAYMENT REQUIRED TO AMORTIZE A LOAN

| TERM AMOUNT | 1 year | 2 years | 3 years | 4 years | 5 years | 6 years | 7 years | 8 years | 9 years | 10 years | 11 years | 12 years |
|---|---|---|---|---|---|---|---|---|---|---|---|---|
| 50 | 4.38 | 2.29 | 1.59 | 1.25 | 1.04 | .91 | .81 | .74 | .68 | .64 | .60 | .57 |
| 100 | 8.75 | 4.57 | 3.18 | 2.49 | 2.08 | 1.81 | 1.61 | 1.47 | 1.36 | 1.27 | 1.20 | 1.14 |
| 200 | 17.50 | 9.14 | 6.36 | 4.98 | 4.16 | 3.61 | 3.22 | 2.94 | 2.71 | 2.54 | 2.40 | 2.28 |
| 300 | 26.24 | 13.71 | 9.54 | 7.47 | 6.23 | 5.41 | 4.83 | 4.40 | 4.07 | 3.81 | 3.59 | 3.42 |
| 400 | 34.99 | 18.28 | 12.72 | 9.96 | 8.31 | 7.22 | 6.44 | 5.87 | 5.42 | 5.07 | 4.79 | 4.56 |
| 500 | 43.73 | 22.85 | 15.90 | 12.45 | 10.38 | 9.02 | 8.05 | 7.33 | 6.78 | 6.34 | 5.99 | 5.70 |
| 600 | 52.48 | 27.42 | 19.08 | 14.94 | 12.46 | 10.82 | 9.66 | 8.80 | 8.13 | 7.61 | 7.18 | 6.83 |
| 700 | 61.22 | 31.98 | 22.26 | 17.42 | 14.54 | 12.62 | 11.27 | 10.26 | 9.49 | 8.87 | 8.38 | 7.97 |
| 800 | 69.97 | 36.55 | 25.44 | 19.91 | 16.61 | 14.43 | 12.88 | 11.73 | 10.84 | 10.14 | 9.57 | 9.11 |
| 900 | 78.71 | 41.12 | 28.62 | 22.40 | 18.69 | 16.23 | 14.49 | 13.19 | 12.19 | 11.41 | 10.77 | 10.25 |
| 1000 | 87.46 | 45.69 | 31.80 | 24.89 | 20.76 | 18.03 | 16.09 | 14.66 | 13.55 | 12.67 | 11.97 | 11.39 |
| 2000 | 174.91 | 91.37 | 63.60 | 49.78 | 41.52 | 36.06 | 32.18 | 29.31 | 27.09 | 25.34 | 23.93 | 22.77 |
| 3000 | 262.36 | 137.06 | 95.40 | 74.66 | 62.28 | 54.08 | 48.27 | 43.96 | 40.63 | 38.01 | 35.89 | 34.15 |
| 4000 | 349.81 | 182.74 | 127.20 | 99.55 | 83.04 | 72.11 | 64.36 | 58.61 | 54.18 | 50.68 | 47.85 | 45.53 |
| 5000 | 437.26 | 228.43 | 159.00 | 124.43 | 103.80 | 90.13 | 80.45 | 73.26 | 67.72 | 63.34 | 59.81 | 56.91 |
| 6000 | 524.71 | 274.11 | 190.80 | 149.32 | 124.56 | 108.16 | 96.54 | 87.91 | 81.26 | 76.01 | 71.77 | 68.29 |
| 7000 | 612.17 | 319.80 | 222.60 | 174.20 | 145.31 | 126.18 | 112.63 | 102.56 | 94.81 | 88.68 | 83.73 | 79.67 |
| 8000 | 699.62 | 365.48 | 254.40 | 199.09 | 166.07 | 144.21 | 128.72 | 117.21 | 108.35 | 101.35 | 95.69 | 91.05 |
| 9000 | 787.07 | 411.17 | 286.20 | 223.97 | 186.83 | 162.23 | 144.81 | 131.86 | 121.89 | 114.01 | 107.65 | 102.43 |
| 10000 | 874.52 | 456.85 | 318.00 | 248.86 | 207.59 | 180.26 | 160.90 | 146.51 | 135.43 | 126.68 | 119.61 | 113.81 |
| 11000 | 961.97 | 502.54 | 349.80 | 273.74 | 228.35 | 198.29 | 176.98 | 161.16 | 148.98 | 139.35 | 131.57 | 125.19 |
| 12000 | 1049.42 | 548.22 | 381.60 | 298.63 | 249.11 | 216.31 | 193.07 | 175.81 | 162.52 | 152.02 | 143.53 | 136.57 |
| 13000 | 1136.87 | 593.91 | 413.40 | 323.51 | 269.86 | 234.34 | 209.16 | 190.46 | 176.06 | 164.68 | 155.50 | 147.95 |
| 14000 | 1224.33 | 639.59 | 445.20 | 348.40 | 290.62 | 252.36 | 225.25 | 205.11 | 189.61 | 177.35 | 167.46 | 159.33 |
| 15000 | 1311.78 | 685.28 | 477.00 | 373.28 | 311.38 | 270.39 | 241.34 | 219.76 | 203.15 | 190.02 | 179.42 | 170.71 |
| 16000 | 1399.23 | 730.96 | 508.80 | 398.17 | 332.14 | 288.41 | 257.43 | 234.41 | 216.69 | 202.69 | 191.38 | 182.09 |
| 17000 | 1486.68 | 776.65 | 540.60 | 423.05 | 352.90 | 306.44 | 273.52 | 249.06 | 230.23 | 215.35 | 203.34 | 193.47 |
| 18000 | 1574.13 | 822.33 | 572.40 | 447.94 | 373.66 | 324.46 | 289.61 | 263.71 | 243.78 | 228.02 | 215.30 | 204.85 |
| 19000 | 1661.58 | 868.02 | 604.20 | 472.82 | 394.41 | 342.49 | 305.70 | 278.36 | 257.32 | 240.69 | 227.26 | 216.23 |
| 20000 | 1749.03 | 913.70 | 636.00 | 497.71 | 415.17 | 360.52 | 321.79 | 293.01 | 270.86 | 253.36 | 239.22 | 227.61 |
| 21000 | 1836.49 | 959.38 | 667.80 | 522.59 | 435.93 | 378.54 | 337.88 | 307.66 | 284.41 | 266.02 | 251.18 | 238.99 |
| 22000 | 1923.94 | 1005.07 | 699.60 | 547.48 | 456.69 | 396.57 | 353.96 | 322.31 | 297.95 | 278.69 | 263.14 | 250.37 |
| 23000 | 2011.39 | 1050.75 | 731.40 | 572.36 | 477.45 | 414.59 | 370.05 | 336.96 | 311.49 | 291.36 | 275.10 | 261.75 |
| 24000 | 2098.84 | 1096.44 | 763.20 | 597.25 | 498.21 | 432.62 | 386.14 | 351.61 | 325.03 | 304.03 | 287.06 | 273.13 |
| 25000 | 2186.29 | 1142.12 | 795.00 | 622.13 | 518.96 | 450.64 | 402.23 | 366.26 | 338.58 | 316.69 | 299.03 | 284.51 |
| 26000 | 2273.74 | 1187.81 | 826.80 | 647.02 | 539.72 | 468.67 | 418.32 | 380.91 | 352.12 | 329.36 | 310.99 | 295.89 |
| 27000 | 2361.19 | 1233.49 | 858.60 | 671.90 | 560.48 | 486.69 | 434.41 | 395.56 | 365.66 | 342.03 | 322.95 | 307.27 |
| 28000 | 2448.65 | 1279.18 | 890.40 | 696.79 | 581.24 | 504.72 | 450.50 | 410.21 | 379.21 | 354.70 | 334.91 | 318.65 |
| 29000 | 2536.10 | 1324.86 | 922.20 | 721.67 | 602.00 | 522.75 | 466.59 | 424.86 | 392.75 | 367.36 | 346.87 | 330.03 |
| 30000 | 2623.55 | 1370.55 | 954.00 | 746.56 | 622.76 | 540.77 | 482.68 | 439.51 | 406.29 | 380.03 | 358.58 | 341.41 |
| 31000 | 2711.00 | 1416.23 | 985.80 | 771.44 | 643.51 | 558.80 | 498.77 | 454.16 | 419.84 | 392.70 | 370.79 | 352.79 |
| 32000 | 2798.45 | 1461.92 | 1017.60 | 796.33 | 664.27 | 576.82 | 514.86 | 468.81 | 433.38 | 405.37 | 382.75 | 364.17 |
| 33000 | 2885.90 | 1507.60 | 1049.40 | 821.21 | 685.03 | 594.85 | 530.94 | 483.46 | 446.92 | 418.04 | 394.71 | 375.56 |
| 34000 | 2973.36 | 1553.29 | 1081.20 | 846.10 | 705.79 | 612.87 | 547.03 | 498.11 | 460.46 | 430.70 | 406.67 | 386.94 |
| 35000 | 3060.81 | 1598.97 | 1113.00 | 870.98 | 726.55 | 630.90 | 563.12 | 512.76 | 474.01 | 443.37 | 418.63 | 398.32 |
| 36000 | 3148.26 | 1644.66 | 1144.80 | 895.87 | 747.31 | 648.92 | 579.21 | 527.41 | 487.55 | 456.04 | 430.59 | 409.70 |
| 37000 | 3235.71 | 1690.34 | 1176.60 | 920.75 | 768.06 | 666.95 | 595.30 | 542.06 | 501.09 | 468.71 | 442.55 | 421.08 |
| 38000 | 3323.16 | 1736.03 | 1208.39 | 945.64 | 788.82 | 684.98 | 611.39 | 556.71 | 514.64 | 481.37 | 454.52 | 432.46 |
| 39000 | 3410.61 | 1781.71 | 1240.19 | 970.52 | 809.58 | 703.00 | 627.48 | 571.36 | 528.18 | 494.04 | 466.48 | 443.84 |
| 40000 | 3498.06 | 1827.39 | 1271.99 | 995.41 | 830.34 | 721.03 | 643.57 | 586.01 | 541.72 | 506.71 | 478.44 | 455.22 |
| 41000 | 3585.52 | 1873.08 | 1303.79 | 1020.29 | 851.10 | 739.05 | 659.66 | 600.66 | 555.26 | 519.38 | 490.40 | 466.60 |
| 42000 | 3672.97 | 1918.76 | 1335.59 | 1045.18 | 871.86 | 757.08 | 675.75 | 615.31 | 568.81 | 532.04 | 502.36 | 477.98 |
| 43000 | 3760.42 | 1964.45 | 1367.39 | 1070.06 | 892.61 | 775.10 | 691.84 | 629.96 | 582.35 | 544.71 | 514.32 | 489.36 |
| 44000 | 3847.87 | 2010.13 | 1399.19 | 1094.95 | 913.37 | 793.13 | 707.92 | 644.61 | 595.89 | 557.38 | 526.28 | 500.74 |
| 45000 | 3935.32 | 2055.82 | 1430.99 | 1119.83 | 934.13 | 811.15 | 724.01 | 659.26 | 609.44 | 570.05 | 538.24 | 512.12 |
| 46000 | 4022.77 | 2101.50 | 1462.79 | 1144.72 | 954.89 | 829.18 | 740.10 | 673.91 | 622.98 | 582.71 | 550.20 | 523.50 |
| 47000 | 4110.22 | 2147.19 | 1494.59 | 1169.60 | 975.65 | 847.21 | 756.19 | 688.56 | 636.52 | 595.38 | 562.16 | 534.88 |
| 48000 | 4197.68 | 2192.87 | 1526.39 | 1194.49 | 996.41 | 865.23 | 772.28 | 703.21 | 650.06 | 608.05 | 574.12 | 546.26 |
| 49000 | 4285.13 | 2238.56 | 1558.19 | 1219.37 | 1017.16 | 883.26 | 788.37 | 717.86 | 663.61 | 620.72 | 586.08 | 557.64 |
| 50000 | 4372.58 | 2284.24 | 1589.99 | 1244.26 | 1037.92 | 901.28 | 804.46 | 732.52 | 677.15 | 633.38 | 598.05 | 569.02 |
| 55000 | 4809.84 | 2512.67 | 1748.99 | 1368.68 | 1141.71 | 991.41 | 884.90 | 805.77 | 744.86 | 696.72 | 657.85 | 625.92 |
| 60000 | 5247.09 | 2741.09 | 1907.99 | 1493.11 | 1245.51 | 1081.54 | 965.35 | 879.02 | 812.58 | 760.06 | 717.65 | 682.82 |
| 65000 | 5684.35 | 2969.51 | 2066.99 | 1617.53 | 1349.30 | 1171.66 | 1045.80 | 952.27 | 880.29 | 823.40 | 777.46 | 739.72 |
| 70000 | 6121.61 | 3197.94 | 2225.99 | 1741.96 | 1453.09 | 1261.79 | 1126.24 | 1025.52 | 948.01 | 886.74 | 837.26 | 796.63 |
| 75000 | 6558.87 | 3426.36 | 2384.98 | 1866.38 | 1556.88 | 1351.92 | 1206.69 | 1098.77 | 1015.72 | 950.07 | 897.07 | 853.53 |
| 80000 | 6996.12 | 3654.78 | 2543.98 | 1990.81 | 1660.67 | 1442.05 | 1287.13 | 1172.02 | 1083.44 | 1013.41 | 956.87 | 910.43 |
| 85000 | 7433.38 | 3883.21 | 2702.98 | 2115.23 | 1764.47 | 1532.18 | 1367.58 | 1245.27 | 1151.15 | 1076.75 | 1016.67 | 967.33 |
| 90000 | 7870.64 | 4111.63 | 2861.98 | 2239.66 | 1868.26 | 1622.30 | 1448.02 | 1318.52 | 1218.87 | 1140.09 | 1076.48 | 1024.23 |
| 95000 | 8307.90 | 4340.06 | 3020.98 | 2364.08 | 1972.05 | 1712.43 | 1528.47 | 1391.77 | 1286.58 | 1203.42 | 1136.28 | 1081.13 |
| 100000 | 8745.15 | 4568.48 | 3179.98 | 2488.51 | 2075.84 | 1802.56 | 1608.91 | 1465.03 | 1354.30 | 1266.76 | 1196.09 | 1138.04 |

## PAYMENT REQUIRED TO AMORTIZE A LOAN

| TERM AMOUNT | 13 year | 14 years | 15 years | 16 years | 17 years | 18 years | 19 years | 20 years | 25 years | 30 years | 35 years | 40 years |
|---|---|---|---|---|---|---|---|---|---|---|---|---|
| 50 | .55 | .53 | .51 | .50 | .48 | .47 | .46 | .45 | .42 | .41 | .40 | .39 |
| 100 | 1.09 | 1.05 | 1.02 | .99 | .96 | .94 | .92 | .90 | .84 | .81 | .79 | .78 |
| 200 | 2.18 | 2.10 | 2.03 | 1.97 | 1.92 | 1.88 | 1.84 | 1.80 | 1.68 | 1.61 | 1.57 | 1.55 |
| 300 | 3.27 | 3.15 | 3.05 | 2.96 | 2.88 | 2.81 | 2.76 | 2.70 | 2.52 | 2.42 | 2.36 | 2.32 |
| 400 | 4.36 | 4.20 | 4.06 | 3.94 | 3.84 | 3.75 | 3.67 | 3.60 | 3.36 | 3.22 | 3.14 | 3.09 |
| 500 | 5.45 | 5.25 | 5.08 | 4.93 | 4.80 | 4.69 | 4.59 | 4.50 | 4.20 | 4.03 | 3.92 | 3.86 |
| 600 | 6.54 | 6.30 | 6.09 | 5.91 | 5.76 | 5.62 | 5.51 | 5.40 | 5.04 | 4.83 | 4.71 | 4.63 |
| 700 | 7.63 | 7.35 | 7.10 | 6.90 | 6.72 | 6.56 | 6.42 | 6.30 | 5.88 | 5.64 | 5.49 | 5.40 |
| 800 | 8.72 | 8.40 | 8.12 | 7.88 | 7.68 | 7.50 | 7.34 | 7.20 | 6.72 | 6.44 | 6.28 | 6.18 |
| 900 | 9.81 | 9.45 | 9.13 | 8.87 | 8.63 | 8.43 | 8.26 | 8.09 | 7.56 | 7.25 | 7.06 | 6.95 |
| 1000 | 10.90 | 10.49 | 10.15 | 9.85 | 9.59 | 9.37 | 9.17 | 9.00 | 8.40 | 8.05 | 7.84 | 7.72 |
| 2000 | 21.80 | 20.98 | 20.29 | 19.70 | 19.18 | 18.73 | 18.34 | 18.00 | 16.79 | 16.10 | 15.68 | 15.43 |
| 3000 | 32.70 | 31.47 | 30.43 | 29.54 | 28.77 | 28.10 | 27.51 | 27.00 | 25.18 | 24.14 | 23.52 | 23.15 |
| 4000 | 43.59 | 41.96 | 40.58 | 39.39 | 38.36 | 37.46 | 36.68 | 35.99 | 33.57 | 32.19 | 31.36 | 30.86 |
| 5000 | 54.49 | 52.45 | 50.72 | 49.23 | 47.95 | 46.83 | 45.85 | 44.99 | 41.96 | 40.24 | 39.20 | 38.57 |
| 6000 | 65.39 | 62.94 | 60.86 | 59.08 | 57.53 | 56.19 | 55.02 | 53.99 | 50.36 | 48.28 | 47.04 | 46.29 |
| 7000 | 76.28 | 73.43 | 71.00 | 68.92 | 67.12 | 65.56 | 64.19 | 62.99 | 58.75 | 56.33 | 54.88 | 54.00 |
| 8000 | 87.18 | 83.92 | 81.15 | 78.77 | 76.71 | 74.92 | 73.36 | 71.98 | 67.14 | 64.37 | 62.72 | 61.71 |
| 9000 | 98.08 | 94.41 | 91.29 | 88.61 | 86.30 | 84.29 | 82.53 | 80.98 | 75.53 | 72.42 | 70.56 | 69.43 |
| 10000 | 108.97 | 104.90 | 101.43 | 98.46 | 95.89 | 93.65 | 91.69 | 89.98 | 83.92 | 80.47 | 78.40 | 77.14 |
| 11000 | 119.87 | 115.39 | 111.57 | 108.30 | 105.47 | 103.01 | 100.86 | 98.97 | 92.32 | 88.51 | 86.24 | 84.85 |
| 12000 | 130.77 | 125.88 | 121.72 | 118.15 | 115.06 | 112.38 | 110.03 | 107.97 | 100.71 | 96.56 | 94.08 | 92.57 |
| 13000 | 141.66 | 136.37 | 131.86 | 127.99 | 124.65 | 121.74 | 119.20 | 116.97 | 109.10 | 104.61 | 101.92 | 100.28 |
| 14000 | 152.56 | 146.86 | 142.00 | 137.84 | 134.24 | 131.11 | 128.37 | 125.97 | 117.49 | 112.65 | 109.76 | 108.00 |
| 15000 | 163.46 | 157.35 | 152.14 | 147.68 | 143.83 | 140.47 | 137.54 | 134.96 | 125.88 | 120.70 | 117.60 | 115.71 |
| 16000 | 174.35 | 167.84 | 162.29 | 157.53 | 153.41 | 149.84 | 146.71 | 143.96 | 134.28 | 128.74 | 125.44 | 123.42 |
| 17000 | 185.25 | 178.32 | 172.43 | 167.37 | 163.00 | 159.20 | 155.88 | 152.96 | 142.67 | 136.79 | 133.28 | 131.14 |
| 18000 | 196.15 | 188.81 | 182.57 | 177.22 | 172.59 | 168.57 | 165.05 | 161.96 | 151.06 | 144.84 | 141.12 | 138.85 |
| 19000 | 207.04 | 199.30 | 192.72 | 187.06 | 182.18 | 177.93 | 174.22 | 170.95 | 159.45 | 152.88 | 148.96 | 146.56 |
| 20000 | 217.94 | 209.79 | 202.86 | 196.91 | 191.77 | 187.29 | 183.38 | 179.95 | 167.84 | 160.93 | 156.80 | 154.28 |
| 21000 | 228.84 | 220.28 | 213.00 | 206.75 | 201.35 | 196.66 | 192.55 | 188.95 | 176.24 | 168.98 | 164.64 | 161.99 |
| 22000 | 239.73 | 230.77 | 223.14 | 216.60 | 210.94 | 206.02 | 201.72 | 197.94 | 184.63 | 177.02 | 172.48 | 169.70 |
| 23000 | 250.63 | 241.26 | 233.29 | 226.44 | 220.53 | 215.39 | 210.89 | 206.94 | 193.02 | 185.07 | 180.32 | 177.42 |
| 24000 | 261.53 | 251.75 | 243.43 | 236.29 | 230.12 | 224.75 | 220.06 | 215.94 | 201.41 | 193.11 | 188.16 | 185.13 |
| 25000 | 272.43 | 262.24 | 253.57 | 246.13 | 239.71 | 234.12 | 229.23 | 224.94 | 209.80 | 201.16 | 196.00 | 192.85 |
| 26000 | 283.32 | 272.73 | 263.71 | 255.98 | 249.29 | 243.48 | 238.40 | 233.93 | 218.20 | 209.21 | 203.84 | 200.56 |
| 27000 | 294.22 | 283.22 | 273.86 | 265.82 | 258.88 | 252.85 | 247.57 | 242.93 | 226.59 | 217.25 | 211.68 | 208.27 |
| 28000 | 305.12 | 293.71 | 284.00 | 275.67 | 268.47 | 262.21 | 256.74 | 251.93 | 234.98 | 225.30 | 219.52 | 215.99 |
| 29000 | 316.01 | 304.20 | 294.14 | 285.51 | 278.06 | 271.57 | 265.91 | 260.93 | 243.37 | 233.35 | 227.36 | 223.70 |
| 30000 | 326.91 | 314.69 | 304.28 | 295.36 | 287.65 | 280.94 | 275.07 | 269.92 | 251.76 | 241.39 | 235.20 | 231.41 |
| 31000 | 337.81 | 325.18 | 314.43 | 305.20 | 297.23 | 290.30 | 284.24 | 278.92 | 260.16 | 249.44 | 243.04 | 239.13 |
| 32000 | 348.70 | 335.67 | 324.57 | 315.05 | 306.82 | 299.67 | 293.41 | 287.92 | 268.55 | 257.48 | 250.88 | 246.84 |
| 33000 | 359.60 | 346.15 | 334.71 | 324.90 | 316.41 | 309.03 | 302.58 | 296.91 | 276.94 | 265.53 | 258.72 | 254.55 |
| 34000 | 370.50 | 356.64 | 344.86 | 334.74 | 326.00 | 318.40 | 311.75 | 305.91 | 285.33 | 273.58 | 266.56 | 262.27 |
| 35000 | 381.39 | 367.13 | 355.00 | 344.59 | 335.59 | 327.76 | 320.92 | 314.91 | 293.72 | 281.62 | 274.40 | 269.98 |
| 36000 | 392.29 | 377.62 | 365.14 | 354.43 | 345.17 | 337.13 | 330.09 | 323.91 | 302.12 | 289.67 | 282.24 | 277.70 |
| 37000 | 403.19 | 388.11 | 375.28 | 364.28 | 354.76 | 346.49 | 339.26 | 332.90 | 310.51 | 297.72 | 290.08 | 285.41 |
| 38000 | 414.08 | 398.60 | 385.43 | 374.12 | 364.35 | 355.85 | 348.43 | 341.90 | 318.90 | 305.76 | 297.92 | 293.12 |
| 39000 | 424.98 | 409.09 | 395.57 | 383.97 | 373.94 | 365.22 | 357.59 | 350.90 | 327.29 | 313.81 | 305.76 | 300.84 |
| 40000 | 435.88 | 419.58 | 405.71 | 393.81 | 383.53 | 374.58 | 366.76 | 359.90 | 335.68 | 321.85 | 313.60 | 308.55 |
| 41000 | 446.77 | 430.07 | 415.85 | 403.66 | 393.11 | 383.95 | 375.93 | 368.89 | 344.08 | 329.90 | 321.44 | 316.26 |
| 42000 | 457.67 | 440.56 | 426.00 | 413.50 | 402.70 | 393.31 | 385.10 | 377.89 | 352.47 | 337.95 | 329.28 | 323.98 |
| 43000 | 468.57 | 451.05 | 436.14 | 423.35 | 412.29 | 402.68 | 394.27 | 386.89 | 360.86 | 345.99 | 337.12 | 331.69 |
| 44000 | 479.46 | 461.54 | 446.28 | 433.19 | 421.88 | 412.04 | 403.44 | 395.88 | 369.25 | 354.04 | 344.96 | 339.40 |
| 45000 | 490.36 | 472.03 | 456.42 | 443.04 | 431.47 | 421.41 | 412.61 | 404.88 | 377.64 | 362.09 | 352.80 | 347.12 |
| 46000 | 501.26 | 482.52 | 466.57 | 452.88 | 441.05 | 430.77 | 421.78 | 413.88 | 386.04 | 370.13 | 360.64 | 354.83 |
| 47000 | 512.15 | 493.01 | 476.71 | 462.73 | 450.64 | 440.13 | 430.95 | 422.88 | 394.43 | 378.18 | 368.48 | 362.54 |
| 48000 | 523.05 | 503.50 | 486.85 | 472.57 | 460.23 | 449.50 | 440.12 | 431.87 | 402.82 | 386.22 | 376.32 | 370.26 |
| 49000 | 533.95 | 513.98 | 497.00 | 482.42 | 469.82 | 458.86 | 449.28 | 440.87 | 411.21 | 394.27 | 384.16 | 377.97 |
| 50000 | 544.85 | 524.47 | 507.14 | 492.26 | 479.41 | 468.23 | 458.45 | 449.87 | 419.60 | 402.32 | 392.00 | 385.69 |
| 55000 | 599.33 | 576.92 | 557.85 | 541.49 | 527.35 | 515.05 | 504.30 | 494.85 | 461.56 | 442.55 | 431.20 | 424.25 |
| 60000 | 653.81 | 629.37 | 608.56 | 590.71 | 575.29 | 561.87 | 550.14 | 539.84 | 503.52 | 482.78 | 470.40 | 462.82 |
| 65000 | 708.30 | 681.81 | 659.28 | 639.94 | 623.23 | 608.69 | 595.99 | 584.83 | 545.48 | 523.01 | 509.60 | 501.39 |
| 70000 | 762.78 | 734.26 | 709.99 | 689.17 | 671.17 | 655.52 | 641.83 | 629.81 | 587.44 | 563.24 | 548.80 | 539.96 |
| 75000 | 817.27 | 786.71 | 760.70 | 738.39 | 719.11 | 702.34 | 687.68 | 674.80 | 629.40 | 603.47 | 588.00 | 578.53 |
| 80000 | 871.75 | 839.16 | 811.42 | 787.62 | 767.05 | 749.16 | 733.52 | 719.79 | 671.36 | 643.70 | 627.20 | 617.09 |
| 85000 | 926.23 | 891.60 | 862.13 | 836.84 | 814.99 | 795.98 | 779.37 | 764.77 | 713.32 | 683.93 | 666.40 | 655.66 |
| 90000 | 980.72 | 944.05 | 912.84 | 886.07 | 862.93 | 842.81 | 825.21 | 809.76 | 755.28 | 724.17 | 705.60 | 694.23 |
| 95000 | 1035.20 | 996.50 | 963.56 | 935.30 | 910.87 | 889.63 | 871.06 | 854.74 | 797.24 | 764.40 | 744.80 | 732.80 |
| 100000 | 1089.69 | 1048.94 | 1014.27 | 984.52 | 958.81 | 936.45 | 916.90 | 899.73 | 839.20 | 804.63 | 784.00 | 771.37 |

# 9.50% MONTHLY
## PAYMENT REQUIRED TO AMORTIZE A LOAN

| TERM<br>AMOUNT | 1<br>year | 2<br>years | 3<br>years | 4<br>years | 5<br>years | 6<br>years | 7<br>years | 8<br>years | 9<br>years | 10<br>years | 11<br>years | 12<br>years |
|---|---|---|---|---|---|---|---|---|---|---|---|---|
| 50 | 4.39 | 2.30 | 1.61 | 1.26 | 1.06 | .92 | .82 | .75 | .70 | .65 | .62 | .59 |
| 100 | 8.77 | 4.60 | 3.21 | 2.52 | 2.11 | 1.83 | 1.64 | 1.50 | 1.39 | 1.30 | 1.23 | 1.17 |
| 200 | 17.54 | 9.19 | 6.41 | 5.03 | 4.21 | 3.66 | 3.27 | 2.99 | 2.77 | 2.59 | 2.45 | 2.34 |
| 300 | 26.31 | 13.78 | 9.61 | 7.54 | 6.31 | 5.49 | 4.91 | 4.48 | 4.15 | 3.89 | 3.68 | 3.50 |
| 400 | 35.08 | 18.37 | 12.82 | 10.05 | 8.41 | 7.31 | 6.54 | 5.97 | 5.53 | 5.18 | 4.90 | 4.67 |
| 500 | 43.85 | 22.96 | 16.02 | 12.57 | 10.51 | 9.14 | 8.18 | 7.46 | 6.91 | 6.47 | 6.12 | 5.84 |
| 600 | 52.62 | 27.55 | 19.22 | 15.08 | 12.61 | 10.97 | 9.81 | 8.95 | 8.29 | 7.77 | 7.35 | 7.00 |
| 700 | 61.38 | 32.15 | 22.43 | 17.59 | 14.71 | 12.80 | 11.45 | 10.44 | 9.67 | 9.06 | 8.57 | 8.17 |
| 800 | 70.15 | 36.74 | 25.63 | 20.10 | 16.81 | 14.62 | 13.08 | 11.93 | 11.05 | 10.36 | 9.80 | 9.34 |
| 900 | 78.92 | 41.33 | 28.83 | 22.62 | 18.91 | 16.45 | 14.71 | 13.42 | 12.43 | 11.65 | 11.02 | 10.50 |
| 1000 | 87.69 | 45.92 | 32.04 | 25.13 | 21.01 | 18.28 | 16.35 | 14.92 | 13.81 | 12.94 | 12.24 | 11.67 |
| 2000 | 175.37 | 91.83 | 64.07 | 50.25 | 42.01 | 36.55 | 32.69 | 29.83 | 27.62 | 25.88 | 24.48 | 23.33 |
| 3000 | 263.04 | 137.75 | 96.10 | 75.37 | 63.01 | 54.83 | 49.04 | 44.74 | 41.43 | 38.82 | 36.72 | 35.00 |
| 4000 | 350.74 | 183.66 | 128.14 | 100.50 | 84.01 | 73.10 | 65.38 | 59.65 | 55.24 | 51.76 | 48.96 | 46.66 |
| 5000 | 438.42 | 229.58 | 160.17 | 125.62 | 105.01 | 91.38 | 81.72 | 74.56 | 69.05 | 64.70 | 61.20 | 58.32 |
| 6000 | 526.11 | 275.49 | 192.20 | 150.74 | 126.02 | 109.65 | 98.07 | 89.47 | 82.86 | 77.64 | 73.44 | 69.99 |
| 7000 | 613.79 | 321.41 | 224.24 | 175.87 | 147.02 | 127.93 | 114.41 | 104.38 | 96.67 | 90.58 | 85.68 | 81.65 |
| 8000 | 701.47 | 367.32 | 256.27 | 200.99 | 168.02 | 146.20 | 130.76 | 119.29 | 110.48 | 103.52 | 97.91 | 93.31 |
| 9000 | 789.16 | 413.24 | 288.30 | 226.11 | 189.02 | 164.48 | 147.10 | 134.20 | 124.29 | 116.46 | 110.15 | 104.98 |
| 10000 | 876.84 | 459.15 | 320.33 | 251.24 | 210.02 | 182.75 | 163.44 | 149.11 | 138.10 | 129.40 | 122.39 | 116.64 |
| 11000 | 964.52 | 505.06 | 352.37 | 276.36 | 231.03 | 201.03 | 179.79 | 164.02 | 151.91 | 142.34 | 134.63 | 128.31 |
| 12000 | 1052.21 | 550.98 | 384.40 | 301.48 | 252.03 | 219.30 | 196.13 | 178.94 | 165.72 | 155.28 | 146.87 | 139.97 |
| 13000 | 1139.89 | 596.89 | 416.43 | 326.61 | 273.03 | 237.58 | 212.48 | 193.85 | 179.53 | 168.22 | 159.11 | 151.63 |
| 14000 | 1227.57 | 642.81 | 448.47 | 351.73 | 294.03 | 255.85 | 228.82 | 208.76 | 193.34 | 181.16 | 171.35 | 163.30 |
| 15000 | 1315.26 | 688.72 | 480.50 | 376.85 | 315.03 | 274.13 | 245.16 | 223.67 | 207.15 | 194.10 | 183.58 | 174.96 |
| 16000 | 1402.94 | 734.64 | 512.53 | 401.98 | 336.03 | 292.40 | 261.51 | 238.58 | 220.95 | 207.04 | 195.82 | 186.62 |
| 17000 | 1490.62 | 780.55 | 544.57 | 427.10 | 357.04 | 310.67 | 277.85 | 253.49 | 234.76 | 219.98 | 208.06 | 198.29 |
| 18000 | 1578.31 | 826.47 | 576.60 | 452.22 | 378.04 | 328.95 | 294.20 | 268.40 | 248.57 | 232.92 | 220.30 | 209.95 |
| 19000 | 1665.99 | 872.38 | 608.63 | 477.34 | 399.04 | 347.22 | 310.54 | 283.31 | 262.38 | 245.86 | 232.54 | 221.62 |
| 20000 | 1753.68 | 918.29 | 640.66 | 502.47 | 420.04 | 365.50 | 326.88 | 298.22 | 276.19 | 258.80 | 244.78 | 233.28 |
| 21000 | 1841.36 | 964.21 | 672.70 | 527.59 | 441.04 | 383.77 | 343.23 | 313.13 | 290.00 | 271.74 | 257.02 | 244.94 |
| 22000 | 1929.04 | 1010.12 | 704.73 | 552.71 | 462.05 | 402.05 | 359.57 | 328.04 | 303.81 | 284.68 | 269.26 | 256.61 |
| 23000 | 2016.73 | 1056.04 | 736.76 | 577.84 | 483.05 | 420.32 | 375.92 | 342.96 | 317.62 | 297.62 | 281.49 | 268.27 |
| 24000 | 2104.41 | 1101.95 | 768.80 | 602.96 | 504.05 | 438.60 | 392.26 | 357.87 | 331.43 | 310.56 | 293.73 | 279.93 |
| 25000 | 2192.09 | 1147.87 | 800.83 | 628.08 | 525.05 | 456.87 | 408.60 | 372.78 | 345.24 | 323.50 | 305.97 | 291.60 |
| 26000 | 2279.78 | 1193.78 | 832.86 | 653.21 | 546.05 | 475.15 | 424.95 | 387.69 | 359.05 | 336.44 | 318.21 | 303.26 |
| 27000 | 2367.46 | 1239.70 | 864.89 | 678.33 | 567.06 | 493.42 | 441.29 | 402.60 | 372.86 | 349.38 | 330.45 | 314.93 |
| 28000 | 2455.14 | 1285.61 | 896.93 | 703.45 | 588.06 | 511.70 | 457.64 | 417.51 | 386.67 | 362.32 | 342.69 | 326.59 |
| 29000 | 2542.83 | 1331.53 | 928.96 | 728.58 | 609.06 | 529.97 | 473.98 | 432.42 | 400.48 | 375.26 | 354.93 | 338.25 |
| 30000 | 2630.51 | 1377.44 | 960.99 | 753.70 | 630.06 | 548.25 | 490.32 | 447.33 | 414.29 | 388.20 | 367.16 | 349.92 |
| 31000 | 2718.19 | 1423.35 | 993.03 | 778.82 | 651.06 | 566.52 | 506.67 | 462.24 | 428.10 | 401.14 | 379.40 | 361.58 |
| 32000 | 2805.88 | 1469.27 | 1025.06 | 803.95 | 672.06 | 584.80 | 523.01 | 477.15 | 441.90 | 414.08 | 391.64 | 373.24 |
| 33000 | 2893.56 | 1515.18 | 1057.09 | 829.07 | 693.07 | 603.07 | 539.36 | 492.06 | 455.71 | 427.02 | 403.88 | 384.91 |
| 34000 | 2981.24 | 1561.10 | 1089.13 | 854.19 | 714.07 | 621.34 | 555.70 | 506.98 | 469.52 | 439.96 | 416.12 | 396.57 |
| 35000 | 3068.93 | 1607.01 | 1121.16 | 879.31 | 735.07 | 639.62 | 572.04 | 521.89 | 483.33 | 452.90 | 428.36 | 408.24 |
| 36000 | 3156.61 | 1652.93 | 1153.19 | 904.44 | 756.07 | 657.89 | 588.39 | 536.80 | 497.14 | 465.84 | 440.60 | 419.90 |
| 37000 | 3244.29 | 1698.84 | 1185.22 | 929.56 | 777.07 | 676.17 | 604.73 | 551.71 | 510.95 | 478.78 | 452.83 | 431.56 |
| 38000 | 3331.98 | 1744.76 | 1217.26 | 954.68 | 798.08 | 694.44 | 621.08 | 566.62 | 524.76 | 491.72 | 465.07 | 443.23 |
| 39000 | 3419.66 | 1790.67 | 1249.29 | 979.81 | 819.08 | 712.72 | 637.42 | 581.53 | 538.57 | 504.66 | 477.31 | 454.89 |
| 40000 | 3507.35 | 1836.58 | 1281.32 | 1004.93 | 840.08 | 730.99 | 653.76 | 596.44 | 552.38 | 517.60 | 489.55 | 466.55 |
| 41000 | 3595.03 | 1882.50 | 1313.36 | 1030.05 | 861.08 | 749.27 | 670.11 | 611.35 | 566.19 | 530.53 | 501.79 | 478.22 |
| 42000 | 3682.71 | 1928.41 | 1345.39 | 1055.18 | 882.08 | 767.54 | 686.45 | 626.26 | 580.00 | 543.47 | 514.03 | 489.88 |
| 43000 | 3770.40 | 1974.33 | 1377.42 | 1080.30 | 903.09 | 785.82 | 702.80 | 641.17 | 593.81 | 556.41 | 526.27 | 501.55 |
| 44000 | 3858.08 | 2020.24 | 1409.45 | 1105.42 | 924.09 | 804.09 | 719.14 | 656.08 | 607.62 | 569.35 | 538.51 | 513.21 |
| 45000 | 3945.76 | 2066.16 | 1441.49 | 1130.55 | 945.09 | 822.37 | 735.48 | 670.99 | 621.43 | 582.29 | 550.74 | 524.87 |
| 46000 | 4033.45 | 2112.07 | 1473.52 | 1155.67 | 966.09 | 840.64 | 751.83 | 685.91 | 635.24 | 595.23 | 562.98 | 536.54 |
| 47000 | 4121.13 | 2157.99 | 1505.55 | 1180.79 | 987.09 | 858.92 | 768.17 | 700.82 | 649.04 | 608.17 | 575.22 | 548.20 |
| 48000 | 4208.81 | 2203.90 | 1537.59 | 1205.92 | 1008.09 | 877.19 | 784.52 | 715.73 | 662.85 | 621.11 | 587.46 | 559.86 |
| 49000 | 4296.50 | 2249.82 | 1569.62 | 1231.04 | 1029.10 | 895.46 | 800.86 | 730.64 | 676.66 | 634.05 | 599.70 | 571.53 |
| 50000 | 4384.18 | 2295.73 | 1601.65 | 1256.16 | 1050.10 | 913.74 | 817.20 | 745.55 | 690.47 | 646.99 | 611.94 | 583.19 |
| 55000 | 4822.60 | 2525.30 | 1761.82 | 1381.78 | 1155.11 | 1005.11 | 898.92 | 820.10 | 759.52 | 711.69 | 673.13 | 641.51 |
| 60000 | 5261.02 | 2754.87 | 1921.98 | 1507.39 | 1260.12 | 1096.49 | 980.64 | 894.66 | 828.57 | 776.39 | 734.32 | 699.83 |
| 65000 | 5699.43 | 2984.45 | 2082.15 | 1633.01 | 1365.13 | 1187.86 | 1062.36 | 969.21 | 897.61 | 841.09 | 795.52 | 758.15 |
| 70000 | 6137.85 | 3214.02 | 2242.31 | 1758.62 | 1470.14 | 1279.23 | 1144.08 | 1043.77 | 966.66 | 905.79 | 856.71 | 816.47 |
| 75000 | 6576.27 | 3443.59 | 2402.48 | 1884.24 | 1575.14 | 1370.61 | 1225.80 | 1118.32 | 1035.71 | 970.49 | 917.90 | 874.78 |
| 80000 | 7014.69 | 3673.16 | 2562.64 | 2009.86 | 1680.15 | 1461.98 | 1307.52 | 1192.88 | 1104.75 | 1035.19 | 979.10 | 933.10 |
| 85000 | 7453.10 | 3902.74 | 2722.81 | 2135.47 | 1785.16 | 1553.35 | 1389.24 | 1267.43 | 1173.80 | 1099.88 | 1040.29 | 991.42 |
| 90000 | 7891.52 | 4132.31 | 2882.97 | 2261.09 | 1890.17 | 1644.73 | 1470.96 | 1341.98 | 1242.85 | 1164.58 | 1101.48 | 1049.74 |
| 95000 | 8329.94 | 4361.88 | 3043.14 | 2386.70 | 1995.18 | 1736.10 | 1552.68 | 1416.54 | 1311.89 | 1229.28 | 1162.68 | 1108.06 |
| 100000 | 8768.36 | 4591.45 | 3203.30 | 2512.32 | 2100.19 | 1827.47 | 1634.40 | 1491.09 | 1380.94 | 1293.98 | 1223.87 | 1166.38 |

206

## PAYMENT REQUIRED TO AMORTIZE A LOAN

| TERM<br>AMOUNT | 13<br>year | 14<br>years | 15<br>years | 16<br>years | 17<br>years | 18<br>years | 19<br>years | 20<br>years | 25<br>years | 30<br>years | 35<br>years | 40<br>years |
|---|---|---|---|---|---|---|---|---|---|---|---|---|
| 50 | .56 | .54 | .53 | .51 | .50 | .49 | .48 | .47 | .44 | .43 | .42 | .41 |
| 100 | 1.12 | 1.08 | 1.05 | 1.02 | .99 | .97 | .95 | .94 | .88 | .85 | .83 | .82 |
| 200 | 2.24 | 2.16 | 2.09 | 2.03 | 1.98 | 1.94 | 1.90 | 1.87 | 1.75 | 1.69 | 1.65 | 1.63 |
| 300 | 3.36 | 3.24 | 3.14 | 3.05 | 2.97 | 2.91 | 2.85 | 2.80 | 2.63 | 2.53 | 2.47 | 2.44 |
| 400 | 4.48 | 4.32 | 4.18 | 4.06 | 3.96 | 3.88 | 3.80 | 3.73 | 3.50 | 3.37 | 3.29 | 3.25 |
| 500 | 5.60 | 5.40 | 5.23 | 5.08 | 4.95 | 4.84 | 4.75 | 4.67 | 4.37 | 4.21 | 4.11 | 4.06 |
| 600 | 6.72 | 6.48 | 6.27 | 6.09 | 5.94 | 5.81 | 5.70 | 5.60 | 5.25 | 5.05 | 4.93 | 4.87 |
| 700 | 7.84 | 7.55 | 7.31 | 7.11 | 6.93 | 6.78 | 6.65 | 6.53 | 6.12 | 5.89 | 5.76 | 5.68 |
| 800 | 8.95 | 8.63 | 8.36 | 8.12 | 7.92 | 7.75 | 7.60 | 7.46 | 6.99 | 6.73 | 6.58 | 6.49 |
| 900 | 10.07 | 9.71 | 9.40 | 9.14 | 8.91 | 8.72 | 8.54 | 8.39 | 7.87 | 7.57 | 7.40 | 7.30 |
| 1000 | 11.19 | 10.79 | 10.45 | 10.15 | 9.90 | 9.68 | 9.49 | 9.33 | 8.74 | 8.41 | 8.22 | 8.11 |
| 2000 | 22.38 | 21.57 | 20.89 | 20.30 | 19.80 | 19.36 | 18.98 | 18.65 | 17.48 | 16.82 | 16.44 | 16.21 |
| 3000 | 33.56 | 32.36 | 31.33 | 30.45 | 29.70 | 29.04 | 28.47 | 27.97 | 26.22 | 25.23 | 24.65 | 24.31 |
| 4000 | 44.75 | 43.., | 41.77 | 40.60 | 39.60 | 38.72 | 37.96 | 37.29 | 34.95 | 33.64 | 32.87 | 32.41 |
| 5000 | 55.93 | 53.92 | 52.22 | 50.75 | 49.49 | 48.40 | 47.45 | 46.61 | 43.69 | 42.05 | 41.09 | 40.51 |
| 6000 | 67.12 | 64.71 | 62.66 | 60.90 | 59.39 | 58.08 | 56.94 | 55.93 | 52.43 | 50.46 | 49.30 | 48.61 |
| 7000 | 78.31 | 75.49 | 73.10 | 71.05 | 69.29 | 67.76 | 66.42 | 65.25 | 61.16 | 58.86 | 57.52 | 56.71 |
| 8000 | 89.49 | 86.27 | 83.54 | 81.20 | 79.19 | 77.44 | 75.91 | 74.58 | 69.90 | 67.27 | 65.73 | 64.81 |
| 9000 | 100.68 | 97.06 | 93.99 | 91.35 | 89.09 | 87.12 | 85.40 | 83.90 | 78.64 | 75.68 | 73.95 | 72.91 |
| 10000 | 111.86 | 107.84 | 104.43 | 101.50 | 98.98 | 96.80 | 94.89 | 93.22 | 87.37 | 84.09 | 82.17 | 81.01 |
| 11000 | 123.05 | 118.63 | 114.87 | 111.65 | 108.88 | 106.48 | 104.38 | 102.54 | 96.11 | 92.50 | 90.38 | 89.11 |
| 12000 | 134.23 | 129.41 | 125.31 | 121.80 | 118.78 | 116.15 | 113.87 | 111.86 | 104.85 | 100.91 | 98.60 | 97.21 |
| 13000 | 145.42 | 140.19 | 135.75 | 131.95 | 128.68 | 125.83 | 123.35 | 121.18 | 113.59 | 109.32 | 106.81 | 105.31 |
| 14000 | 156.61 | 150.98 | 146.20 | 142.10 | 138.57 | 135.51 | 132.84 | 130.50 | 122.32 | 117.72 | 115.03 | 113.41 |
| 15000 | 167.79 | 161.76 | 156.64 | 152.25 | 148.47 | 145.19 | 142.33 | 139.82 | 131.06 | 126.13 | 123.25 | 121.51 |
| 16000 | 178.98 | 172.54 | 167.08 | 162.40 | 158.37 | 154.87 | 151.82 | 149.15 | 139.80 | 134.54 | 131.46 | 129.61 |
| 17000 | 190.16 | 183.33 | 177.52 | 172.55 | 168.27 | 164.55 | 161.31 | 158.47 | 148.53 | 142.95 | 139.68 | 137.72 |
| 18000 | 201.35 | 194.11 | 187.97 | 182.70 | 178.17 | 174.23 | 170.80 | 167.79 | 157.27 | 151.36 | 147.90 | 145.82 |
| 19000 | 212.53 | 204.89 | 198.41 | 192.85 | 188.06 | 183.91 | 180.28 | 177.11 | 166.01 | 159.77 | 156.11 | 153.92 |
| 20000 | 223.72 | 215.68 | 208.85 | 203.00 | 197.96 | 193.59 | 189.77 | 186.43 | 174.74 | 168.18 | 164.33 | 162.02 |
| 21000 | 234.91 | 226.46 | 219.29 | 213.15 | 207.86 | 203.27 | 199.26 | 195.75 | 183.48 | 176.58 | 172.54 | 170.12 |
| 22000 | 246.09 | 237.25 | 229.73 | 223.30 | 217.76 | 212.95 | 208.75 | 205.07 | 192.22 | 184.99 | 180.76 | 178.22 |
| 23000 | 257.28 | 248.03 | 240.18 | 233.45 | 227.65 | 222.62 | 218.24 | 214.40 | 200.96 | 193.40 | 188.98 | 186.32 |
| 24000 | 268.46 | 258.81 | 250.62 | 243.60 | 237.55 | 232.30 | 227.73 | 223.72 | 209.69 | 201.81 | 197.19 | 194.42 |
| 25000 | 279.65 | 269.60 | 261.06 | 253.75 | 247.45 | 241.98 | 237.21 | 233.04 | 218.43 | 210.22 | 205.41 | 202.52 |
| 26000 | 290.83 | 280.38 | 271.50 | 263.90 | 257.35 | 251.66 | 246.70 | 242.36 | 227.17 | 218.63 | 213.62 | 210.62 |
| 27000 | 302.02 | 291.16 | 281.95 | 274.05 | 267.25 | 261.34 | 256.19 | 251.68 | 235.90 | 227.04 | 221.84 | 218.72 |
| 28000 | 313.21 | 301.95 | 292.39 | 284.20 | 277.14 | 271.02 | 265.68 | 261.00 | 244.64 | 235.44 | 230.06 | 226.82 |
| 29000 | 324.39 | 312.73 | 302.83 | 294.35 | 287.04 | 280.70 | 275.17 | 270.32 | 253.38 | 243.85 | 238.27 | 234.92 |
| 30000 | 335.58 | 323.52 | 313.27 | 304.50 | 296.94 | 290.38 | 284.66 | 279.64 | 262.11 | 252.26 | 246.49 | 243.02 |
| 31000 | 346.76 | 334.30 | 323.71 | 314.65 | 306.84 | 300.06 | 294.15 | 288.97 | 270.85 | 260.67 | 254.70 | 251.12 |
| 32000 | 357.95 | 345.08 | 334.16 | 324.80 | 316.73 | 309.74 | 303.63 | 298.29 | 279.59 | 269.08 | 262.92 | 259.22 |
| 33000 | 369.13 | 355.87 | 344.60 | 334.95 | 326.63 | 319.42 | 313.12 | 307.61 | 288.32 | 277.49 | 271.14 | 267.33 |
| 34000 | 380.32 | 366.65 | 355.04 | 345.10 | 336.53 | 329.09 | 322.61 | 316.93 | 297.06 | 285.90 | 279.35 | 275.43 |
| 35000 | 391.51 | 377.43 | 365.48 | 355.25 | 346.43 | 338.77 | 332.10 | 326.25 | 305.80 | 294.30 | 287.57 | 283.53 |
| 36000 | 402.69 | 388.22 | 375.93 | 365.40 | 356.33 | 348.45 | 341.59 | 335.57 | 314.54 | 302.71 | 295.79 | 291.63 |
| 37000 | 413.88 | 399.00 | 386.37 | 375.55 | 366.22 | 358.13 | 351.08 | 344.89 | 323.27 | 311.12 | 304.00 | 299.73 |
| 38000 | 425.06 | 409.78 | 396.81 | 385.70 | 376.12 | 367.81 | 360.56 | 354.21 | 332.01 | 319.53 | 312.22 | 307.83 |
| 39000 | 436.25 | 420.57 | 407.25 | 395.85 | 386.02 | 377.49 | 370.05 | 363.54 | 340.75 | 327.94 | 320.43 | 315.93 |
| 40000 | 447.43 | 431.35 | 417.69 | 406.00 | 395.92 | 387.17 | 379.54 | 372.86 | 349.48 | 336.35 | 328.65 | 324.04 |
| 41000 | 458.62 | 442.14 | 428.14 | 416.15 | 405.82 | 396.85 | 389.03 | 382.18 | 358.22 | 344.76 | 336.87 | 332.13 |
| 42000 | 469.81 | 452.92 | 438.58 | 426.30 | 415.71 | 406.53 | 398.52 | 391.50 | 366.96 | 353.16 | 345.08 | 340.23 |
| 43000 | 480.99 | 463.70 | 449.02 | 436.45 | 425.61 | 416.21 | 408.01 | 400.82 | 375.69 | 361.57 | 353.30 | 348.33 |
| 44000 | 492.18 | 474.49 | 459.46 | 446.60 | 435.51 | 425.89 | 417.49 | 410.14 | 384.43 | 369.98 | 361.51 | 356.43 |
| 45000 | 503.36 | 485.27 | 469.91 | 456.75 | 445.41 | 435.57 | 426.98 | 419.46 | 393.17 | 378.39 | 369.73 | 364.53 |
| 46000 | 514.55 | 496.05 | 480.35 | 466.90 | 455.30 | 445.24 | 436.47 | 428.79 | 401.91 | 386.80 | 377.95 | 372.63 |
| 47000 | 525.73 | 506.84 | 490.79 | 477.05 | 465.20 | 454.92 | 445.96 | 438.11 | 410.64 | 395.21 | 386.16 | 380.73 |
| 48000 | 536.92 | 517.62 | 501.23 | 487.20 | 475.10 | 464.60 | 455.45 | 447.43 | 419.38 | 403.62 | 394.38 | 388.83 |
| 49000 | 548.11 | 528.41 | 511.68 | 497.35 | 485.00 | 474.28 | 464.94 | 456.75 | 428.12 | 412.02 | 402.59 | 396.94 |
| 50000 | 559.29 | 539.19 | 522.12 | 507.50 | 494.90 | 483.96 | 474.42 | 466.07 | 436.85 | 420.43 | 410.81 | 405.04 |
| 55000 | 615.22 | 593.11 | 574.33 | 558.25 | 544.38 | 532.36 | 521.87 | 512.68 | 480.54 | 462.47 | 451.89 | 445.54 |
| 60000 | 671.15 | 647.03 | 626.54 | 609.00 | 593.87 | 580.75 | 569.31 | 559.28 | 524.22 | 504.52 | 492.97 | 486.04 |
| 65000 | 727.08 | 700.94 | 678.75 | 659.75 | 643.36 | 629.15 | 616.75 | 605.89 | 567.91 | 546.56 | 534.05 | 526.55 |
| 70000 | 783.01 | 754.86 | 730.96 | 710.50 | 692.85 | 677.54 | 664.19 | 652.50 | 611.59 | 588.60 | 575.13 | 567.05 |
| 75000 | 838.93 | 808.78 | 783.17 | 761.25 | 742.34 | 725.94 | 711.63 | 699.10 | 655.28 | 630.65 | 616.21 | 607.55 |
| 80000 | 894.86 | 862.70 | 835.38 | 812.00 | 791.83 | 774.33 | 759.08 | 745.71 | 698.96 | 672.69 | 657.29 | 648.05 |
| 85000 | 950.79 | 916.62 | 887.60 | 862.75 | 841.32 | 822.73 | 806.52 | 792.32 | 742.65 | 714.73 | 698.37 | 688.56 |
| 90000 | 1006.72 | 970.54 | 939.81 | 913.50 | 890.81 | 871.13 | 853.96 | 838.92 | 786.33 | 756.77 | 739.46 | 729.06 |
| 95000 | 1062.65 | 1024.45 | 992.02 | 964.25 | 940.30 | 919.52 | 901.40 | 885.53 | 830.02 | 798.82 | 780.54 | 769.56 |
| 100000 | 1118.58 | 1078.37 | 1044.23 | 1014.99 | 989.79 | 967.92 | 948.84 | 932.14 | 873.70 | 840.86 | 821.62 | 810.07 |

# MONTHLY

## PAYMENT REQUIRED TO AMORTIZE A LOAN

| TERM AMOUNT | 1 year | 2 years | 3 years | 4 years | 5 years | 6 years | 7 years | 8 years | 9 years | 10 years | 11 years | 12 years |
|---|---|---|---|---|---|---|---|---|---|---|---|---|
| 50 | 4.40 | 2.31 | 1.62 | 1.27 | 1.07 | .93 | .84 | .76 | .71 | .67 | 63 | 60 |
| 100 | 8.80 | 4.62 | 3.23 | 2.54 | 2.13 | 1.86 | 1.67 | 1.52 | 1.41 | 1.33 | 1.26 | 1.20 |
| 200 | 17.59 | 9.23 | 6.46 | 5.08 | 4.25 | 3.71 | 3.33 | 3.04 | 2.82 | 2.65 | 2.51 | 2.40 |
| 300 | 26.38 | 13.85 | 9.69 | 7.61 | 6.38 | 5.56 | 4.99 | 4.56 | 4.23 | 3.97 | 3.76 | 3.59 |
| 400 | 35.17 | 18.46 | 12.91 | 10.15 | 8.50 | 7.42 | 6.65 | 6.07 | 5.64 | 5.29 | 5.01 | 4.79 |
| 500 | 43.96 | 23.08 | 16.14 | 12.69 | 10.63 | 9.27 | 8.31 | 7.59 | 7.04 | 6.61 | 6.26 | 5.98 |
| 600 | 52.75 | 27.69 | 19.37 | 15.22 | 12.75 | 11.12 | 9.97 | 9.11 | 8.45 | 7.93 | 7.52 | 7.18 |
| 700 | 61.55 | 32.31 | 22.59 | 17.76 | 14.88 | 12.97 | 11.63 | 10.63 | 9.86 | 9.26 | 8.77 | 8.37 |
| 800 | 70.34 | 36.92 | 25.82 | 20.30 | 17.00 | 14.83 | 13.29 | 12.14 | 11.27 | 10.58 | 10.02 | 9.57 |
| 900 | 79.13 | 41.54 | 29.05 | 22.83 | 19.13 | 16.68 | 14.95 | 13.66 | 12.68 | 11.90 | 11.27 | 10.76 |
| 1000 | 87.92 | 46.15 | 32.27 | 25.37 | 21.25 | 18.53 | 16.61 | 15.18 | 14.08 | 13.22 | 12.52 | 11.96 |
| 2000 | 175.84 | 92.29 | 64.54 | 50.73 | 42.50 | 37.06 | 33.21 | 30.35 | 28.16 | 26.44 | 25.04 | 23.91 |
| 3000 | 263.75 | 138.44 | 96.81 | 76.09 | 63.75 | 55.58 | 49.81 | 45.53 | 42.24 | 39.65 | 37.56 | 35.86 |
| 4000 | 351.67 | 184.58 | 129.07 | 101.46 | 84.99 | 74.11 | 66.41 | 60.70 | 56.32 | 52.87 | 50.08 | 47.81 |
| 5000 | 439.58 | 230.73 | 161.34 | 126.82 | 106.24 | 92.63 | 83.01 | 75.88 | 70.40 | 66.08 | 62.60 | 59.76 |
| 6000 | 527.50 | 276.87 | 193.61 | 152.18 | 127.49 | 111.16 | 99.61 | 91.05 | 84.48 | 79.30 | 75.12 | 71.71 |
| 7000 | 615.42 | 323.02 | 225.88 | 177.54 | 148.73 | 129.69 | 116.21 | 106.22 | 98.56 | 92.51 | 87.64 | 83.66 |
| 8000 | 703.33 | 369.16 | 258.14 | 202.91 | 169.98 | 148.21 | 132.81 | 121.40 | 112.63 | 105.73 | 100.16 | 95.61 |
| 9000 | 791.25 | 415.31 | 290.41 | 228.27 | 191.23 | 166.74 | 149.42 | 136.57 | 126.71 | 118.94 | 112.68 | 107.56 |
| 10000 | 879.16 | 461.45 | 322.68 | 253.63 | 212.48 | 185.26 | 166.02 | 151.75 | 140.79 | 132.16 | 125.20 | 119.51 |
| 11000 | 967.08 | 507.60 | 354.94 | 278.99 | 233.72 | 203.79 | 182.62 | 166.92 | 154.87 | 145.37 | 137.72 | 131.46 |
| 12000 | 1055.00 | 553.74 | 387.21 | 304.36 | 254.97 | 222.32 | 199.22 | 182.09 | 168.95 | 158.59 | 150.24 | 143.41 |
| 13000 | 1142.91 | 599.89 | 419.48 | 329.72 | 276.22 | 240.84 | 215.82 | 197.27 | 183.03 | 171.80 | 162.76 | 155.37 |
| 14000 | 1230.83 | 646.03 | 451.75 | 355.08 | 297.46 | 259.37 | 232.42 | 212.44 | 197.11 | 185.02 | 175.28 | 167.32 |
| 15000 | 1318.74 | 692.18 | 484.01 | 380.44 | 318.71 | 277.89 | 249.02 | 227.62 | 211.19 | 198.23 | 187.80 | 179.27 |
| 16000 | 1406.66 | 738.32 | 516.28 | 405.81 | 339.96 | 296.42 | 265.62 | 242.79 | 225.26 | 211.45 | 200.32 | 191.22 |
| 17000 | 1494.58 | 784.47 | 548.55 | 431.17 | 361.20 | 314.94 | 282.23 | 257.97 | 239.34 | 224.66 | 212.84 | 203.17 |
| 18000 | 1582.49 | 830.61 | 580.81 | 456.53 | 382.45 | 333.47 | 298.83 | 273.14 | 253.42 | 237.88 | 225.36 | 215.12 |
| 19000 | 1670.41 | 876.76 | 613.08 | 481.89 | 403.70 | 352.00 | 315.43 | 288.31 | 267.50 | 251.09 | 237.88 | 227.07 |
| 20000 | 1758.32 | 922.90 | 645.35 | 507.26 | 424.95 | 370.52 | 332.03 | 303.49 | 281.58 | 264.31 | 250.40 | 239.02 |
| 21000 | 1846.24 | 969.05 | 677.62 | 532.62 | 446.19 | 389.05 | 348.63 | 318.66 | 295.66 | 277.52 | 262.92 | 250.97 |
| 22000 | 1934.15 | 1015.19 | 709.88 | 557.98 | 467.44 | 407.57 | 365.23 | 333.84 | 309.74 | 290.74 | 275.44 | 262.92 |
| 23000 | 2022.07 | 1061.34 | 742.15 | 583.34 | 488.69 | 426.10 | 381.83 | 349.01 | 323.81 | 303.95 | 287.96 | 274.87 |
| 24000 | 2109.99 | 1107.48 | 774.42 | 608.71 | 509.93 | 444.63 | 398.43 | 364.18 | 337.89 | 317.17 | 300.48 | 286.82 |
| 25000 | 2197.90 | 1153.63 | 806.68 | 634.07 | 531.18 | 463.15 | 415.03 | 379.36 | 351.97 | 330.38 | 313.00 | 298.77 |
| 26000 | 2285.82 | 1199.77 | 838.95 | 659.43 | 552.43 | 481.68 | 431.64 | 394.53 | 366.05 | 343.60 | 325.52 | 310.73 |
| 27000 | 2373.73 | 1245.92 | 871.22 | 684.79 | 573.68 | 500.20 | 448.24 | 409.71 | 380.13 | 356.81 | 338.04 | 322.68 |
| 28000 | 2461.65 | 1292.06 | 903.49 | 710.16 | 594.92 | 518.73 | 464.84 | 424.88 | 394.21 | 370.03 | 350.56 | 334.63 |
| 29000 | 2549.57 | 1338.21 | 935.75 | 735.52 | 616.17 | 537.25 | 481.44 | 440.06 | 408.29 | 383.24 | 363.08 | 346.58 |
| 30000 | 2637.48 | 1384.35 | 968.02 | 760.88 | 637.42 | 555.78 | 498.04 | 455.23 | 422.37 | 396.46 | 375.60 | 358.53 |
| 31000 | 2725.40 | 1430.50 | 1000.29 | 786.25 | 658.66 | 574.31 | 514.64 | 470.40 | 436.44 | 409.67 | 388.12 | 370.48 |
| 32000 | 2813.31 | 1476.64 | 1032.56 | 811.61 | 679.91 | 592.83 | 531.24 | 485.58 | 450.52 | 422.89 | 400.64 | 382.43 |
| 33000 | 2901.23 | 1522.79 | 1064.82 | 836.97 | 701.16 | 611.36 | 547.84 | 500.75 | 464.60 | 436.10 | 413.16 | 394.38 |
| 34000 | 2989.15 | 1568.93 | 1097.09 | 862.33 | 722.40 | 629.88 | 564.45 | 515.93 | 478.68 | 449.32 | 425.68 | 406.33 |
| 35000 | 3077.06 | 1615.08 | 1129.36 | 887.70 | 743.65 | 648.41 | 581.05 | 531.10 | 492.76 | 462.53 | 438.20 | 418.28 |
| 36000 | 3164.98 | 1661.22 | 1161.62 | 913.06 | 764.90 | 666.94 | 597.65 | 546.27 | 506.84 | 475.75 | 450.72 | 430.23 |
| 37000 | 3252.89 | 1707.37 | 1193.89 | 938.42 | 786.15 | 685.46 | 614.25 | 561.45 | 520.92 | 488.96 | 463.24 | 442.18 |
| 38000 | 3340.81 | 1753.51 | 1226.16 | 963.78 | 807.39 | 703.99 | 630.85 | 576.62 | 535.00 | 502.18 | 475.76 | 454.13 |
| 39000 | 3428.72 | 1799.66 | 1258.43 | 989.15 | 828.64 | 722.51 | 647.45 | 591.80 | 549.07 | 515.39 | 488.28 | 466.09 |
| 40000 | 3516.64 | 1845.80 | 1290.69 | 1014.51 | 849.89 | 741.04 | 664.05 | 606.97 | 563.15 | 528.61 | 500.80 | 478.04 |
| 41000 | 3604.56 | 1891.95 | 1322.96 | 1039.87 | 871.13 | 759.56 | 680.65 | 622.15 | 577.23 | 541.82 | 513.32 | 489.99 |
| 42000 | 3692.47 | 1938.09 | 1355.23 | 1065.23 | 892.38 | 778.09 | 697.25 | 637.32 | 591.31 | 555.04 | 525.84 | 501.94 |
| 43000 | 3780.39 | 1984.24 | 1387.49 | 1090.60 | 913.63 | 796.62 | 713.86 | 652.49 | 605.39 | 568.25 | 538.36 | 513.89 |
| 44000 | 3868.30 | 2030.38 | 1419.76 | 1115.96 | 934.87 | 815.14 | 730.46 | 667.67 | 619.47 | 581.47 | 550.88 | 525.84 |
| 45000 | 3956.22 | 2076.53 | 1452.03 | 1141.32 | 956.12 | 833.67 | 747.06 | 682.84 | 633.55 | 594.68 | 563.40 | 537.79 |
| 46000 | 4044.14 | 2122.67 | 1484.30 | 1166.68 | 977.37 | 852.19 | 763.66 | 698.02 | 647.62 | 607.90 | 575.92 | 549.74 |
| 47000 | 4132.05 | 2168.82 | 1516.56 | 1192.05 | 998.62 | 870.72 | 780.26 | 713.19 | 661.70 | 621.11 | 588.44 | 561.69 |
| 48000 | 4219.97 | 2214.96 | 1548.83 | 1217.41 | 1019.86 | 889.25 | 796.86 | 728.36 | 675.78 | 634.33 | 600.96 | 573.64 |
| 49000 | 4307.88 | 2261.11 | 1581.10 | 1242.77 | 1041.11 | 907.77 | 813.46 | 743.54 | 689.86 | 647.54 | 613.48 | 585.59 |
| 50000 | 4395.80 | 2307.25 | 1613.36 | 1268.13 | 1062.36 | 926.30 | 830.06 | 758.71 | 703.94 | 660.76 | 626.00 | 597.54 |
| 55000 | 4835.38 | 2537.98 | 1774.70 | 1394.95 | 1168.59 | 1018.93 | 913.07 | 834.58 | 774.33 | 726.83 | 688.60 | 657.30 |
| 60000 | 5274.96 | 2768.70 | 1936.04 | 1521.76 | 1274.83 | 1111.56 | 996.08 | 910.45 | 844.73 | 792.91 | 751.20 | 717.05 |
| 65000 | 5714.54 | 2999.43 | 2097.37 | 1648.57 | 1381.06 | 1204.18 | 1079.08 | 986.33 | 915.12 | 858.98 | 813.80 | 776.81 |
| 70000 | 6154.12 | 3230.15 | 2258.71 | 1775.39 | 1487.30 | 1296.81 | 1162.09 | 1062.20 | 985.51 | 925.06 | 876.40 | 836.56 |
| 75000 | 6593.70 | 3460.87 | 2420.04 | 1902.20 | 1593.53 | 1389.44 | 1245.09 | 1138.07 | 1055.91 | 991.14 | 939.00 | 896.31 |
| 80000 | 7033.28 | 3691.60 | 2581.38 | 2029.01 | 1699.77 | 1482.07 | 1328.10 | 1213.94 | 1126.30 | 1057.21 | 1001.60 | 956.07 |
| 85000 | 7472.86 | 3922.32 | 2742.72 | 2155.82 | 1806.00 | 1574.70 | 1411.11 | 1289.81 | 1196.69 | 1123.29 | 1064.19 | 1015.82 |
| 90000 | 7912.43 | 4153.05 | 2904.05 | 2282.64 | 1912.24 | 1667.33 | 1494.11 | 1365.68 | 1267.09 | 1189.36 | 1126.79 | 1075.58 |
| 95000 | 8352.01 | 4383.77 | 3065.39 | 2409.45 | 2018.47 | 1759.96 | 1577.12 | 1441.55 | 1337.48 | 1255.44 | 1189.39 | 1135.33 |
| 100000 | 8791.59 | 4614.50 | 3226.72 | 2536.26 | 2124.71 | 1852.59 | 1660.12 | 1517.42 | 1407.87 | 1321.51 | 1251.99 | 1195.08 |

## PAYMENT REQUIRED TO AMORTIZE A LOAN

| TERM<br>AMOUNT | 13<br>year | 14<br>years | 15<br>years | 16<br>years | 17<br>years | 18<br>years | 19<br>years | 20<br>years | 25<br>years | 30<br>years | 35<br>years | 40<br>years |
|---|---|---|---|---|---|---|---|---|---|---|---|---|
| 50 | .58 | .56 | .54 | .53 | .52 | .50 | .50 | .49 | .46 | .44 | .43 | .43 |
| 100 | 1.15 | 1.11 | 1.08 | 1.05 | 1.03 | 1.00 | .99 | .97 | .91 | .88 | .86 | .85 |
| 200 | 2.30 | 2.22 | 2.15 | 2.10 | 2.05 | 2.00 | 1.97 | 1.94 | 1.82 | 1.76 | 1.72 | 1.70 |
| 300 | 3.45 | 3.33 | 3.23 | 3.14 | 3.07 | 3.00 | 2.95 | 2.90 | 2.73 | 2.64 | 2.58 | 2.55 |
| 400 | 4.60 | 4.44 | 4.30 | 4.19 | 4.09 | 4.00 | 3.93 | 3.87 | 3.64 | 3.52 | 3.44 | 3.40 |
| 500 | 5.74 | 5.55 | 5.38 | 5.23 | 5.11 | 5.00 | 4.91 | 4.83 | 4.55 | 4.39 | 4.30 | 4.25 |
| 600 | 6.89 | 6.65 | 6.45 | 6.28 | 6.13 | 6.00 | 5.89 | 5.80 | 5.46 | 5.27 | 5.16 | 5.10 |
| 700 | 8.04 | 7.76 | 7.53 | 7.33 | 7.15 | 7.00 | 6.87 | 6.76 | 6.37 | 6.15 | 6.02 | 5.95 |
| 800 | 9.19 | 8.87 | 8.60 | 8.37 | 8.17 | 8.00 | 7.86 | 7.73 | 7.27 | 7.03 | 6.88 | 6.80 |
| 900 | 10.34 | 9.98 | 9.68 | 9.42 | 9.20 | 9.00 | 8.84 | 8.69 | 8.18 | 7.90 | 7.74 | 7.65 |
| 1000 | 11.48 | 11.09 | 10.75 | 10.46 | 10.22 | 10.00 | 9.82 | 9.66 | 9.09 | 8.78 | 8.60 | 8.50 |
| 2000 | 22.96 | 22.17 | 21.50 | 20.92 | 20.43 | 20.00 | 19.63 | 19.31 | 18.18 | 17.56 | 17.20 | 16.99 |
| 3000 | 34.44 | 33.25 | 32.24 | 31.38 | 30.64 | 30.00 | 29.44 | 28.96 | 27.27 | 26.33 | 25.80 | 25.48 |
| 4000 | 45.92 | 44.33 | 42.99 | 41.84 | 40.85 | 40.00 | 39.26 | 38.61 | 36.35 | 35.11 | 34.39 | 33.97 |
| 5000 | 57.40 | 55.42 | 53.74 | 52.30 | 51.07 | 50.00 | 49.07 | 48.26 | 45.44 | 43.88 | 42.99 | 42.46 |
| 6000 | 68.88 | 66.50 | 64.48 | 62.76 | 61.28 | 60.00 | 58.88 | 57.91 | 54.53 | 52.66 | 51.59 | 50.95 |
| 7000 | 80.35 | 77.58 | 75.23 | 73.22 | 71.49 | 69.99 | 68.69 | 67.56 | 63.61 | 61.44 | 60.18 | 59.45 |
| 8000 | 91.83 | 88.66 | 85.97 | 83.68 | 81.70 | 79.99 | 78.51 | 77.21 | 72.70 | 70.21 | 68.78 | 67.94 |
| 9000 | 103.31 | 99.74 | 96.72 | 94.14 | 91.91 | 89.99 | 88.32 | 86.86 | 81.79 | 78.99 | 77.38 | 76.43 |
| 10000 | 114.79 | 110.83 | 107.47 | 104.60 | 102.13 | 99.99 | 98.13 | 96.51 | 90.88 | 87.76 | 85.97 | 84.92 |
| 11000 | 126.27 | 121.91 | 118.21 | 115.05 | 112.34 | 109.99 | 107.94 | 106.16 | 99.96 | 96.54 | 94.57 | 93.41 |
| 12000 | 137.75 | 132.99 | 128.96 | 125.51 | 122.55 | 119.99 | 117.76 | 115.81 | 109.05 | 105.31 | 103.17 | 101.90 |
| 13000 | 149.23 | 144.07 | 139.70 | 135.97 | 132.76 | 129.98 | 127.57 | 125.46 | 118.14 | 114.09 | 111.76 | 110.39 |
| 14000 | 160.70 | 155.15 | 150.45 | 146.43 | 142.97 | 139.98 | 137.38 | 135.11 | 127.22 | 122.87 | 120.36 | 118.89 |
| 15000 | 172.18 | 166.24 | 161.20 | 156.89 | 153.19 | 149.98 | 147.19 | 144.76 | 136.31 | 131.64 | 128.96 | 127.38 |
| 16000 | 183.66 | 177.32 | 171.94 | 167.35 | 163.40 | 159.98 | 157.01 | 154.41 | 145.40 | 140.42 | 137.55 | 135.87 |
| 17000 | 195.14 | 188.40 | 182.69 | 177.81 | 173.61 | 169.98 | 166.82 | 164.06 | 154.48 | 149.19 | 146.15 | 144.36 |
| 18000 | 206.62 | 199.48 | 193.43 | 188.27 | 183.82 | 179.98 | 176.63 | 173.71 | 163.57 | 157.97 | 154.75 | 152.85 |
| 19000 | 218.10 | 210.56 | 204.18 | 198.73 | 194.03 | 189.98 | 186.44 | 183.36 | 172.66 | 166.74 | 163.34 | 161.34 |
| 20000 | 229.57 | 221.65 | 214.93 | 209.19 | 204.25 | 199.97 | 196.26 | 193.01 | 181.75 | 175.52 | 171.94 | 169.83 |
| 21000 | 241.05 | 232.73 | 225.67 | 219.64 | 214.46 | 209.97 | 206.07 | 202.66 | 190.83 | 184.30 | 180.54 | 178.33 |
| 22000 | 252.53 | 243.81 | 236.42 | 230.10 | 224.67 | 219.97 | 215.88 | 212.31 | 199.92 | 193.07 | 189.13 | 186.82 |
| 23000 | 264.01 | 254.89 | 247.16 | 240.56 | 234.88 | 229.97 | 225.69 | 221.96 | 209.01 | 201.85 | 197.73 | 195.31 |
| 24000 | 275.49 | 265.97 | 257.91 | 251.02 | 245.10 | 239.97 | 235.51 | 231.61 | 218.09 | 210.62 | 206.33 | 203.80 |
| 25000 | 286.97 | 277.06 | 268.66 | 261.48 | 255.31 | 249.97 | 245.32 | 241.26 | 227.18 | 219.40 | 214.92 | 212.29 |
| 26000 | 298.45 | 288.14 | 279.40 | 271.94 | 265.52 | 259.96 | 255.13 | 250.91 | 236.27 | 228.17 | 223.52 | 220.78 |
| 27000 | 309.92 | 299.22 | 290.15 | 282.40 | 275.73 | 269.96 | 264.94 | 260.56 | 245.35 | 236.95 | 232.12 | 229.27 |
| 28000 | 321.40 | 310.30 | 300.89 | 292.86 | 285.94 | 279.96 | 274.76 | 270.21 | 254.44 | 245.73 | 240.71 | 237.77 |
| 29000 | 332.88 | 321.38 | 311.64 | 303.32 | 296.16 | 289.96 | 284.57 | 279.86 | 263.53 | 254.50 | 249.31 | 246.26 |
| 30000 | 344.36 | 332.47 | 322.39 | 313.78 | 306.37 | 299.96 | 294.38 | 289.51 | 272.62 | 263.28 | 257.91 | 254.75 |
| 31000 | 355.84 | 343.55 | 333.13 | 324.23 | 316.58 | 309.96 | 304.20 | 299.16 | 281.70 | 272.05 | 266.50 | 263.24 |
| 32000 | 367.32 | 354.63 | 343.88 | 334.69 | 326.79 | 319.95 | 314.01 | 308.81 | 290.79 | 280.83 | 275.10 | 271.73 |
| 33000 | 378.79 | 365.71 | 354.62 | 345.15 | 337.00 | 329.95 | 323.82 | 318.46 | 299.88 | 289.60 | 283.70 | 280.22 |
| 34000 | 390.27 | 376.79 | 365.37 | 355.61 | 347.22 | 339.95 | 333.63 | 328.11 | 308.96 | 298.38 | 292.29 | 288.71 |
| 35000 | 401.75 | 387.88 | 376.12 | 366.07 | 357.43 | 349.95 | 343.45 | 337.76 | 318.05 | 307.16 | 300.89 | 297.21 |
| 36000 | 413.23 | 398.96 | 386.86 | 376.53 | 367.64 | 359.95 | 353.26 | 347.41 | 327.14 | 315.93 | 309.49 | 305.70 |
| 37000 | 424.71 | 410.04 | 397.61 | 386.99 | 377.85 | 369.95 | 363.07 | 357.06 | 336.22 | 324.71 | 318.08 | 314.19 |
| 38000 | 436.19 | 421.12 | 408.35 | 397.45 | 388.06 | 379.95 | 372.88 | 366.71 | 345.31 | 333.48 | 326.68 | 322.68 |
| 39000 | 447.67 | 432.20 | 419.10 | 407.91 | 398.28 | 389.94 | 382.70 | 376.36 | 354.40 | 342.26 | 335.28 | 331.17 |
| 40000 | 459.14 | 443.29 | 429.85 | 418.37 | 408.49 | 399.94 | 392.51 | 386.01 | 363.49 | 351.03 | 343.87 | 339.66 |
| 41000 | 470.62 | 454.37 | 440.59 | 428.82 | 418.70 | 409.94 | 402.32 | 395.66 | 372.57 | 359.81 | 352.47 | 348.15 |
| 42000 | 482.10 | 465.45 | 451.34 | 439.28 | 428.91 | 419.94 | 412.13 | 405.31 | 381.66 | 368.59 | 361.07 | 356.65 |
| 43000 | 493.58 | 476.53 | 462.09 | 449.74 | 439.13 | 429.94 | 421.95 | 414.96 | 390.75 | 377.36 | 369.66 | 365.14 |
| 44000 | 505.06 | 487.61 | 472.83 | 460.20 | 449.34 | 439.94 | 431.76 | 424.61 | 399.83 | 386.14 | 378.26 | 373.63 |
| 45000 | 516.54 | 498.70 | 483.58 | 470.66 | 459.55 | 449.93 | 441.57 | 434.26 | 408.92 | 394.91 | 386.86 | 382.12 |
| 46000 | 528.02 | 509.78 | 494.32 | 481.12 | 469.76 | 459.93 | 451.38 | 443.91 | 418.01 | 403.69 | 395.45 | 390.61 |
| 47000 | 539.49 | 520.86 | 505.07 | 491.58 | 479.97 | 469.93 | 461.20 | 453.57 | 427.09 | 412.46 | 404.05 | 399.10 |
| 48000 | 550.97 | 531.94 | 515.82 | 502.04 | 490.19 | 479.93 | 471.01 | 463.22 | 436.18 | 421.24 | 412.65 | 407.60 |
| 49000 | 562.45 | 543.02 | 526.56 | 512.50 | 500.40 | 489.93 | 480.82 | 472.87 | 445.27 | 430.02 | 421.24 | 416.09 |
| 50000 | 573.93 | 554.11 | 537.31 | 522.96 | 510.61 | 499.93 | 490.63 | 482.52 | 454.36 | 438.79 | 429.84 | 424.58 |
| 55000 | 631.32 | 609.52 | 591.04 | 575.25 | 561.67 | 549.92 | 539.70 | 530.77 | 499.79 | 482.67 | 472.82 | 467.04 |
| 60000 | 688.71 | 664.93 | 644.77 | 627.55 | 612.73 | 599.91 | 588.76 | 579.02 | 545.23 | 526.55 | 515.81 | 509.49 |
| 65000 | 746.11 | 720.34 | 698.50 | 679.84 | 663.79 | 649.90 | 637.82 | 627.27 | 590.66 | 570.43 | 558.79 | 551.95 |
| 70000 | 803.50 | 775.75 | 752.23 | 732.14 | 714.85 | 699.90 | 686.89 | 675.52 | 636.10 | 614.31 | 601.78 | 594.41 |
| 75000 | 860.89 | 831.16 | 805.96 | 784.43 | 765.91 | 749.89 | 735.95 | 723.77 | 681.53 | 658.18 | 644.76 | 636.86 |
| 80000 | 918.28 | 886.57 | 859.69 | 836.73 | 816.97 | 799.88 | 785.01 | 772.02 | 726.97 | 702.06 | 687.74 | 679.32 |
| 85000 | 975.68 | 941.98 | 913.42 | 889.02 | 868.03 | 849.87 | 834.08 | 820.27 | 772.40 | 745.94 | 730.73 | 721.78 |
| 90000 | 1033.07 | 997.39 | 967.15 | 941.32 | 919.09 | 899.86 | 883.14 | 868.52 | 817.84 | 789.82 | 773.71 | 764.24 |
| 95000 | 1090.46 | 1052.80 | 1020.88 | 993.61 | 970.15 | 949.86 | 932.20 | 916.78 | 863.27 | 833.70 | 816.69 | 806.69 |
| 100000 | 1147.85 | 1108.21 | 1074.61 | 1045.91 | 1021.22 | 999.85 | 981.26 | 965.03 | 908.71 | 877.58 | 859.68 | 849.15 |

# MONTHLY

## PAYMENT REQUIRED TO AMORTIZE A LOAN

| TERM AMOUNT | 1 year | 2 years | 3 years | 4 years | 5 years | 6 years | 7 years | 8 years | 9 years | 10 years | 11 years | 12 years |
|---|---|---|---|---|---|---|---|---|---|---|---|---|
| 50 | 4.41 | 2.32 | 1.63 | 1.29 | 1.08 | .94 | .85 | .78 | .72 | .68 | .65 | .62 |
| 100 | 8.82 | 4.64 | 3.26 | 2.57 | 2.15 | 1.88 | 1.69 | 1.55 | 1.44 | 1.35 | 1.29 | 1.23 |
| 200 | 17.63 | 9.28 | 6.51 | 5.13 | 4.30 | 3.76 | 3.38 | 3.09 | 2.88 | 2.70 | 2.57 | 2.45 |
| 300 | 26.45 | 13.92 | 9.76 | 7.69 | 6.45 | 5.64 | 5.06 | 4.64 | 4.31 | 4.05 | 3.85 | 3.68 |
| 400 | 35.26 | 18.56 | 13.01 | 10.25 | 8.60 | 7.52 | 6.75 | 6.18 | 5.75 | 5.40 | 5.13 | 4.90 |
| 500 | 44.08 | 23.19 | 16.26 | 12.81 | 10.75 | 9.39 | 8.44 | 7.73 | 7.18 | 6.75 | 6.41 | 6.13 |
| 600 | 52.89 | 27.83 | 19.51 | 15.37 | 12.90 | 11.27 | 10.12 | 9.27 | 8.62 | 8.10 | 7.69 | 7.35 |
| 700 | 61.71 | 32.47 | 22.76 | 17.93 | 15.05 | 13.15 | 11.81 | 10.81 | 10.05 | 9.45 | 8.97 | 8.57 |
| 800 | 70.52 | 37.11 | 26.01 | 20.49 | 17.20 | 15.03 | 13.49 | 12.36 | 11.49 | 10.80 | 10.25 | 9.80 |
| 900 | 79.34 | 41.74 | 29.26 | 23.05 | 19.35 | 16.91 | 15.18 | 13.90 | 12.92 | 12.15 | 11.53 | 11.02 |
| 1000 | 88.15 | 46.38 | 32.51 | 25.61 | 21.50 | 18.78 | 16.87 | 15.45 | 14.36 | 13.50 | 12.81 | 12.25 |
| 2000 | 176.30 | 92.76 | 65.01 | 51.21 | 42.99 | 37.56 | 33.73 | 30.89 | 28.71 | 26.99 | 25.61 | 24.49 |
| 3000 | 264.45 | 139.13 | 97.51 | 76.82 | 64.49 | 56.34 | 50.59 | 46.33 | 43.06 | 40.49 | 38.42 | 36.73 |
| 4000 | 352.60 | 185.51 | 130.01 | 102.42 | 85.98 | 75.12 | 67.45 | 61.77 | 57.41 | 53.98 | 51.22 | 48.97 |
| 5000 | 440.75 | 231.89 | 162.52 | 128.02 | 107.47 | 93.90 | 84.31 | 77.21 | 71.76 | 67.47 | 64.03 | 61.21 |
| 6000 | 528.90 | 278.26 | 195.02 | 153.63 | 128.97 | 112.68 | 101.17 | 92.65 | 86.11 | 80.97 | 76.83 | 73.45 |
| 7000 | 617.05 | 324.64 | 227.52 | 179.23 | 150.46 | 131.46 | 118.03 | 108.09 | 100.46 | 94.46 | 89.64 | 85.69 |
| 8000 | 705.19 | 371.01 | 260.02 | 204.83 | 171.96 | 150.24 | 134.89 | 123.53 | 114.81 | 107.95 | 102.44 | 97.94 |
| 9000 | 793.34 | 417.39 | 292.53 | 230.44 | 193.45 | 169.02 | 151.75 | 138.97 | 129.16 | 121.45 | 115.25 | 110.18 |
| 10000 | 881.49 | 463.77 | 325.03 | 256.04 | 214.94 | 187.79 | 168.61 | 154.41 | 143.51 | 134.94 | 128.05 | 122.42 |
| 11000 | 969.64 | 510.14 | 357.53 | 281.64 | 236.44 | 206.57 | 185.47 | 169.85 | 157.86 | 148.43 | 140.85 | 134.66 |
| 12000 | 1057.79 | 556.52 | 390.03 | 307.25 | 257.93 | 225.35 | 202.33 | 185.29 | 172.22 | 161.93 | 153.66 | 146.90 |
| 13000 | 1145.94 | 602.89 | 422.54 | 332.85 | 279.43 | 244.13 | 219.19 | 200.73 | 186.57 | 175.42 | 166.46 | 159.14 |
| 14000 | 1234.09 | 649.27 | 455.04 | 358.45 | 300.92 | 262.91 | 236.05 | 216.17 | 200.92 | 188.91 | 179.27 | 171.38 |
| 15000 | 1322.23 | 695.65 | 487.54 | 384.06 | 322.41 | 281.69 | 252.92 | 231.61 | 215.27 | 202.41 | 192.07 | 183.63 |
| 16000 | 1410.38 | 742.02 | 520.04 | 409.66 | 343.91 | 300.47 | 269.78 | 247.05 | 229.62 | 215.90 | 204.88 | 195.87 |
| 17000 | 1498.53 | 788.40 | 552.55 | 435.26 | 365.40 | 319.25 | 286.64 | 262.49 | 243.97 | 229.39 | 217.68 | 208.11 |
| 18000 | 1586.68 | 834.77 | 585.05 | 460.87 | 386.90 | 338.03 | 303.50 | 277.93 | 258.32 | 242.89 | 230.49 | 220.35 |
| 19000 | 1674.83 | 881.15 | 617.55 | 486.47 | 408.39 | 356.81 | 320.34 | 293.37 | 272.67 | 256.38 | 243.29 | 232.59 |
| 20000 | 1762.98 | 927.53 | 650.05 | 512.07 | 429.88 | 375.58 | 337.22 | 308.81 | 287.02 | 269.87 | 256.09 | 244.83 |
| 21000 | 1851.13 | 973.90 | 682.56 | 537.68 | 451.38 | 394.36 | 354.08 | 324.25 | 301.37 | 283.37 | 268.90 | 257.07 |
| 22000 | 1939.27 | 1020.28 | 715.06 | 563.28 | 472.87 | 413.14 | 370.94 | 339.69 | 315.72 | 296.86 | 281.70 | 269.32 |
| 23000 | 2027.42 | 1066.65 | 747.56 | 588.88 | 494.36 | 431.92 | 387.80 | 355.13 | 330.07 | 310.36 | 294.51 | 281.56 |
| 24000 | 2115.57 | 1113.03 | 780.06 | 614.49 | 515.86 | 450.70 | 404.66 | 370.57 | 344.43 | 323.85 | 307.31 | 293.80 |
| 25000 | 2203.72 | 1159.41 | 812.57 | 640.09 | 537.35 | 469.48 | 421.52 | 386.01 | 358.78 | 337.34 | 320.12 | 306.04 |
| 26000 | 2291.87 | 1205.78 | 845.07 | 665.69 | 558.85 | 488.26 | 438.38 | 401.45 | 373.13 | 350.84 | 332.92 | 318.28 |
| 27000 | 2380.02 | 1252.16 | 877.57 | 691.30 | 580.34 | 507.04 | 455.24 | 416.89 | 387.48 | 364.33 | 345.73 | 330.52 |
| 28000 | 2468.17 | 1298.53 | 910.07 | 716.90 | 601.83 | 525.82 | 472.10 | 432.33 | 401.83 | 377.82 | 358.53 | 342.76 |
| 29000 | 2556.31 | 1344.91 | 942.58 | 742.50 | 623.33 | 544.60 | 488.96 | 447.77 | 416.18 | 391.32 | 371.33 | 355.01 |
| 30000 | 2644.46 | 1391.29 | 975.08 | 768.11 | 644.82 | 563.37 | 505.83 | 463.21 | 430.53 | 404.81 | 384.14 | 367.25 |
| 31000 | 2732.41 | 1437.66 | 1007.58 | 793.71 | 666.32 | 582.15 | 522.69 | 478.65 | 444.88 | 418.30 | 396.94 | 379.49 |
| 32000 | 2820.76 | 1484.04 | 1040.08 | 819.31 | 687.81 | 600.93 | 539.55 | 494.09 | 459.23 | 431.80 | 409.75 | 391.73 |
| 33000 | 2908.91 | 1530.41 | 1072.59 | 844.92 | 709.30 | 619.71 | 556.41 | 509.53 | 473.58 | 445.29 | 422.55 | 403.97 |
| 34000 | 2997.06 | 1576.79 | 1105.09 | 870.52 | 730.80 | 638.49 | 573.27 | 524.97 | 487.93 | 458.78 | 435.36 | 416.21 |
| 35000 | 3085.21 | 1623.17 | 1137.59 | 896.12 | 752.29 | 657.27 | 590.13 | 540.41 | 502.29 | 472.28 | 448.16 | 428.45 |
| 36000 | 3173.35 | 1669.54 | 1170.09 | 921.73 | 773.79 | 676.05 | 606.99 | 555.85 | 516.64 | 485.77 | 460.97 | 440.70 |
| 37000 | 3261.50 | 1715.92 | 1202.60 | 947.33 | 795.28 | 694.83 | 623.85 | 571.29 | 530.99 | 499.26 | 473.77 | 452.94 |
| 38000 | 3349.65 | 1762.29 | 1235.10 | 972.93 | 816.77 | 713.61 | 640.71 | 586.73 | 545.34 | 512.76 | 486.57 | 465.18 |
| 39000 | 3437.80 | 1808.67 | 1267.60 | 998.54 | 838.27 | 732.38 | 657.57 | 602.17 | 559.69 | 526.25 | 499.38 | 477.42 |
| 40000 | 3525.95 | 1855.05 | 1300.10 | 1024.14 | 859.76 | 751.16 | 674.43 | 617.61 | 574.04 | 539.74 | 512.18 | 489.66 |
| 41000 | 3614.10 | 1901.42 | 1332.61 | 1049.74 | 881.25 | 769.94 | 691.29 | 633.05 | 588.39 | 553.24 | 524.99 | 501.90 |
| 42000 | 3702.25 | 1947.80 | 1365.11 | 1075.35 | 902.75 | 788.72 | 708.15 | 648.49 | 602.74 | 566.73 | 537.79 | 514.14 |
| 43000 | 3790.39 | 1994.17 | 1397.61 | 1100.95 | 924.24 | 807.50 | 725.01 | 663.93 | 617.09 | 580.23 | 550.60 | 526.39 |
| 44000 | 3878.54 | 2040.55 | 1430.11 | 1126.55 | 945.74 | 826.28 | 741.87 | 679.37 | 631.44 | 593.72 | 563.40 | 538.63 |
| 45000 | 3966.69 | 2086.93 | 1462.61 | 1152.16 | 967.23 | 845.06 | 758.74 | 694.81 | 645.79 | 607.21 | 576.21 | 550.87 |
| 46000 | 4054.84 | 2133.30 | 1495.12 | 1177.76 | 988.72 | 863.84 | 775.60 | 710.25 | 660.14 | 620.71 | 589.01 | 563.11 |
| 47000 | 4142.99 | 2179.68 | 1527.62 | 1203.36 | 1010.22 | 882.62 | 792.46 | 725.69 | 674.50 | 634.20 | 601.81 | 575.35 |
| 48000 | 4231.14 | 2226.06 | 1560.12 | 1228.97 | 1031.71 | 901.40 | 809.32 | 741.13 | 688.85 | 647.69 | 614.62 | 587.59 |
| 49000 | 4319.29 | 2272.43 | 1592.62 | 1254.57 | 1053.21 | 920.17 | 826.18 | 756.57 | 703.20 | 661.19 | 627.42 | 599.83 |
| 50000 | 4407.44 | 2318.81 | 1625.13 | 1280.17 | 1074.70 | 938.95 | 843.04 | 772.01 | 717.55 | 674.68 | 640.23 | 612.08 |
| 55000 | 4848.18 | 2550.69 | 1787.64 | 1408.19 | 1182.17 | 1032.85 | 927.34 | 849.21 | 789.30 | 742.15 | 704.25 | 673.28 |
| 60000 | 5288.92 | 2782.57 | 1950.15 | 1536.21 | 1289.64 | 1126.74 | 1011.65 | 926.41 | 861.06 | 809.61 | 768.27 | 734.49 |
| 65000 | 5729.66 | 3014.45 | 2112.66 | 1664.22 | 1397.11 | 1220.64 | 1095.95 | 1003.61 | 932.81 | 877.08 | 832.29 | 795.70 |
| 70000 | 6170.41 | 3246.33 | 2275.18 | 1792.24 | 1504.58 | 1314.53 | 1180.25 | 1080.81 | 1004.57 | 944.55 | 896.32 | 856.90 |
| 75000 | 6611.15 | 3478.21 | 2437.69 | 1920.26 | 1612.05 | 1408.43 | 1264.56 | 1158.01 | 1076.32 | 1012.02 | 960.34 | 918.11 |
| 80000 | 7051.89 | 3710.09 | 2600.20 | 2048.28 | 1719.52 | 1502.32 | 1348.86 | 1235.21 | 1148.07 | 1079.49 | 1024.36 | 979.32 |
| 85000 | 7492.64 | 3941.97 | 2762.71 | 2176.29 | 1826.99 | 1596.22 | 1433.16 | 1312.41 | 1219.83 | 1146.95 | 1088.38 | 1040.52 |
| 90000 | 7933.38 | 4173.85 | 2925.22 | 2304.31 | 1934.46 | 1690.11 | 1517.47 | 1389.61 | 1291.58 | 1214.42 | 1152.41 | 1101.73 |
| 95000 | 8374.12 | 4405.73 | 3087.74 | 2432.33 | 2041.93 | 1784.01 | 1601.77 | 1466.81 | 1363.34 | 1281.89 | 1216.43 | 1162.94 |
| 100000 | 8814.87 | 4637.61 | 3250.25 | 2560.34 | 2149.40 | 1877.90 | 1686.07 | 1544.01 | 1435.09 | 1349.36 | 1280.45 | 1224.15 |

# MONTHLY  10.50%

## PAYMENT REQUIRED TO AMORTIZE A LOAN

| TERM / AMOUNT | 13 year | 14 years | 15 years | 16 years | 17 years | 18 years | 19 years | 20 years | 25 years | 30 years | 35 years | 40 years |
|---|---|---|---|---|---|---|---|---|---|---|---|---|
| 50 | .59 | .57 | .56 | .54 | .53 | .52 | .51 | .50 | .48 | 46 | .45 | .45 |
| 100 | 1.18 | 1.14 | 1.11 | 1.08 | 1.06 | 1.04 | 1.02 | 1.00 | .95 | .92 | .90 | .89 |
| 200 | 2.36 | 2.28 | 2.22 | 2.16 | 2.11 | 2.07 | 2.03 | 2.00 | 1.89 | 1.83 | 1.80 | 1.78 |
| 300 | 3.54 | 3.42 | 3.32 | 3.24 | 3.16 | 3.10 | 3.05 | 3.00 | 2.84 | 2.75 | 2.70 | 2.67 |
| 400 | 4.72 | 4.56 | 4.43 | 4.31 | 4.22 | 4.13 | 4.06 | 4.00 | 3.78 | 3.66 | 3.60 | 3.56 |
| 500 | 5.89 | 5.70 | 5.53 | 5.39 | 5.27 | 5.17 | 5.08 | 5.00 | 4.73 | 4.58 | 4.50 | 4.45 |
| 600 | 7.07 | 6.84 | 6.64 | 6.47 | 6.32 | 6.20 | 6.09 | 6.00 | 5.67 | 5.49 | 5.39 | 5.34 |
| 700 | 8.25 | 7.97 | 7.74 | 7.55 | 7.38 | 7.23 | 7.10 | 6.99 | 6.61 | 6.41 | 6.29 | 6.22 |
| 800 | 9.43 | 9.11 | 8.85 | 8.62 | 8.43 | 8.26 | 8.12 | 7.99 | 7.56 | 7.32 | 7.19 | 7.11 |
| 900 | 10.60 | 10.25 | 9.95 | 9.70 | 9.48 | 9.30 | 9.13 | 8.99 | 8.50 | 8.24 | 8.09 | 8.00 |
| 1000 | 11.78 | 11.39 | 11.06 | 10.78 | 10.54 | 10.33 | 10.15 | 9.99 | 9.45 | 9.15 | 8.99 | 8.89 |
| 2000 | 23.56 | 22.77 | 22.11 | 21.55 | 21.07 | 20.65 | 20.29 | 19.97 | 18.89 | 18.30 | 17.97 | 17.78 |
| 3000 | 35.33 | 34.16 | 33.17 | 32.32 | 31.60 | 30.97 | 30.43 | 29.96 | 28.33 | 27.45 | 26.95 | 26.66 |
| 4000 | 47.11 | 45.54 | 44.22 | 43.09 | 42.13 | 41.29 | 40.57 | 39.94 | 37.77 | 36.59 | 35.93 | 35.55 |
| 5000 | 58.88 | 56.93 | 55.27 | 53.87 | 52.66 | 51.62 | 50.71 | 49.92 | 47.21 | 45.74 | 44.91 | 44.43 |
| 6000 | 70.66 | 68.31 | 66.33 | 64.64 | 63.19 | 61.94 | 60.85 | 59.91 | 56.66 | 54.89 | 53.89 | 53.32 |
| 7000 | 82.43 | 79.70 | 77.38 | 75.41 | 73.72 | 72.26 | 70.99 | 69.89 | 66.10 | 64.04 | 62.87 | 62.20 |
| 8000 | 94.21 | 91.08 | 88.44 | 86.18 | 84.25 | 82.58 | 81.14 | 79.88 | 75.54 | 73.18 | 71.86 | 71.09 |
| 9000 | 105.98 | 102.46 | 99.49 | 96.96 | 94.78 | 92.91 | 91.28 | 89.86 | 84.98 | 82.33 | 80.84 | 79.98 |
| 10000 | 117.76 | 113.85 | 110.54 | 107.73 | 105.31 | 103.23 | 101.42 | 99.84 | 94.42 | 91.48 | 89.82 | 88.86 |
| 11000 | 129.53 | 125.23 | 121.60 | 118.50 | 115.84 | 113.55 | 111.56 | 109.83 | 103.86 | 100.63 | 98.80 | 97.75 |
| 12000 | 141.31 | 136.62 | 132.65 | 129.27 | 126.37 | 123.87 | 121.70 | 119.81 | 113.31 | 109.77 | 107.78 | 106.63 |
| 13000 | 153.08 | 148.00 | 143.71 | 140.05 | 136.91 | 134.19 | 131.84 | 129.79 | 122.75 | 118.92 | 116.76 | 115.52 |
| 14000 | 164.86 | 159.39 | 154.76 | 150.82 | 147.44 | 144.52 | 141.98 | 139.78 | 132.19 | 128.07 | 125.74 | 124.40 |
| 15000 | 176.63 | 170.77 | 165.81 | 161.59 | 157.97 | 154.84 | 152.13 | 149.76 | 141.63 | 137.22 | 134.73 | 133.29 |
| 16000 | 188.41 | 182.15 | 176.87 | 172.36 | 168.50 | 165.16 | 162.27 | 159.75 | 151.07 | 146.36 | 143.71 | 142.18 |
| 17000 | 200.18 | 193.54 | 187.92 | 183.14 | 179.03 | 175.48 | 172.41 | 169.73 | 160.52 | 155.51 | 152.69 | 151.06 |
| 18000 | 211.96 | 204.92 | 198.98 | 193.91 | 189.56 | 185.81 | 182.55 | 179.71 | 169.96 | 164.66 | 161.67 | 159.95 |
| 19000 | 223.73 | 216.31 | 210.03 | 204.68 | 200.09 | 196.13 | 192.69 | 189.70 | 179.40 | 173.81 | 170.65 | 168.83 |
| 20000 | 235.51 | 227.69 | 221.08 | 215.45 | 210.62 | 206.45 | 202.83 | 199.68 | 188.84 | 182.95 | 179.63 | 177.72 |
| 21000 | 247.28 | 239.08 | 232.14 | 226.23 | 221.15 | 216.77 | 212.97 | 209.66 | 198.28 | 192.10 | 188.61 | 186.60 |
| 22000 | 259.06 | 250.46 | 243.19 | 237.00 | 231.68 | 227.10 | 223.12 | 219.65 | 207.72 | 201.25 | 197.59 | 195.49 |
| 23000 | 270.83 | 261.84 | 254.25 | 247.77 | 242.21 | 237.42 | 233.26 | 229.63 | 217.17 | 210.40 | 206.58 | 204.38 |
| 24000 | 282.61 | 273.23 | 265.30 | 258.54 | 252.74 | 247.74 | 243.40 | 239.62 | 226.61 | 219.54 | 215.56 | 213.26 |
| 25000 | 294.38 | 284.61 | 276.35 | 269.32 | 263.28 | 258.06 | 253.54 | 249.60 | 236.05 | 228.69 | 224.54 | 222.15 |
| 26000 | 306.16 | 296.00 | 287.41 | 280.09 | 273.81 | 268.38 | 263.68 | 259.58 | 245.49 | 237.84 | 233.52 | 231.03 |
| 27000 | 317.93 | 307.38 | 298.46 | 290.86 | 284.34 | 278.71 | 273.82 | 269.57 | 254.93 | 246.98 | 242.50 | 239.92 |
| 28000 | 329.71 | 318.77 | 309.52 | 301.63 | 294.87 | 289.03 | 283.96 | 279.55 | 264.38 | 256.13 | 251.48 | 248.80 |
| 29000 | 341.48 | 330.15 | 320.57 | 312.41 | 305.40 | 299.35 | 294.11 | 289.54 | 273.82 | 265.28 | 260.46 | 257.69 |
| 30000 | 353.26 | 341.54 | 331.62 | 323.18 | 315.93 | 309.67 | 304.25 | 299.52 | 283.26 | 274.43 | 269.45 | 266.58 |
| 31000 | 365.03 | 352.92 | 342.68 | 333.95 | 326.46 | 320.00 | 314.39 | 309.50 | 292.70 | 283.57 | 278.43 | 275.46 |
| 32000 | 376.81 | 364.30 | 353.73 | 344.72 | 336.99 | 330.32 | 324.53 | 319.49 | 302.14 | 292.72 | 287.41 | 284.35 |
| 33000 | 388.58 | 375.69 | 364.79 | 355.50 | 347.52 | 340.64 | 334.67 | 329.47 | 311.58 | 301.87 | 296.39 | 293.23 |
| 34000 | 400.36 | 387.07 | 375.84 | 366.27 | 358.05 | 350.96 | 344.81 | 339.45 | 321.03 | 311.02 | 305.37 | 302.12 |
| 35000 | 412.13 | 398.46 | 386.89 | 377.04 | 368.58 | 361.28 | 354.95 | 349.44 | 330.47 | 320.16 | 314.35 | 311.00 |
| 36000 | 423.91 | 409.84 | 397.95 | 387.81 | 379.11 | 371.61 | 365.10 | 359.42 | 339.91 | 329.31 | 323.33 | 319.89 |
| 37000 | 435.68 | 421.23 | 409.00 | 398.58 | 389.65 | 381.93 | 375.24 | 369.41 | 349.35 | 338.46 | 332.31 | 328.78 |
| 38000 | 447.46 | 432.61 | 420.06 | 409.36 | 400.18 | 392.25 | 385.38 | 379.39 | 358.79 | 347.61 | 341.30 | 337.66 |
| 39000 | 459.23 | 443.99 | 431.11 | 420.13 | 410.71 | 402.57 | 395.52 | 389.37 | 368.24 | 356.75 | 350.28 | 346.55 |
| 40000 | 471.01 | 455.38 | 442.16 | 430.90 | 421.24 | 412.90 | 405.66 | 399.36 | 377.68 | 365.90 | 359.26 | 355.43 |
| 41000 | 482.78 | 466.76 | 453.22 | 441.67 | 431.77 | 423.22 | 415.80 | 409.34 | 387.12 | 375.05 | 368.24 | 364.32 |
| 42000 | 494.56 | 478.15 | 464.27 | 452.45 | 442.30 | 433.54 | 425.94 | 419.32 | 396.56 | 384.20 | 377.22 | 373.20 |
| 43000 | 506.33 | 489.53 | 475.33 | 463.22 | 452.83 | 443.86 | 436.08 | 429.31 | 406.00 | 393.34 | 386.20 | 382.09 |
| 44000 | 518.11 | 500.92 | 486.38 | 473.99 | 463.36 | 454.19 | 446.23 | 439.29 | 415.44 | 402.49 | 395.18 | 390.98 |
| 45000 | 529.88 | 512.30 | 497.43 | 484.76 | 473.89 | 464.51 | 456.37 | 449.28 | 424.89 | 411.64 | 404.17 | 399.86 |
| 46000 | 541.66 | 523.68 | 508.49 | 495.54 | 484.42 | 474.83 | 466.51 | 459.26 | 434.33 | 420.79 | 413.15 | 408.75 |
| 47000 | 553.43 | 535.07 | 519.54 | 506.31 | 494.95 | 485.15 | 476.65 | 469.24 | 443.77 | 429.93 | 422.13 | 417.63 |
| 48000 | 565.21 | 546.45 | 530.60 | 517.08 | 505.48 | 495.47 | 486.79 | 479.23 | 453.21 | 439.08 | 431.11 | 426.52 |
| 49000 | 576.98 | 557.84 | 541.65 | 527.85 | 516.01 | 505.80 | 496.93 | 489.21 | 462.65 | 448.23 | 440.09 | 435.40 |
| 50000 | 588.76 | 569.22 | 552.70 | 538.63 | 526.55 | 516.12 | 507.07 | 499.19 | 472.10 | 457.37 | 449.07 | 444.29 |
| 55000 | 647.63 | 626.14 | 607.97 | 592.49 | 579.20 | 567.73 | 557.78 | 549.11 | 519.30 | 503.11 | 493.98 | 488.72 |
| 60000 | 706.51 | 683.07 | 663.24 | 646.35 | 631.85 | 619.34 | 608.49 | 599.03 | 566.51 | 548.85 | 538.89 | 533.15 |
| 65000 | 765.38 | 739.99 | 718.51 | 700.21 | 684.51 | 670.95 | 659.20 | 648.95 | 613.72 | 594.59 | 583.79 | 577.58 |
| 70000 | 824.26 | 796.91 | 773.78 | 754.07 | 737.16 | 722.56 | 709.90 | 698.87 | 660.93 | 640.32 | 628.70 | 622.00 |
| 75000 | 883.13 | 853.83 | 829.05 | 807.94 | 789.82 | 774.18 | 760.61 | 748.79 | 708.14 | 686.06 | 673.61 | 666.43 |
| 80000 | 942.01 | 910.75 | 884.32 | 861.80 | 842.47 | 825.79 | 811.32 | 798.71 | 755.35 | 731.80 | 718.51 | 710.86 |
| 85000 | 1000.88 | 967.67 | 939.59 | 915.66 | 895.12 | 877.40 | 862.02 | 848.63 | 802.56 | 777.53 | 763.42 | 755.29 |
| 90000 | 1059.76 | 1024.60 | 994.86 | 969.52 | 947.78 | 929.01 | 912.73 | 898.55 | 849.77 | 823.27 | 808.33 | 799.72 |
| 95000 | 1118.63 | 1081.52 | 1050.13 | 1023.39 | 1000.43 | 980.62 | 963.44 | 948.47 | 896.98 | 869.01 | 853.23 | 844.15 |
| 100000 | 1177.51 | 1138.44 | 1105.40 | 1077.25 | 1053.09 | 1032.23 | 1014.14 | 998.38 | 944.19 | 914.74 | 898.14 | 888.58 |

211

# MONTHLY
## PAYMENT REQUIRED TO AMORTIZE A LOAN

| TERM AMOUNT | 1 year | 2 years | 3 years | 4 years | 5 years | 6 years | 7 years | 8 years | 9 years | 10 years | 11 years | 12 years |
|---|---|---|---|---|---|---|---|---|---|---|---|---|
| 50 | 4.42 | 2.34 | 1.64 | 1.30 | 1.09 | .96 | .86 | .79 | .74 | .69 | .66 | .63 |
| 100 | 8.84 | 4.67 | 3.28 | 2.59 | 2.18 | 1.91 | 1.72 | 1.58 | 1.47 | 1.38 | 1.31 | 1.26 |
| 200 | 17.68 | 9.33 | 6.55 | 5.17 | 4.35 | 3.81 | 3.43 | 3.15 | 2.93 | 2.76 | 2.62 | 2.51 |
| 300 | 26.52 | 13.99 | 9.83 | 7.76 | 6.53 | 5.72 | 5.14 | 4.72 | 4.39 | 4.14 | 3.93 | 3.77 |
| 400 | 35.36 | 18.65 | 13.10 | 10.34 | 8.70 | 7.62 | 6.85 | 6.29 | 5.86 | 5.52 | 5.24 | 5.02 |
| 500 | 44.20 | 23.31 | 16.37 | 12.93 | 10.88 | 9.52 | 8.57 | 7.86 | 7.32 | 6.89 | 6.55 | 6.27 |
| 600 | 53.03 | 27.97 | 19.65 | 15.51 | 13.05 | 11.43 | 10.28 | 9.43 | 8.78 | 8.27 | 7.86 | 7.53 |
| 700 | 61.87 | 32.63 | 22.92 | 18.10 | 15.22 | 13.33 | 11.99 | 11.00 | 10.24 | 9.65 | 9.17 | 8.78 |
| 800 | 70.71 | 37.29 | 26.20 | 20.68 | 17.40 | 15.23 | 13.70 | 12.57 | 11.71 | 11.03 | 10.48 | 10.03 |
| 900 | 79.55 | 41.95 | 29.47 | 23.27 | 19.57 | 17.14 | 15.42 | 14.14 | 13.17 | 12.40 | 11.79 | 11.29 |
| 1000 | 88.39 | 46.61 | 32.74 | 25.85 | 21.75 | 19.04 | 17.13 | 15.71 | 14.63 | 13.78 | 13.10 | 12.54 |
| 2000 | 176.77 | 93.22 | 65.48 | 51.70 | 43.49 | 38.07 | 34.25 | 31.42 | 29.26 | 27.56 | 26.19 | 25.08 |
| 3000 | 265.15 | 139.83 | 98.22 | 77.54 | 65.23 | 57.11 | 51.37 | 47.13 | 43.88 | 41.33 | 39.28 | 37.61 |
| 4000 | 353.53 | 186.44 | 130.96 | 103.39 | 86.97 | 76.14 | 68.49 | 62.84 | 58.51 | 55.11 | 52.37 | 50.15 |
| 5000 | 441.91 | 233.04 | 163.70 | 129.23 | 108.72 | 95.18 | 85.62 | 78.55 | 73.13 | 68.88 | 65.47 | 62.68 |
| 6000 | 530.29 | 279.65 | 196.44 | 155.08 | 130.46 | 114.21 | 102.74 | 94.26 | 87.76 | 82.66 | 78.56 | 75.22 |
| 7000 | 618.68 | 326.26 | 229.18 | 180.92 | 152.20 | 133.24 | 119.86 | 109.96 | 102.39 | 96.43 | 91.65 | 87.75 |
| 8000 | 707.06 | 372.87 | 261.91 | 206.77 | 173.94 | 152.28 | 136.98 | 125.67 | 117.01 | 110.21 | 104.74 | 100.29 |
| 9000 | 795.44 | 419.48 | 294.65 | 232.61 | 195.69 | 171.31 | 154.11 | 141.38 | 131.64 | 123.98 | 117.84 | 112.82 |
| 10000 | 883.82 | 466.08 | 327.39 | 258.46 | 217.43 | 190.35 | 171.23 | 157.09 | 146.26 | 137.76 | 130.93 | 125.36 |
| 11000 | 972.20 | 512.69 | 360.13 | 284.31 | 239.17 | 209.38 | 188.35 | 172.80 | 160.89 | 151.53 | 144.02 | 137.90 |
| 12000 | 1060.58 | 559.30 | 392.87 | 310.15 | 260.91 | 228.41 | 205.47 | 188.51 | 175.52 | 165.31 | 157.11 | 150.43 |
| 13000 | 1148.97 | 605.91 | 425.61 | 336.00 | 282.66 | 247.45 | 222.60 | 204.21 | 190.14 | 179.08 | 170.21 | 162.97 |
| 14000 | 1237.35 | 652.51 | 458.35 | 361.84 | 304.40 | 266.48 | 239.72 | 219.92 | 204.77 | 192.86 | 183.30 | 175.50 |
| 15000 | 1325.73 | 699.12 | 491.09 | 387.69 | 326.14 | 285.52 | 256.84 | 235.63 | 219.39 | 206.63 | 196.39 | 188.04 |
| 16000 | 1414.11 | 745.73 | 523.82 | 413.53 | 347.88 | 304.55 | 273.96 | 251.34 | 234.02 | 220.41 | 209.48 | 200.57 |
| 17000 | 1502.49 | 792.34 | 556.56 | 439.38 | 369.63 | 323.58 | 291.09 | 267.05 | 248.64 | 234.18 | 222.57 | 213.11 |
| 18000 | 1590.87 | 838.95 | 589.30 | 465.22 | 391.37 | 342.62 | 308.21 | 282.76 | 263.27 | 247.96 | 235.67 | 225.64 |
| 19000 | 1679.26 | 885.55 | 622.04 | 491.07 | 413.11 | 361.65 | 325.33 | 298.47 | 277.90 | 261.73 | 248.76 | 238.18 |
| 20000 | 1767.64 | 932.16 | 654.78 | 516.92 | 434.85 | 380.69 | 342.45 | 314.17 | 292.52 | 275.51 | 261.85 | 250.72 |
| 21000 | 1856.02 | 978.77 | 687.52 | 542.76 | 456.60 | 399.72 | 359.58 | 329.88 | 307.15 | 289.28 | 274.94 | 263.25 |
| 22000 | 1944.40 | 1025.38 | 720.26 | 568.61 | 478.34 | 418.75 | 376.70 | 345.59 | 321.77 | 303.06 | 288.04 | 275.79 |
| 23000 | 2032.78 | 1071.99 | 753.00 | 594.45 | 500.08 | 437.79 | 393.82 | 361.30 | 336.40 | 316.83 | 301.13 | 288.32 |
| 24000 | 2121.16 | 1118.59 | 785.73 | 620.30 | 521.82 | 456.82 | 410.94 | 377.01 | 351.03 | 330.61 | 314.22 | 300.86 |
| 25000 | 2209.55 | 1165.20 | 818.47 | 646.14 | 543.57 | 475.86 | 428.07 | 392.72 | 365.65 | 344.38 | 327.31 | 313.39 |
| 26000 | 2297.93 | 1211.81 | 851.21 | 671.99 | 565.31 | 494.89 | 445.19 | 408.42 | 380.28 | 358.16 | 340.41 | 325.93 |
| 27000 | 2386.31 | 1258.42 | 883.95 | 697.83 | 587.05 | 513.93 | 462.31 | 424.13 | 394.90 | 371.93 | 353.50 | 338.46 |
| 28000 | 2474.69 | 1305.02 | 916.69 | 723.68 | 608.79 | 532.96 | 479.43 | 439.84 | 409.53 | 385.71 | 366.59 | 351.00 |
| 29000 | 2563.07 | 1351.63 | 949.43 | 749.53 | 630.54 | 551.99 | 496.56 | 455.55 | 424.15 | 399.48 | 379.68 | 363.54 |
| 30000 | 2651.45 | 1398.24 | 982.17 | 775.37 | 652.28 | 571.03 | 513.68 | 471.26 | 438.78 | 413.26 | 392.78 | 376.07 |
| 31000 | 2739.84 | 1444.85 | 1014.91 | 801.22 | 674.02 | 590.06 | 530.80 | 486.97 | 453.41 | 427.03 | 405.87 | 388.61 |
| 32000 | 2828.22 | 1491.46 | 1047.64 | 827.06 | 695.76 | 609.10 | 547.92 | 502.67 | 468.03 | 440.81 | 418.96 | 401.14 |
| 33000 | 2916.60 | 1538.06 | 1080.38 | 852.91 | 717.50 | 628.13 | 565.05 | 518.38 | 482.66 | 454.58 | 432.05 | 413.68 |
| 34000 | 3004.98 | 1584.67 | 1113.12 | 878.75 | 739.25 | 647.16 | 582.17 | 534.09 | 497.28 | 468.36 | 445.14 | 426.21 |
| 35000 | 3093.36 | 1631.28 | 1145.86 | 904.60 | 760.99 | 666.20 | 599.29 | 549.80 | 511.91 | 482.13 | 458.24 | 438.75 |
| 36000 | 3181.74 | 1677.89 | 1178.60 | 930.44 | 782.73 | 685.23 | 616.41 | 565.51 | 526.54 | 495.91 | 471.33 | 451.28 |
| 37000 | 3270.13 | 1724.50 | 1211.34 | 956.29 | 804.47 | 704.27 | 633.54 | 581.22 | 541.16 | 509.68 | 484.42 | 463.82 |
| 38000 | 3358.51 | 1771.10 | 1244.08 | 982.13 | 826.22 | 723.30 | 650.66 | 596.93 | 555.79 | 523.46 | 497.51 | 476.36 |
| 39000 | 3446.89 | 1817.71 | 1276.82 | 1007.98 | 847.96 | 742.33 | 667.78 | 612.63 | 570.41 | 537.23 | 510.61 | 488.89 |
| 40000 | 3535.27 | 1864.32 | 1309.55 | 1033.83 | 869.70 | 761.37 | 684.90 | 628.34 | 585.04 | 551.01 | 523.70 | 501.43 |
| 41000 | 3623.65 | 1910.93 | 1342.29 | 1059.67 | 891.44 | 780.40 | 702.02 | 644.05 | 599.67 | 564.78 | 536.79 | 513.96 |
| 42000 | 3712.03 | 1957.53 | 1375.03 | 1085.52 | 913.19 | 799.44 | 719.15 | 659.76 | 614.29 | 578.56 | 549.88 | 526.50 |
| 43000 | 3800.42 | 2004.14 | 1407.77 | 1111.36 | 934.93 | 818.47 | 736.27 | 675.47 | 628.92 | 592.33 | 562.98 | 539.03 |
| 44000 | 3888.80 | 2050.75 | 1440.51 | 1137.21 | 956.67 | 837.50 | 753.39 | 691.18 | 643.54 | 606.11 | 576.07 | 551.57 |
| 45000 | 3977.18 | 2097.36 | 1473.25 | 1163.05 | 978.41 | 856.54 | 770.51 | 706.88 | 658.17 | 619.88 | 589.16 | 564.10 |
| 46000 | 4065.56 | 2143.97 | 1505.99 | 1188.90 | 1000.16 | 875.57 | 787.64 | 722.59 | 672.79 | 633.66 | 602.25 | 576.64 |
| 47000 | 4153.94 | 2190.57 | 1538.72 | 1214.74 | 1021.90 | 894.61 | 804.76 | 738.30 | 687.42 | 647.43 | 615.35 | 589.18 |
| 48000 | 4242.32 | 2237.18 | 1571.46 | 1240.59 | 1043.64 | 913.64 | 821.88 | 754.01 | 702.05 | 661.21 | 628.44 | 601.71 |
| 49000 | 4330.71 | 2283.79 | 1604.20 | 1266.44 | 1065.38 | 932.67 | 839.00 | 769.72 | 716.67 | 674.98 | 641.53 | 614.25 |
| 50000 | 4419.09 | 2330.40 | 1636.94 | 1292.28 | 1087.13 | 951.71 | 856.13 | 785.43 | 731.30 | 688.76 | 654.62 | 626.78 |
| 55000 | 4861.00 | 2563.44 | 1800.63 | 1421.51 | 1195.84 | 1046.88 | 941.74 | 863.97 | 804.43 | 757.63 | 720.08 | 689.46 |
| 60000 | 5302.90 | 2796.48 | 1964.33 | 1550.74 | 1304.55 | 1142.05 | 1027.35 | 942.51 | 877.56 | 826.51 | 785.55 | 752.14 |
| 65000 | 5744.81 | 3029.51 | 2128.02 | 1679.96 | 1413.26 | 1237.22 | 1112.96 | 1021.05 | 950.69 | 895.38 | 851.01 | 814.82 |
| 70000 | 6186.72 | 3262.55 | 2291.72 | 1809.19 | 1521.97 | 1332.39 | 1198.58 | 1099.59 | 1023.82 | 964.26 | 916.47 | 877.49 |
| 75000 | 6628.63 | 3495.59 | 2455.41 | 1938.42 | 1630.69 | 1427.56 | 1284.19 | 1178.14 | 1096.94 | 1033.13 | 981.93 | 940.17 |
| 80000 | 7070.54 | 3728.63 | 2619.10 | 2067.65 | 1739.40 | 1522.73 | 1369.80 | 1256.68 | 1170.07 | 1102.01 | 1047.39 | 1002.85 |
| 85000 | 7512.45 | 3961.67 | 2782.80 | 2196.87 | 1848.11 | 1617.90 | 1455.41 | 1335.22 | 1243.20 | 1170.88 | 1112.85 | 1065.53 |
| 90000 | 7954.35 | 4194.71 | 2946.49 | 2326.10 | 1956.82 | 1713.07 | 1541.02 | 1413.76 | 1316.33 | 1239.76 | 1178.32 | 1128.20 |
| 95000 | 8396.26 | 4427.75 | 3110.18 | 2455.33 | 2065.54 | 1808.24 | 1626.64 | 1492.31 | 1389.46 | 1308.63 | 1243.78 | 1190.88 |
| 100000 | 8838.17 | 4660.79 | 3273.88 | 2584.56 | 2174.25 | 1903.41 | 1712.25 | 1570.85 | 1462.59 | 1377.51 | 1309.24 | 1253.56 |

# MONTHLY

## PAYMENT REQUIRED TO AMORTIZE A LOAN

| TERM AMOUNT | 13 year | 14 years | 15 years | 16 years | 17 years | 18 years | 19 years | 20 years | 25 years | 30 years | 35 years | 40 years |
|---|---|---|---|---|---|---|---|---|---|---|---|---|
| 50 | .61 | .59 | .57 | .56 | .55 | .54 | .53 | .52 | .50 | .48 | .47 | .47 |
| 100 | 1.21 | 1.17 | 1.14 | 1.11 | 1.09 | 1.07 | 1.05 | 1.04 | .99 | .96 | .94 | .93 |
| 200 | 2.42 | 2.34 | 2.28 | 2.22 | 2.18 | 2.14 | 2.10 | 2.07 | 1.97 | 1.91 | 1.88 | 1.86 |
| 300 | 3.63 | 3.51 | 3.41 | 3.33 | 3.26 | 3.20 | 3.15 | 3.10 | 2.95 | 2.86 | 2.82 | 2.79 |
| 400 | 4.84 | 4.68 | 4.55 | 4.44 | 4.35 | 4.27 | 4.19 | 4.13 | 3.93 | 3.81 | 3.75 | 3.72 |
| 500 | 6.04 | 5.85 | 5.69 | 5.55 | 5.43 | 5.33 | 5.24 | 5.17 | 4.91 | 4.77 | 4.69 | 4.65 |
| 600 | 7.25 | 7.02 | 6.82 | 6.66 | 6.52 | 6.40 | 6.29 | 6.20 | 5.89 | 5.72 | 5.63 | 5.57 |
| 700 | 8.46 | 8.19 | 7.96 | 7.77 | 7.60 | 7.46 | 7.34 | 7.23 | 6.87 | 6.67 | 6.56 | 6.50 |
| 800 | 9.67 | 9.36 | 9.10 | 8.88 | 8.69 | 8.53 | 8.38 | 8.26 | 7.85 | 7.62 | 7.50 | 7.43 |
| 900 | 10.87 | 10.53 | 10.23 | 9.99 | 9.77 | 9.59 | 9.43 | 9.29 | 8.83 | 8.58 | 8.44 | 8.36 |
| 1000 | 12.08 | 11.70 | 11.37 | 11.10 | 10.86 | 10.66 | 10.48 | 10.33 | 9.81 | 9.53 | 9.37 | 9.29 |
| 2000 | 24.16 | 23.39 | 22.74 | 22.19 | 21.71 | 21.31 | 20.95 | 20.65 | 19.61 | 19.05 | 18.74 | 18.57 |
| 3000 | 36.23 | 35.08 | 34.10 | 33.28 | 32.57 | 31.96 | 31.43 | 30.97 | 29.41 | 28.57 | 28.11 | 27.85 |
| 4000 | 48.31 | 46.77 | 45.47 | 44.37 | 43.42 | 42.61 | 41.90 | 41.29 | 39.21 | 38.10 | 37.48 | 37.14 |
| 5000 | 60.38 | 58.46 | 56.83 | 55.46 | 54.27 | 53.26 | 52.38 | 51.61 | 49.01 | 47.62 | 46.85 | 46.42 |
| 6000 | 72.46 | 70.15 | 68.20 | 66.55 | 65.13 | 63.91 | 62.85 | 61.94 | 58.81 | 57.14 | 56.22 | 55.70 |
| 7000 | 84.53 | 81.84 | 79.57 | 77.64 | 75.98 | 74.56 | 73.33 | 72.26 | 68.61 | 66.67 | 65.59 | 64.99 |
| 8000 | 96.61 | 93.53 | 90.93 | 88.73 | 86.84 | 85.21 | 83.80 | 82.58 | 78.41 | 76.19 | 74.96 | 74.27 |
| 9000 | 108.68 | 105.22 | 102.30 | 99.82 | 97.69 | 95.86 | 94.28 | 92.90 | 88.22 | 85.71 | 84.33 | 83.55 |
| 10000 | 120.76 | 116.91 | 113.66 | 110.91 | 108.54 | 106.51 | 104.75 | 103.22 | 98.02 | 95.24 | 93.70 | 92.83 |
| 11000 | 132.83 | 128.60 | 125.03 | 122.00 | 119.40 | 117.16 | 115.23 | 113.55 | 107.82 | 104.76 | 103.07 | 102.12 |
| 12000 | 144.91 | 140.29 | 136.40 | 133.09 | 130.25 | 127.81 | 125.70 | 123.87 | 117.62 | 114.28 | 112.44 | 111.40 |
| 13000 | 156.98 | 151.98 | 147.76 | 144.18 | 141.10 | 138.46 | 136.18 | 134.19 | 127.42 | 123.81 | 121.81 | 120.68 |
| 14000 | 169.06 | 163.67 | 159.13 | 155.27 | 151.96 | 149.11 | 146.65 | 144.51 | 137.22 | 133.33 | 131.18 | 129.97 |
| 15000 | 181.13 | 175.36 | 170.49 | 166.36 | 162.81 | 159.76 | 157.12 | 154.83 | 147.02 | 142.85 | 140.55 | 139.25 |
| 16000 | 193.21 | 187.05 | 181.86 | 177.45 | 173.67 | 170.41 | 167.60 | 165.16 | 156.82 | 152.38 | 149.92 | 148.53 |
| 17000 | 205.28 | 198.74 | 193.23 | 188.54 | 184.52 | 181.06 | 178.07 | 175.48 | 166.62 | 161.90 | 159.29 | 157.82 |
| 18000 | 217.36 | 210.43 | 204.59 | 199.63 | 195.37 | 191.71 | 188.55 | 185.80 | 176.43 | 171.42 | 168.66 | 167.10 |
| 19000 | 229.44 | 222.13 | 215.96 | 210.72 | 206.23 | 202.36 | 199.02 | 196.12 | 186.23 | 180.95 | 178.03 | 176.38 |
| 20000 | 241.51 | 233.82 | 227.32 | 221.81 | 217.08 | 213.01 | 209.50 | 206.44 | 196.03 | 190.47 | 187.40 | 185.66 |
| 21000 | 253.59 | 245.51 | 238.69 | 232.90 | 227.93 | 223.67 | 219.97 | 216.76 | 205.83 | 199.99 | 196.77 | 194.95 |
| 22000 | 265.66 | 257.20 | 250.06 | 243.99 | 238.79 | 234.32 | 230.45 | 227.09 | 215.63 | 209.52 | 206.14 | 204.23 |
| 23000 | 277.74 | 268.89 | 261.42 | 255.08 | 249.64 | 244.97 | 240.92 | 237.41 | 225.43 | 219.04 | 215.51 | 213.51 |
| 24000 | 289.81 | 280.58 | 272.79 | 266.17 | 260.50 | 255.62 | 251.40 | 247.73 | 235.23 | 228.56 | 224.87 | 222.80 |
| 25000 | 301.89 | 292.27 | 284.15 | 277.26 | 271.35 | 266.27 | 261.87 | 258.05 | 245.03 | 238.09 | 234.24 | 232.08 |
| 26000 | 313.96 | 303.96 | 295.52 | 288.35 | 282.20 | 276.92 | 272.35 | 268.37 | 254.83 | 247.61 | 243.61 | 241.36 |
| 27000 | 326.04 | 315.65 | 306.89 | 299.44 | 293.06 | 287.57 | 282.82 | 278.70 | 264.64 | 257.13 | 252.98 | 250.64 |
| 28000 | 338.11 | 327.34 | 318.25 | 310.53 | 303.91 | 298.22 | 293.29 | 289.02 | 274.44 | 266.66 | 262.35 | 259.93 |
| 29000 | 350.19 | 339.03 | 329.62 | 321.62 | 314.77 | 308.87 | 303.77 | 299.34 | 284.24 | 276.18 | 271.72 | 269.21 |
| 30000 | 362.26 | 350.72 | 340.98 | 332.71 | 325.62 | 319.52 | 314.24 | 309.66 | 294.04 | 285.70 | 281.09 | 278.49 |
| 31000 | 374.34 | 362.41 | 352.35 | 343.80 | 336.47 | 330.17 | 324.72 | 319.98 | 303.84 | 295.23 | 290.46 | 287.78 |
| 32000 | 386.41 | 374.10 | 363.72 | 354.89 | 347.33 | 340.82 | 335.19 | 330.31 | 313.64 | 304.75 | 299.83 | 297.06 |
| 33000 | 398.49 | 385.79 | 375.08 | 365.98 | 358.18 | 351.47 | 345.67 | 340.63 | 323.44 | 314.27 | 309.20 | 306.34 |
| 34000 | 410.56 | 397.48 | 386.45 | 377.07 | 369.03 | 362.12 | 356.14 | 350.95 | 333.24 | 323.79 | 318.57 | 315.63 |
| 35000 | 422.64 | 409.17 | 397.81 | 388.16 | 379.89 | 372.77 | 366.62 | 361.27 | 343.04 | 333.32 | 327.94 | 324.91 |
| 36000 | 434.71 | 420.86 | 409.18 | 399.25 | 390.74 | 383.42 | 377.09 | 371.59 | 352.85 | 342.84 | 337.31 | 334.19 |
| 37000 | 446.79 | 432.56 | 420.55 | 410.34 | 401.60 | 394.07 | 387.57 | 381.91 | 362.65 | 352.36 | 346.68 | 343.47 |
| 38000 | 458.87 | 444.25 | 431.91 | 421.43 | 412.45 | 404.72 | 398.04 | 392.24 | 372.45 | 361.89 | 356.05 | 352.76 |
| 39000 | 470.94 | 455.94 | 443.28 | 432.52 | 423.30 | 415.37 | 408.52 | 402.56 | 382.25 | 371.41 | 365.42 | 362.04 |
| 40000 | 483.02 | 467.63 | 454.64 | 443.61 | 434.16 | 426.02 | 418.99 | 412.88 | 392.05 | 380.93 | 374.79 | 371.32 |
| 41000 | 495.09 | 479.32 | 466.01 | 454.70 | 445.01 | 436.68 | 429.47 | 423.20 | 401.85 | 390.46 | 384.16 | 380.61 |
| 42000 | 507.17 | 491.01 | 477.38 | 465.79 | 455.86 | 447.33 | 439.94 | 433.52 | 411.65 | 399.98 | 393.53 | 389.89 |
| 43000 | 519.24 | 502.70 | 488.74 | 476.88 | 466.72 | 457.98 | 450.41 | 443.85 | 421.45 | 409.50 | 402.90 | 399.17 |
| 44000 | 531.32 | 514.39 | 500.11 | 487.97 | 477.57 | 468.63 | 460.89 | 454.17 | 431.25 | 419.03 | 412.27 | 408.45 |
| 45000 | 543.39 | 526.08 | 511.47 | 499.06 | 488.43 | 479.28 | 471.36 | 464.49 | 441.06 | 428.55 | 421.64 | 417.74 |
| 46000 | 555.47 | 537.77 | 522.84 | 510.15 | 499.28 | 489.93 | 481.84 | 474.81 | 450.86 | 438.07 | 431.01 | 427.02 |
| 47000 | 567.54 | 549.46 | 534.21 | 521.24 | 510.13 | 500.58 | 492.31 | 485.13 | 460.66 | 447.60 | 440.38 | 436.30 |
| 48000 | 579.62 | 561.15 | 545.57 | 532.33 | 520.99 | 511.23 | 502.79 | 495.46 | 470.46 | 457.12 | 449.74 | 445.59 |
| 49000 | 591.69 | 572.84 | 556.94 | 543.42 | 531.84 | 521.88 | 513.26 | 505.78 | 480.26 | 466.64 | 459.11 | 454.87 |
| 50000 | 603.77 | 584.53 | 568.30 | 554.51 | 542.70 | 532.53 | 523.74 | 516.10 | 490.06 | 476.17 | 468.48 | 464.15 |
| 55000 | 664.15 | 642.98 | 625.13 | 609.96 | 596.96 | 585.78 | 576.11 | 567.71 | 539.07 | 523.78 | 515.33 | 510.57 |
| 60000 | 724.52 | 701.44 | 681.96 | 665.41 | 651.23 | 639.03 | 628.48 | 619.32 | 588.07 | 571.40 | 562.18 | 556.98 |
| 65000 | 784.90 | 759.89 | 738.79 | 720.86 | 705.50 | 692.29 | 680.86 | 670.93 | 637.08 | 619.02 | 609.03 | 603.40 |
| 70000 | 845.27 | 818.34 | 795.62 | 776.31 | 759.77 | 745.54 | 733.23 | 722.54 | 686.08 | 666.63 | 655.88 | 649.81 |
| 75000 | 905.65 | 876.80 | 852.45 | 831.76 | 814.04 | 798.79 | 785.60 | 774.15 | 735.09 | 714.25 | 702.72 | 696.23 |
| 80000 | 966.03 | 935.25 | 909.28 | 887.21 | 868.31 | 852.04 | 837.98 | 825.76 | 784.10 | 761.86 | 749.57 | 742.64 |
| 85000 | 1026.40 | 993.70 | 966.11 | 942.66 | 922.58 | 905.30 | 890.35 | 877.37 | 833.10 | 809.48 | 796.42 | 789.06 |
| 90000 | 1086.78 | 1052.15 | 1022.94 | 998.11 | 976.85 | 958.55 | 942.72 | 928.97 | 882.11 | 857.10 | 843.27 | 835.47 |
| 95000 | 1147.16 | 1110.61 | 1079.77 | 1053.56 | 1031.12 | 1011.80 | 995.10 | 980.58 | 931.11 | 904.71 | 890.11 | 881.88 |
| 100000 | 1207.53 | 1169.06 | 1136.60 | 1109.01 | 1085.39 | 1065.05 | 1047.47 | 1032.19 | 980.12 | 952.33 | 936.96 | 928.30 |

# MONTHLY

### PAYMENT REQUIRED TO AMORTIZE A LOAN

| TERM AMOUNT | 1 year | 2 years | 3 years | 4 years | 5 years | 6 years | 7 years | 8 years | 9 years | 10 years | 11 years | 12 years |
|---|---|---|---|---|---|---|---|---|---|---|---|---|
| 50 | 4.44 | 2.35 | 1.65 | 1.31 | 1.10 | .97 | .87 | .80 | .75 | .71 | .67 | .65 |
| 100 | 8.87 | 4.69 | 3.30 | 2.61 | 2.20 | 1.93 | 1.74 | 1.60 | 1.50 | 1.41 | 1.34 | 1.29 |
| 200 | 17.73 | 9.37 | 6.60 | 5.22 | 4.40 | 3.86 | 3.48 | 3.20 | 2.99 | 2.82 | 2.68 | 2.57 |
| 300 | 26.59 | 14.06 | 9.90 | 7.83 | 6.60 | 5.79 | 5.22 | 4.80 | 4.48 | 4.22 | 4.02 | 3.85 |
| 400 | 35.45 | 18.74 | 13.20 | 10.44 | 8.80 | 7.72 | 6.96 | 6.40 | 5.97 | 5.63 | 5.36 | 5.14 |
| 500 | 44.31 | 23.43 | 16.49 | 13.05 | 11.00 | 9.65 | 8.70 | 7.99 | 7.46 | 7.03 | 6.70 | 6.42 |
| 600 | 53.17 | 28.11 | 19.79 | 15.66 | 13.20 | 11.58 | 10.44 | 9.59 | 8.95 | 8.44 | 8.04 | 7.70 |
| 700 | 62.04 | 32.79 | 23.09 | 18.27 | 15.40 | 13.51 | 12.18 | 11.19 | 10.44 | 9.85 | 9.37 | 8.99 |
| 800 | 70.90 | 37.48 | 26.39 | 20.88 | 17.60 | 15.44 | 13.91 | 12.79 | 11.93 | 11.25 | 10.71 | 10.27 |
| 900 | 79.76 | 42.16 | 29.68 | 23.49 | 19.80 | 17.37 | 15.65 | 14.39 | 13.42 | 12.66 | 12.05 | 11.55 |
| 1000 | 88.62 | 46.85 | 32.98 | 26.09 | 22.00 | 19.30 | 17.39 | 15.98 | 14.91 | 14.06 | 13.39 | 12.84 |
| 2000 | 177.24 | 93.69 | 65.96 | 52.18 | 43.99 | 38.59 | 34.78 | 31.96 | 29.81 | 28.12 | 26.77 | 25.67 |
| 3000 | 265.85 | 140.53 | 98.93 | 78.27 | 65.98 | 57.88 | 52.16 | 47.94 | 44.72 | 42.18 | 40.16 | 38.50 |
| 4000 | 354.47 | 187.37 | 131.91 | 104.36 | 87.98 | 77.17 | 69.55 | 63.92 | 59.62 | 56.24 | 53.54 | 51.34 |
| 5000 | 443.08 | 234.21 | 164.89 | 130.45 | 109.97 | 96.46 | 86.94 | 79.90 | 74.52 | 70.30 | 66.92 | 64.17 |
| 6000 | 531.70 | 281.05 | 197.86 | 156.54 | 131.96 | 115.75 | 104.32 | 95.88 | 89.43 | 84.36 | 80.31 | 77.00 |
| 7000 | 620.31 | 327.89 | 230.84 | 182.63 | 153.95 | 135.04 | 121.71 | 111.86 | 104.33 | 98.42 | 93.69 | 89.84 |
| 8000 | 708.93 | 374.73 | 263.81 | 208.72 | 175.95 | 154.33 | 139.10 | 127.84 | 119.23 | 112.48 | 107.07 | 102.67 |
| 9000 | 797.54 | 421.57 | 296.79 | 234.81 | 197.94 | 173.63 | 156.48 | 143.82 | 134.14 | 126.54 | 120.46 | 115.50 |
| 10000 | 886.16 | 468.41 | 329.77 | 260.90 | 219.93 | 192.92 | 173.87 | 159.80 | 149.04 | 140.60 | 133.84 | 128.34 |
| 11000 | 974.77 | 515.25 | 362.74 | 286.98 | 241.92 | 212.21 | 191.26 | 175.78 | 163.95 | 154.66 | 147.22 | 141.17 |
| 12000 | 1063.39 | 562.09 | 395.72 | 313.07 | 263.92 | 231.50 | 208.64 | 191.76 | 178.85 | 168.72 | 160.61 | 154.00 |
| 13000 | 1152.00 | 608.93 | 428.69 | 339.16 | 285.91 | 250.79 | 226.03 | 207.74 | 193.75 | 182.78 | 173.99 | 166.84 |
| 14000 | 1240.62 | 655.77 | 461.67 | 365.25 | 307.90 | 270.08 | 243.42 | 223.72 | 208.66 | 196.84 | 187.37 | 179.67 |
| 15000 | 1329.23 | 702.61 | 494.65 | 391.34 | 329.89 | 289.37 | 260.80 | 239.70 | 223.56 | 210.90 | 200.76 | 192.50 |
| 16000 | 1417.85 | 749.45 | 527.62 | 417.43 | 351.89 | 308.66 | 278.19 | 255.67 | 238.46 | 224.96 | 214.14 | 205.34 |
| 17000 | 1506.46 | 796.29 | 560.60 | 443.52 | 373.88 | 327.95 | 295.57 | 271.65 | 253.37 | 239.02 | 227.52 | 218.17 |
| 18000 | 1595.08 | 843.13 | 593.57 | 469.61 | 395.87 | 347.25 | 312.96 | 287.63 | 268.27 | 253.08 | 240.91 | 231.00 |
| 19000 | 1683.69 | 889.97 | 626.55 | 495.70 | 417.86 | 366.54 | 330.35 | 303.61 | 283.17 | 267.14 | 254.29 | 243.84 |
| 20000 | 1772.31 | 936.81 | 659.53 | 521.79 | 439.86 | 385.83 | 347.73 | 319.59 | 298.08 | 281.20 | 267.68 | 256.67 |
| 21000 | 1860.92 | 983.65 | 692.50 | 547.87 | 461.85 | 405.12 | 365.12 | 335.57 | 312.98 | 295.26 | 281.06 | 269.50 |
| 22000 | 1949.54 | 1030.49 | 725.48 | 573.96 | 483.84 | 424.41 | 382.51 | 351.55 | 327.89 | 309.31 | 294.44 | 282.33 |
| 23000 | 2038.15 | 1077.33 | 758.45 | 600.05 | 505.83 | 443.70 | 399.89 | 367.53 | 342.79 | 323.37 | 307.83 | 295.17 |
| 24000 | 2126.77 | 1124.17 | 791.43 | 626.14 | 527.83 | 462.99 | 417.28 | 383.51 | 357.69 | 337.43 | 321.21 | 308.00 |
| 25000 | 2215.38 | 1171.01 | 824.41 | 652.23 | 549.82 | 482.28 | 434.67 | 399.49 | 372.60 | 351.49 | 334.59 | 320.83 |
| 26000 | 2304.00 | 1217.85 | 857.38 | 678.32 | 571.81 | 501.58 | 452.05 | 415.47 | 387.50 | 365.55 | 347.98 | 333.67 |
| 27000 | 2392.61 | 1264.69 | 890.36 | 704.41 | 553.81 | 520.87 | 469.44 | 431.45 | 402.40 | 379.61 | 361.36 | 346.50 |
| 28000 | 2481.23 | 1311.53 | 923.33 | 730.50 | 615.80 | 540.16 | 486.83 | 447.43 | 417.31 | 393.67 | 374.74 | 359.33 |
| 29000 | 2569.84 | 1358.37 | 956.31 | 756.59 | 637.79 | 559.45 | 504.21 | 463.41 | 432.21 | 407.73 | 388.13 | 372.17 |
| 30000 | 2658.46 | 1405.21 | 989.29 | 782.68 | 659.78 | 578.74 | 521.60 | 479.39 | 447.11 | 421.79 | 401.51 | 385.00 |
| 31000 | 2747.07 | 1452.05 | 1022.26 | 808.76 | 681.78 | 598.03 | 538.99 | 495.37 | 462.02 | 435.85 | 414.89 | 397.83 |
| 32000 | 2835.69 | 1498.90 | 1055.24 | 834.85 | 703.77 | 617.32 | 556.37 | 511.34 | 476.92 | 449.91 | 428.28 | 410.67 |
| 33000 | 2924.30 | 1545.74 | 1088.21 | 860.94 | 725.76 | 636.61 | 573.76 | 527.32 | 491.83 | 463.97 | 455.04 | 423.50 |
| 34000 | 3012.92 | 1592.58 | 1121.19 | 887.03 | 747.75 | 655.90 | 591.14 | 543.30 | 506.73 | 478.03 | 455.04 | 436.33 |
| 35000 | 3101.53 | 1639.42 | 1154.17 | 913.12 | 769.75 | 675.20 | 608.53 | 559.28 | 521.63 | 492.09 | 468.43 | 449.17 |
| 36000 | 3190.15 | 1686.26 | 1187.14 | 939.21 | 791.74 | 694.49 | 625.92 | 575.26 | 536.54 | 506.15 | 481.81 | 462.00 |
| 37000 | 3278.76 | 1733.10 | 1220.12 | 965.30 | 813.73 | 713.78 | 643.30 | 591.24 | 551.44 | 520.21 | 495.19 | 474.83 |
| 38000 | 3367.38 | 1779.94 | 1253.09 | 991.39 | 835.72 | 733.07 | 660.69 | 607.22 | 566.34 | 534.27 | 508.58 | 487.67 |
| 39000 | 3455.99 | 1826.78 | 1286.07 | 1017.48 | 857.72 | 752.36 | 678.08 | 623.20 | 581.25 | 548.33 | 521.96 | 500.50 |
| 40000 | 3544.61 | 1873.62 | 1319.05 | 1043.57 | 879.71 | 771.65 | 695.46 | 639.18 | 596.15 | 562.39 | 535.35 | 513.33 |
| 41000 | 3633.22 | 1920.46 | 1352.02 | 1069.65 | 901.70 | 790.94 | 712.85 | 655.16 | 611.06 | 576.45 | 548.73 | 526.16 |
| 42000 | 3721.84 | 1967.30 | 1385.00 | 1095.74 | 923.69 | 810.23 | 730.24 | 671.14 | 625.96 | 590.51 | 562.11 | 539.00 |
| 43000 | 3810.45 | 2014.14 | 1417.97 | 1121.83 | 945.69 | 829.52 | 747.62 | 687.12 | 640.86 | 604.57 | 575.50 | 551.83 |
| 44000 | 3899.07 | 2060.98 | 1450.95 | 1147.92 | 967.68 | 848.82 | 765.01 | 703.10 | 655.77 | 618.62 | 588.88 | 564.66 |
| 45000 | 3987.68 | 2107.82 | 1483.93 | 1174.01 | 989.67 | 868.11 | 782.40 | 719.08 | 670.67 | 632.68 | 602.26 | 577.50 |
| 46000 | 4076.30 | 2154.66 | 1516.90 | 1200.10 | 1011.66 | 887.40 | 799.78 | 735.06 | 685.57 | 646.74 | 615.65 | 590.33 |
| 47000 | 4164.91 | 2201.50 | 1549.88 | 1226.19 | 1033.66 | 906.69 | 817.17 | 751.04 | 700.48 | 660.80 | 629.03 | 603.16 |
| 48000 | 4253.53 | 2248.34 | 1582.85 | 1252.28 | 1055.65 | 925.98 | 834.56 | 767.01 | 715.38 | 674.86 | 642.41 | 616.00 |
| 49000 | 4342.14 | 2295.18 | 1615.83 | 1278.37 | 1077.64 | 945.27 | 851.94 | 782.99 | 730.28 | 688.92 | 655.80 | 628.83 |
| 50000 | 4430.76 | 2342.02 | 1648.81 | 1304.46 | 1099.64 | 964.56 | 869.33 | 798.97 | 745.19 | 702.98 | 669.18 | 641.66 |
| 55000 | 4873.83 | 2576.22 | 1813.69 | 1434.90 | 1209.60 | 1061.02 | 956.26 | 878.87 | 819.71 | 773.28 | 736.10 | 705.83 |
| 60000 | 5316.91 | 2810.42 | 1978.57 | 1565.35 | 1319.56 | 1157.47 | 1043.19 | 958.77 | 894.22 | 843.58 | 803.02 | 769.99 |
| 65000 | 5759.98 | 3044.63 | 2143.45 | 1695.79 | 1429.52 | 1253.93 | 1130.12 | 1038.66 | 968.74 | 913.88 | 869.93 | 834.16 |
| 70000 | 6203.06 | 3278.83 | 2308.33 | 1826.24 | 1539.49 | 1350.39 | 1217.06 | 1118.56 | 1043.26 | 984.17 | 936.85 | 898.33 |
| 75000 | 6646.13 | 3513.03 | 2473.21 | 1956.68 | 1649.45 | 1446.84 | 1303.99 | 1198.46 | 1117.78 | 1054.47 | 1003.77 | 962.49 |
| 80000 | 7089.21 | 3747.23 | 2638.09 | 2087.13 | 1759.41 | 1543.30 | 1390.92 | 1278.35 | 1192.30 | 1124.77 | 1070.69 | 1026.66 |
| 85000 | 7532.28 | 3981.43 | 2802.97 | 2217.57 | 1869.38 | 1639.75 | 1477.85 | 1358.25 | 1266.82 | 1195.07 | 1137.60 | 1090.82 |
| 90000 | 7975.36 | 4215.63 | 2967.85 | 2348.02 | 1979.34 | 1736.21 | 1564.79 | 1438.15 | 1341.33 | 1265.36 | 1204.52 | 1154.99 |
| 95000 | 8418.44 | 4449.83 | 3132.73 | 2478.46 | 2089.30 | 1832.66 | 1651.72 | 1518.05 | 1415.85 | 1335.66 | 1271.44 | 1219.16 |
| 100000 | 8861.51 | 4684.04 | 3297.61 | 2608.91 | 2199.27 | 1929.12 | 1738.65 | 1597.94 | 1490.37 | 1405.96 | 1338.36 | 1283.32 |

## PAYMENT REQUIRED TO AMORTIZE A LOAN

| TERM / AMOUNT | 13 year | 14 years | 15 years | 16 years | 17 years | 18 years | 19 years | 20 years | 25 years | 30 years | 35 years | 40 years |
|---|---|---|---|---|---|---|---|---|---|---|---|---|
| 50 | .62 | .61 | .59 | .58 | .56 | .55 | .55 | .54 | .51 | .50 | .49 | .49 |
| 100 | 1.24 | 1.21 | 1.17 | 1.15 | 1.12 | 1.10 | 1.09 | 1.07 | 1.02 | 1.00 | .98 | .97 |
| 200 | 2.48 | 2.41 | 2.34 | 2.29 | 2.24 | 2.20 | 2.17 | 2.14 | 2.04 | 1.99 | 1.96 | 1.94 |
| 300 | 3.72 | 3.61 | 3.51 | 3.43 | 3.36 | 3.30 | 3.25 | 3.20 | 3.05 | 2.98 | 2.93 | 2.91 |
| 400 | 4.96 | 4.81 | 4.68 | 4.57 | 4.48 | 4.40 | 4.33 | 4.27 | 4.07 | 3.97 | 3.91 | 3.88 |
| 500 | 6.19 | 6.01 | 5.85 | 5.71 | 5.60 | 5.50 | 5.41 | 5.34 | 5.09 | 4.96 | 4.89 | 4.85 |
| 600 | 7.43 | 7.21 | 7.01 | 6.85 | 6.71 | 6.59 | 6.49 | 6.40 | 6.10 | 5.95 | 5.86 | 5.81 |
| 700 | 8.67 | 8.41 | 8.18 | 7.99 | 7.83 | 7.69 | 7.57 | 7.47 | 7.12 | 6.94 | 6.84 | 6.78 |
| 800 | 9.91 | 9.61 | 9.35 | 9.13 | 8.95 | 8.79 | 8.65 | 8.54 | 8.14 | 7.93 | 7.81 | 7.75 |
| 900 | 11.15 | 10.81 | 10.52 | 10.28 | 10.07 | 9.69 | 9.74 | 9.60 | 9.15 | 8.92 | 8.79 | 8.72 |
| 1000 | 12.38 | 12.01 | 11.69 | 11.42 | 11.19 | 10.99 | 10.82 | 10.67 | 10.17 | 9.91 | 9.77 | 9.69 |
| 2000 | 24.76 | 24.01 | 23.37 | 22.83 | 22.37 | 21.97 | 21.63 | 21.33 | 20.33 | 19.81 | 19.53 | 19.37 |
| 3000 | 37.14 | 36.01 | 35.05 | 34.24 | 33.55 | 32.95 | 32.44 | 32.00 | 30.50 | 29.71 | 29.29 | 29.05 |
| 4000 | 49.52 | 48.01 | 46.73 | 45.65 | 44.73 | 43.94 | 43.25 | 42.66 | 40.66 | 39.62 | 39.05 | 38.74 |
| 5000 | 61.90 | 60.01 | 58.41 | 57.06 | 55.91 | 54.92 | 54.07 | 53.33 | 50.83 | 49.52 | 48.81 | 48.42 |
| 6000 | 74.28 | 72.01 | 70.10 | 68.47 | 67.09 | 65.90 | 64.88 | 63.99 | 60.99 | 59.42 | 58.57 | 58.10 |
| 7000 | 86.66 | 84.01 | 81.78 | 79.89 | 78.27 | 76.89 | 75.69 | 74.66 | 71.16 | 69.33 | 68.33 | 67.78 |
| 8000 | 99.04 | 96.01 | 93.46 | 91.30 | 89.45 | 87.87 | 86.50 | 85.32 | 81.32 | 79.23 | 78.09 | 77.47 |
| 9000 | 111.42 | 108.01 | 105.14 | 102.71 | 100.63 | 98.85 | 97.31 | 95.98 | 91.49 | 89.13 | 87.85 | 87.15 |
| 10000 | 123.80 | 120.01 | 116.82 | 114.12 | 111.81 | 109.83 | 108.13 | 106.65 | 101.65 | 99.03 | 97.62 | 96.83 |
| 11000 | 136.18 | 132.01 | 128.51 | 125.53 | 123.00 | 120.82 | 118.94 | 117.31 | 111.82 | 108.94 | 107.38 | 106.52 |
| 12000 | 148.56 | 144.01 | 140.19 | 136.94 | 134.18 | 131.80 | 129.75 | 127.98 | 121.98 | 118.84 | 117.14 | 116.20 |
| 13000 | 160.93 | 156.01 | 151.87 | 148.36 | 145.36 | 142.78 | 140.56 | 138.64 | 132.15 | 128.74 | 126.90 | 125.88 |
| 14000 | 173.31 | 168.01 | 163.55 | 159.77 | 156.54 | 153.77 | 151.38 | 149.31 | 142.31 | 138.65 | 136.66 | 135.56 |
| 15000 | 185.69 | 180.01 | 175.23 | 171.18 | 167.72 | 164.75 | 162.19 | 159.97 | 152.48 | 148.55 | 146.42 | 145.25 |
| 16000 | 198.07 | 192.01 | 186.92 | 182.59 | 178.90 | 175.73 | 173.00 | 170.63 | 162.64 | 158.45 | 156.18 | 154.93 |
| 17000 | 210.45 | 204.01 | 198.60 | 194.00 | 190.08 | 186.72 | 183.81 | 181.30 | 172.80 | 168.35 | 165.94 | 164.61 |
| 18000 | 222.83 | 216.01 | 210.28 | 205.41 | 201.26 | 197.70 | 194.62 | 191.96 | 182.97 | 178.26 | 175.70 | 174.30 |
| 19000 | 235.21 | 228.02 | 221.96 | 216.83 | 212.44 | 208.68 | 205.44 | 202.63 | 193.13 | 188.16 | 185.47 | 183.98 |
| 20000 | 247.59 | 240.02 | 233.64 | 228.24 | 223.62 | 219.66 | 216.25 | 213.29 | 203.30 | 198.06 | 195.23 | 193.66 |
| 21000 | 259.97 | 252.02 | 245.32 | 239.65 | 234.81 | 230.65 | 227.06 | 223.96 | 213.46 | 207.97 | 204.99 | 203.34 |
| 22000 | 272.35 | 264.02 | 257.01 | 251.06 | 245.99 | 241.63 | 237.87 | 234.62 | 223.63 | 217.87 | 214.75 | 213.03 |
| 23000 | 284.73 | 276.02 | 268.69 | 262.47 | 257.17 | 252.61 | 248.69 | 245.28 | 233.79 | 227.77 | 224.51 | 222.71 |
| 24000 | 297.11 | 288.02 | 280.37 | 273.88 | 268.35 | 263.60 | 259.50 | 255.95 | 243.96 | 237.67 | 234.27 | 232.39 |
| 25000 | 309.48 | 300.02 | 292.05 | 285.30 | 279.53 | 274.58 | 270.31 | 266.61 | 254.12 | 247.58 | 244.03 | 242.08 |
| 26000 | 321.86 | 312.02 | 303.73 | 296.71 | 290.71 | 285.56 | 281.12 | 277.28 | 264.29 | 257.48 | 253.79 | 251.76 |
| 27000 | 334.24 | 324.02 | 315.42 | 308.12 | 301.89 | 296.54 | 291.93 | 287.94 | 274.45 | 267.38 | 263.55 | 261.44 |
| 28000 | 346.62 | 336.02 | 327.10 | 319.53 | 313.07 | 307.53 | 302.75 | 298.61 | 284.62 | 277.29 | 273.32 | 271.12 |
| 29000 | 359.00 | 348.02 | 338.78 | 330.94 | 324.25 | 318.51 | 313.56 | 309.27 | 294.78 | 287.19 | 283.08 | 280.81 |
| 30000 | 371.38 | 360.02 | 350.46 | 342.35 | 335.43 | 329.49 | 324.37 | 319.93 | 304.95 | 297.09 | 292.84 | 290.49 |
| 31000 | 383.76 | 372.02 | 362.14 | 353.77 | 346.61 | 340.48 | 335.18 | 330.60 | 315.11 | 307.00 | 302.60 | 300.17 |
| 32000 | 396.14 | 384.02 | 373.83 | 365.18 | 357.80 | 351.46 | 345.99 | 341.26 | 325.28 | 316.90 | 312.36 | 309.86 |
| 33000 | 408.52 | 396.02 | 385.51 | 376.59 | 368.98 | 362.44 | 356.81 | 351.93 | 335.44 | 326.80 | 322.12 | 319.54 |
| 34000 | 420.90 | 408.02 | 397.19 | 388.00 | 380.16 | 373.43 | 367.62 | 362.59 | 345.60 | 336.70 | 331.88 | 329.22 |
| 35000 | 433.28 | 420.02 | 408.87 | 399.41 | 391.34 | 384.41 | 378.43 | 373.26 | 355.77 | 346.61 | 341.64 | 338.90- |
| 36000 | 445.66 | 432.02 | 420.55 | 410.82 | 402.52 | 395.39 | 389.24 | 383.92 | 365.93 | 356.51 | 351.40 | 348.59 |
| 37000 | 458.03 | 444.03 | 432.24 | 422.24 | 413.70 | 406.37 | 400.06 | 394.58 | 376.10 | 366.41 | 361.16 | 358.27 |
| 38000 | 470.41 | 456.03 | 443.92 | 433.65 | 424.88 | 417.36 | 410.87 | 405.25 | 386.26 | 376.32 | 370.93 | 367.95 |
| 39000 | 482.79 | 468.03 | 455.60 | 445.06 | 436.06 | 428.34 | 421.68 | 415.91 | 396.43 | 386.22 | 380.69 | 377.63 |
| 40000 | 495.17 | 480.03 | 467.28 | 456.47 | 447.24 | 439.32 | 432.49 | 426.58 | 406.59 | 396.12 | 390.45 | 387.32 |
| 41000 | 507.55 | 492.03 | 478.96 | 467.88 | 458.42 | 450.31 | 443.30 | 437.24 | 416.76 | 406.02 | 400.21 | 397.00 |
| 42000 | 519.93 | 504.03 | 490.64 | 479.29 | 469.61 | 461.29 | 454.12 | 447.91 | 426.92 | 415.93 | 409.97 | 406.68 |
| 43000 | 532.31 | 516.03 | 502.33 | 490.71 | 480.79 | 472.27 | 464.93 | 458.57 | 437.09 | 425.83 | 419.73 | 416.37 |
| 44000 | 544.69 | 528.03 | 514.01 | 502.12 | 491.97 | 483.25 | 475.74 | 469.23 | 447.25 | 435.73 | 429.49 | 426.05 |
| 45000 | 557.07 | 540.03 | 525.69 | 513.53 | 503.15 | 494.24 | 486.55 | 479.90 | 457.42 | 445.64 | 439.25 | 435.73 |
| 46000 | 569.45 | 552.03 | 537.37 | 524.94 | 514.33 | 505.22 | 497.37 | 490.56 | 467.58 | 455.54 | 449.01 | 445.41 |
| 47000 | 581.83 | 564.03 | 549.05 | 536.35 | 525.51 | 516.20 | 508.18 | 501.23 | 477.75 | 465.44 | 458.78 | 455.10 |
| 48000 | 594.21 | 576.03 | 560.74 | 547.76 | 536.69 | 527.19 | 518.99 | 511.89 | 487.91 | 475.34 | 468.54 | 464.78 |
| 49000 | 606.58 | 588.03 | 572.42 | 559.18 | 547.87 | 538.17 | 529.80 | 522.56 | 498.07 | 485.25 | 478.30 | 474.46 |
| 50000 | 618.96 | 600.03 | 584.10 | 570.59 | 559.05 | 549.15 | 540.61 | 533.22 | 508.24 | 495.15 | 488.06 | 484.15 |
| 55000 | 680.86 | 660.04 | 642.51 | 627.65 | 614.96 | 604.07 | 594.67 | 586.54 | 559.06 | 544.67 | 536.86 | 532.56 |
| 60000 | 742.76 | 720.04 | 700.92 | 684.70 | 670.86 | 658.98 | 648.74 | 639.86 | 609.89 | 594.18 | 585.67 | 580.97 |
| 65000 | 804.65 | 780.04 | 759.33 | 741.76 | 726.77 | 713.90 | 702.80 | 693.18 | 660.71 | 643.69 | 634.47 | 629.39 |
| 70000 | 866.55 | 840.04 | 817.74 | 798.82 | 782.67 | 768.81 | 756.86 | 746.51 | 711.53 | 693.21 | 683.28 | 677.80 |
| 75000 | 928.44 | 900.05 | 876.15 | 855.88 | 838.58 | 823.73 | 810.92 | 799.83 | 762.36 | 742.72 | 732.09 | 726.22 |
| 80000 | 990.34 | 960.05 | 934.56 | 912.94 | 894.48 | 878.64 | 864.98 | 853.15 | 813.18 | 792.24 | 780.89 | 774.63 |
| 85000 | 1052.24 | 1020.05 | 992.97 | 970.00 | 950.39 | 933.56 | 919.04 | 906.47 | 864.00 | 841.75 | 829.70 | 823.04 |
| 90000 | 1114.13 | 1080.05 | 1051.38 | 1027.05 | 1006.29 | 988.47 | 973.10 | 959.79 | 914.83 | 891.27 | 878.50 | 871.46 |
| 95000 | 1176.03 | 1140.06 | 1109.79 | 1084.11 | 1062.20 | 1043.39 | 1027.16 | 1013.11 | 965.65 | 940.78 | 927.31 | 919.87 |
| 100000 | 1237.92 | 1200.06 | 1168.19 | 1141.17 | 1118.10 | 1098.30 | 1081.22 | 1066.43 | 1016.47 | 990.30 | 976.11 | 968.29 |

# 12.00%

# MONTHLY
## PAYMENT REQUIRED TO AMORTIZE A LOAN

| TERM<br>AMOUNT | 1<br>year | 2<br>years | 3<br>years | 4<br>years | 5<br>years | 6<br>years | 7<br>years | 8<br>years | 9<br>years | 10<br>years | 11<br>years | 12<br>years |
|---|---|---|---|---|---|---|---|---|---|---|---|---|
| 50 | 4.45 | 2.36 | 1.67 | 1.32 | 1.12 | .98 | .89 | .82 | .76 | .72 | .69 | .66 |
| 100 | 8.89 | 4.71 | 3.33 | 2.64 | 2.23 | 1.96 | 1.77 | 1.63 | 1.52 | 1.44 | 1.37 | 1.32 |
| 200 | 17.77 | 9.42 | 6.65 | 5.27 | 4.45 | 3.92 | 3.54 | 3.26 | 3.04 | 2.87 | 2.74 | 2.63 |
| 300 | 26.66 | 14.13 | 9.97 | 7.91 | 6.68 | 5.87 | 5.30 | 4.88 | 4.56 | 4.31 | 4.11 | 3.95 |
| 400 | 35.54 | 18.83 | 13.29 | 10.54 | 8.90 | 7.83 | 7.07 | 6.51 | 6.08 | 5.74 | 5.48 | 5.26 |
| 500 | 44.43 | 23.54 | 16.61 | 13.17 | 11.13 | 9.78 | 8.83 | 8.13 | 7.60 | 7.18 | 6.84 | 6.57 |
| 600 | 53.31 | 28.25 | 19.93 | 15.81 | 13.35 | 11.74 | 10.60 | 9.76 | 9.12 | 8.61 | 8.21 | 7.89 |
| 700 | 62.20 | 32.96 | 23.26 | 18.44 | 15.58 | 13.69 | 12.36 | 11.38 | 10.63 | 10.05 | 9.58 | 9.20 |
| 800 | 71.08 | 37.66 | 26.58 | 21.07 | 17.80 | 15.65 | 14.13 | 13.01 | 12.15 | 11.48 | 10.95 | 10.51 |
| 900 | 79.97 | 42.37 | 29.90 | 23.71 | 20.03 | 17.60 | 15.89 | 14.63 | 13.67 | 12.92 | 12.32 | 11.83 |
| 1000 | 88.85 | 47.08 | 33.22 | 26.34 | 22.25 | 19.56 | 17.66 | 16.26 | 15.19 | 14.35 | 13.68 | 13.14 |
| 2000 | 177.70 | 94.15 | 66.43 | 52.67 | 44.49 | 39.11 | 35.31 | 32.51 | 30.37 | 28.70 | 27.36 | 26.27 |
| 3000 | 266.55 | 141.23 | 99.65 | 79.01 | 66.74 | 58.66 | 52.96 | 48.76 | 45.56 | 43.05 | 41.04 | 39.41 |
| 4000 | 355.40 | 188.30 | 132.86 | 105.34 | 88.98 | 78.21 | 70.62 | 65.02 | 60.74 | 57.39 | 54.72 | 52.54 |
| 5000 | 444.25 | 235.37 | 166.08 | 131.67 | 111.23 | 97.76 | 88.27 | 81.27 | 75.93 | 71.74 | 68.39 | 65.68 |
| 6000 | 533.10 | 282.45 | 199.29 | 158.01 | 133.47 | 117.31 | 105.92 | 97.52 | 91.11 | 86.09 | 82.07 | 78.81 |
| 7000 | 621.95 | 329.52 | 232.51 | 184.34 | 155.72 | 136.86 | 123.57 | 113.77 | 106.29 | 100.43 | 95.75 | 91.94 |
| 8000 | 710.80 | 376.59 | 265.72 | 210.68 | 177.96 | 156.41 | 141.23 | 130.03 | 121.48 | 114.78 | 109.43 | 105.08 |
| 9000 | 799.64 | 423.67 | 298.93 | 237.01 | 200.21 | 175.96 | 158.88 | 146.28 | 136.66 | 129.13 | 123.11 | 118.21 |
| 10000 | 888.49 | 470.74 | 332.15 | 263.34 | 222.45 | 195.51 | 176.53 | 162.53 | 151.85 | 143.48 | 136.78 | 131.35 |
| 11000 | 977.34 | 517.81 | 365.36 | 289.68 | 244.69 | 215.06 | 194.19 | 178.79 | 167.03 | 157.82 | 150.46 | 144.48 |
| 12000 | 1066.19 | 564.89 | 398.58 | 316.01 | 266.94 | 234.61 | 211.84 | 195.04 | 182.22 | 172.17 | 164.14 | 157.62 |
| 13000 | 1155.04 | 611.96 | 431.79 | 342.34 | 289.18 | 254.16 | 229.49 | 211.29 | 197.40 | 186.52 | 177.82 | 170.75 |
| 14000 | 1243.89 | 659.03 | 465.01 | 368.68 | 311.43 | 273.71 | 247.14 | 227.54 | 212.58 | 200.86 | 191.50 | 183.88 |
| 15000 | 1332.74 | 706.11 | 498.22 | 395.01 | 333.67 | 293.26 | 264.80 | 243.80 | 227.77 | 215.21 | 205.17 | 197.02 |
| 16000 | 1421.59 | 753.18 | 531.43 | 421.35 | 355.92 | 312.81 | 282.45 | 260.05 | 242.95 | 229.56 | 218.85 | 210.15 |
| 17000 | 1510.43 | 800.25 | 564.65 | 447.68 | 378.16 | 332.36 | 300.10 | 276.30 | 258.14 | 243.91 | 232.53 | 223.29 |
| 18000 | 1599.28 | 847.33 | 597.86 | 474.01 | 400.41 | 351.91 | 317.75 | 292.56 | 273.32 | 258.25 | 246.21 | 236.42 |
| 19000 | 1688.13 | 894.40 | 631.08 | 500.35 | 422.65 | 371.46 | 335.41 | 308.81 | 288.51 | 272.60 | 259.88 | 249.55 |
| 20000 | 1776.98 | 941.47 | 664.29 | 526.68 | 444.89 | 391.01 | 353.06 | 325.06 | 303.69 | 286.95 | 273.56 | 262.69 |
| 21000 | 1865.83 | 988.55 | 697.51 | 553.02 | 467.14 | 410.56 | 370.71 | 341.31 | 318.87 | 301.29 | 287.24 | 275.82 |
| 22000 | 1954.68 | 1035.62 | 730.72 | 579.35 | 489.38 | 430.11 | 388.37 | 357.57 | 334.06 | 315.64 | 300.92 | 288.96 |
| 23000 | 2043.53 | 1082.69 | 763.93 | 605.68 | 511.63 | 449.66 | 406.02 | 373.82 | 349.24 | 329.99 | 314.60 | 302.09 |
| 24000 | 2132.38 | 1129.77 | 797.15 | 632.02 | 533.87 | 469.21 | 423.67 | 390.07 | 364.43 | 344.34 | 328.27 | 315.23 |
| 25000 | 2221.22 | 1176.84 | 830.36 | 658.35 | 556.12 | 488.76 | 441.32 | 406.33 | 379.61 | 358.68 | 341.95 | 328.36 |
| 26000 | 2310.07 | 1223.92 | 863.58 | 684.68 | 578.36 | 508.31 | 458.98 | 422.58 | 394.80 | 373.03 | 355.63 | 341.49 |
| 27000 | 2398.92 | 1270.99 | 896.79 | 711.02 | 600.61 | 527.86 | 476.63 | 438.83 | 409.98 | 387.38 | 369.31 | 354.63 |
| 28000 | 2487.77 | 1318.06 | 930.01 | 737.35 | 622.85 | 547.41 | 494.28 | 455.08 | 425.16 | 401.72 | 382.99 | 367.76 |
| 29000 | 2576.62 | 1365.14 | 963.22 | 763.69 | 645.09 | 566.96 | 511.93 | 471.34 | 440.35 | 416.07 | 396.66 | 380.90 |
| 30000 | 2665.47 | 1412.21 | 996.43 | 790.02 | 667.34 | 586.51 | 529.59 | 487.59 | 455.53 | 430.42 | 410.34 | 394.03 |
| 31000 | 2754.32 | 1459.28 | 1029.65 | 816.35 | 689.58 | 606.06 | 547.24 | 503.84 | 470.72 | 444.76 | 424.02 | 407.16 |
| 32000 | 2843.17 | 1506.36 | 1062.86 | 842.69 | 711.83 | 625.61 | 564.89 | 520.10 | 485.90 | 459.11 | 437.70 | 420.30 |
| 33000 | 2932.02 | 1553.43 | 1096.08 | 869.02 | 734.07 | 645.16 | 582.55 | 536.35 | 501.08 | 473.46 | 451.38 | 433.43 |
| 34000 | 3020.86 | 1600.50 | 1129.29 | 895.36 | 756.32 | 664.71 | 600.20 | 552.60 | 516.27 | 487.81 | 465.05 | 446.57 |
| 35000 | 3109.71 | 1647.58 | 1162.51 | 921.69 | 778.56 | 684.26 | 617.85 | 568.85 | 531.45 | 502.15 | 478.73 | 459.70 |
| 36000 | 3198.56 | 1694.65 | 1195.72 | 948.02 | 800.81 | 703.81 | 635.50 | 585.11 | 546.64 | 516.50 | 492.41 | 472.84 |
| 37000 | 3287.41 | 1741.72 | 1228.93 | 974.36 | 823.05 | 723.36 | 653.16 | 601.36 | 561.82 | 530.85 | 506.09 | 485.97 |
| 38000 | 3376.26 | 1788.80 | 1262.15 | 1000.69 | 845.29 | 742.91 | 670.81 | 617.61 | 577.01 | 545.19 | 519.76 | 499.10 |
| 39000 | 3465.11 | 1835.87 | 1295.36 | 1027.02 | 867.54 | 762.46 | 688.46 | 633.87 | 592.19 | 559.54 | 533.44 | 512.24 |
| 40000 | 3553.96 | 1882.94 | 1328.58 | 1053.36 | 889.78 | 782.01 | 706.11 | 650.12 | 607.37 | 573.89 | 547.12 | 525.37 |
| 41000 | 3642.81 | 1930.02 | 1361.79 | 1079.69 | 912.03 | 801.56 | 723.77 | 666.37 | 622.56 | 588.24 | 560.80 | 538.51 |
| 42000 | 3731.65 | 1977.09 | 1395.01 | 1106.03 | 934.27 | 821.11 | 741.42 | 682.62 | 637.74 | 602.58 | 574.48 | 551.64 |
| 43000 | 3820.50 | 2024.16 | 1428.22 | 1132.36 | 956.52 | 840.66 | 759.07 | 698.88 | 652.93 | 616.93 | 588.15 | 564.78 |
| 44000 | 3909.35 | 2071.24 | 1461.43 | 1158.69 | 978.76 | 860.21 | 776.73 | 715.13 | 668.11 | 631.28 | 601.83 | 577.91 |
| 45000 | 3998.20 | 2118.31 | 1494.65 | 1185.03 | 1001.01 | 879.76 | 794.38 | 731.38 | 683.30 | 645.62 | 615.51 | 591.04 |
| 46000 | 4087.05 | 2165.38 | 1527.86 | 1211.36 | 1023.25 | 899.31 | 812.03 | 747.64 | 698.48 | 659.97 | 629.19 | 604.18 |
| 47000 | 4175.90 | 2212.46 | 1561.08 | 1237.70 | 1045.49 | 918.86 | 829.68 | 763.89 | 713.66 | 674.32 | 642.87 | 617.31 |
| 48000 | 4264.75 | 2259.53 | 1594.29 | 1264.03 | 1067.74 | 938.41 | 847.34 | 780.14 | 728.85 | 688.67 | 656.54 | 630.45 |
| 49000 | 4353.60 | 2306.61 | 1627.51 | 1290.36 | 1089.98 | 957.96 | 864.99 | 796.39 | 744.03 | 703.01 | 670.22 | 643.58 |
| 50000 | 4442.44 | 2353.68 | 1660.72 | 1316.70 | 1112.23 | 977.51 | 882.64 | 812.65 | 759.22 | 717.36 | 683.90 | 656.71 |
| 55000 | 4886.69 | 2589.05 | 1826.79 | 1448.37 | 1223.45 | 1075.27 | 970.91 | 893.91 | 835.14 | 789.10 | 752.29 | 722.39 |
| 60000 | 5330.93 | 2824.41 | 1992.86 | 1580.04 | 1334.67 | 1173.02 | 1059.17 | 975.18 | 911.06 | 860.83 | 820.68 | 788.06 |
| 65000 | 5775.18 | 3059.78 | 2158.94 | 1711.70 | 1445.89 | 1270.77 | 1147.43 | 1056.44 | 986.98 | 932.57 | 889.07 | 853.73 |
| 70000 | 6219.42 | 3295.15 | 2325.01 | 1843.37 | 1557.12 | 1368.52 | 1235.70 | 1137.70 | 1062.90 | 1004.30 | 957.46 | 919.40 |
| 75000 | 6663.66 | 3530.52 | 2491.08 | 1975.04 | 1668.34 | 1466.27 | 1323.96 | 1218.97 | 1138.82 | 1076.04 | 1025.85 | 985.07 |
| 80000 | 7107.91 | 3765.88 | 2657.15 | 2106.71 | 1779.56 | 1564.02 | 1412.22 | 1300.23 | 1214.74 | 1147.77 | 1094.24 | 1050.74 |
| 85000 | 7552.15 | 4001.25 | 2823.22 | 2238.38 | 1890.78 | 1661.77 | 1500.49 | 1381.50 | 1290.66 | 1219.51 | 1162.62 | 1116.41 |
| 90000 | 7996.40 | 4236.62 | 2989.29 | 2370.05 | 2002.01 | 1759.52 | 1588.75 | 1462.76 | 1366.59 | 1291.24 | 1231.01 | 1182.08 |
| 95000 | 8440.64 | 4471.98 | 3155.36 | 2501.72 | 2113.23 | 1857.27 | 1677.01 | 1544.02 | 1442.51 | 1362.98 | 1299.40 | 1247.75 |
| 100000 | 8884.88 | 4707.35 | 3321.44 | 2633.39 | 2224.45 | 1955.02 | 1765.28 | 1625.29 | 1518.43 | 1434.71 | 1367.79 | 1313.42 |

# PAYMENT REQUIRED TO AMORTIZE A LOAN

| TERM AMOUNT | 13 year | 14 years | 15 years | 16 years | 17 years | 18 years | 19 years | 20 years | 25 years | 30 years | 35 years | 40 years |
|---|---|---|---|---|---|---|---|---|---|---|---|---|
| 50 | .64 | .62 | .61 | .59 | .58 | .57 | .56 | .56 | .53 | .52 | .51 | .51 |
| 100 | 1.27 | 1.24 | 1.21 | 1.18 | 1.16 | 1.14 | 1.12 | 1.11 | 1.06 | 1.03 | 1.02 | 1.01 |
| 200 | 2.54 | 2.47 | 2.41 | 2.35 | 2.31 | 2.27 | 2.24 | 2.21 | 2.11 | 2.06 | 2.04 | 2.02 |
| 300 | 3.81 | 3.70 | 3.61 | 3.53 | 3.46 | 3.40 | 3.35 | 3.31 | 3.16 | 3.09 | 3.05 | 3.03 |
| 400 | 5.08 | 4.93 | 4.81 | 4.70 | 4.61 | 4.53 | 4.47 | 4.41 | 4.22 | 4.12 | 4.07 | 4.04 |
| 500 | 6.35 | 6.16 | 6.01 | 5.87 | 5.76 | 5.66 | 5.58 | 5.51 | 5.27 | 5.15 | 5.08 | 5.05 |
| 600 | 7.62 | 7.39 | 7.21 | 7.05 | 6.91 | 6.80 | 6.70 | 6.61 | 6.32 | 6.18 | 6.10 | 6.06 |
| 700 | 8.89 | 8.63 | 8.41 | 8.22 | 8.06 | 7.93 | 7.81 | 7.71 | 7.38 | 7.21 | 7.11 | 7.06 |
| 800 | 10.15 | 9.86 | 9.61 | 9.39 | 9.21 | 9.06 | 8.93 | 8.81 | 8.43 | 8.23 | 8.13 | 8.07 |
| 900 | 11.42 | 11.09 | 10.81 | 10.57 | 10.37 | 10.19 | 10.04 | 9.91 | 9.48 | 9.26 | 9.14 | 9.08 |
| 1000 | 12.69 | 12.32 | 12.01 | 11.74 | 11.52 | 11.32 | 11.16 | 11.02 | 10.54 | 10.29 | 10.16 | 10.09 |
| 2000 | 25.38 | 24.63 | 24.01 | 23.48 | 23.03 | 22.64 | 22.31 | 22.03 | 21.07 | 20.58 | 20.32 | 20.17 |
| 3000 | 38.06 | 36.95 | 36.01 | 35.22 | 34.54 | 33.96 | 33.47 | 33.04 | 31.60 | 30.86 | 30.47 | 30.26 |
| 4000 | 50.75 | 49.26 | 48.01 | 46.95 | 46.05 | 45.28 | 44.62 | 44.05 | 42.13 | 41.15 | 40.63 | 40.34 |
| 5000 | 63.44 | 61.58 | 60.01 | 58.69 | 57.57 | 56.60 | 55.77 | 55.06 | 52.67 | 51.44 | 50.78 | 50.43 |
| 6000 | 76.12 | 73.89 | 72.02 | 70.43 | 69.08 | 67.92 | 66.93 | 66.07 | 63.20 | 61.72 | 60.94 | 60.51 |
| 7000 | 88.81 | 86.21 | 84.02 | 82.17 | 80.59 | 79.24 | 78.08 | 77.08 | 73.73 | 72.01 | 71.09 | 70.60 |
| 8000 | 101.50 | 98.52 | 96.02 | 93.90 | 92.10 | 90.56 | 89.24 | 88.09 | 84.26 | 82.29 | 81.25 | 80.68 |
| 9000 | 114.18 | 110.83 | 108.02 | 105.64 | 103.61 | 101.88 | 100.39 | 99.10 | 94.80 | 92.58 | 91.40 | 90.77 |
| 10000 | 126.87 | 123.15 | 120.02 | 117.38 | 115.13 | 113.20 | 111.54 | 110.11 | 105.33 | 102.87 | 101.56 | 100.85 |
| 11000 | 139.56 | 135.46 | 132.02 | 129.11 | 126.64 | 124.52 | 122.70 | 121.12 | 115.86 | 113.15 | 111.72 | 110.94 |
| 12000 | 152.24 | 147.78 | 144.03 | 140.85 | 138.15 | 135.84 | 133.85 | 132.14 | 126.39 | 123.44 | 121.87 | 121.02 |
| 13000 | 164.93 | 160.09 | 156.03 | 152.59 | 149.66 | 147.16 | 145.01 | 143.15 | 136.92 | 133.72 | 132.03 | 131.11 |
| 14000 | 177.62 | 172.41 | 168.03 | 164.33 | 161.18 | 158.48 | 156.16 | 154.16 | 147.46 | 144.01 | 142.18 | 141.19 |
| 15000 | 190.30 | 184.72 | 180.03 | 176.06 | 172.69 | 169.80 | 167.31 | 165.17 | 157.99 | 154.30 | 152.34 | 151.28 |
| 16000 | 202.99 | 197.03 | 192.03 | 187.80 | 184.20 | 181.12 | 178.47 | 176.18 | 168.52 | 164.58 | 162.49 | 161.36 |
| 17000 | 215.68 | 209.35 | 204.03 | 199.54 | 195.71 | 192.44 | 189.62 | 187.19 | 179.05 | 174.87 | 172.65 | 171.45 |
| 18000 | 228.36 | 221.66 | 216.04 | 211.28 | 207.22 | 203.76 | 200.77 | 198.20 | 189.59 | 185.16 | 182.80 | 181.53 |
| 19000 | 241.05 | 233.98 | 228.04 | 223.01 | 218.74 | 215.08 | 211.93 | 209.21 | 200.12 | 195.44 | 192.96 | 191.62 |
| 20000 | 253.74 | 246.29 | 240.04 | 234.75 | 230.25 | 226.40 | 223.08 | 220.22 | 210.65 | 205.73 | 203.11 | 201.70 |
| 21000 | 266.42 | 258.61 | 252.04 | 246.49 | 241.76 | 237.71 | 234.24 | 231.23 | 221.18 | 216.01 | 213.27 | 211.79 |
| 22000 | 279.11 | 270.92 | 264.04 | 258.22 | 253.27 | 249.03 | 245.39 | 242.24 | 231.71 | 226.30 | 223.43 | 221.87 |
| 23000 | 291.80 | 283.23 | 276.04 | 269.96 | 264.78 | 260.35 | 256.54 | 253.25 | 242.25 | 236.59 | 233.58 | 231.96 |
| 24000 | 304.48 | 295.55 | 288.05 | 281.70 | 276.30 | 271.67 | 267.70 | 264.26 | 252.78 | 246.87 | 243.74 | 242.04 |
| 25000 | 317.17 | 307.86 | 300.05 | 293.44 | 287.81 | 282.99 | 278.85 | 275.28 | 263.31 | 257.16 | 253.89 | 252.13 |
| 26000 | 329.86 | 320.18 | 312.05 | 305.17 | 299.32 | 294.31 | 290.01 | 286.29 | 273.84 | 267.44 | 264.05 | 262.21 |
| 27000 | 342.54 | 332.49 | 324.05 | 316.91 | 310.83 | 305.63 | 301.16 | 297.30 | 284.38 | 277.73 | 274.20 | 272.30 |
| 28000 | 355.23 | 344.81 | 336.05 | 328.65 | 322.35 | 316.95 | 312.31 | 308.31 | 294.91 | 288.02 | 284.36 | 282.38 |
| 29000 | 367.92 | 357.12 | 348.05 | 340.39 | 333.86 | 328.27 | 323.47 | 319.32 | 305.44 | 298.30 | 294.51 | 292.47 |
| 30000 | 380.60 | 369.43 | 360.06 | 352.12 | 345.37 | 339.59 | 334.62 | 330.33 | 315.97 | 308.59 | 304.67 | 302.55 |
| 31000 | 393.29 | 381.75 | 372.06 | 363.86 | 356.88 | 350.91 | 345.77 | 341.34 | 326.50 | 318.87 | 314.83 | 312.64 |
| 32000 | 405.98 | 394.06 | 384.06 | 375.60 | 368.39 | 362.23 | 356.93 | 352.35 | 337.04 | 329.16 | 324.98 | 322.72 |
| 33000 | 418.66 | 406.38 | 396.06 | 387.33 | 379.91 | 373.55 | 368.08 | 363.36 | 347.57 | 339.45 | 335.14 | 332.81 |
| 34000 | 431.35 | 418.69 | 408.06 | 399.07 | 391.42 | 384.87 | 379.24 | 374.37 | 358.10 | 349.73 | 345.29 | 342.89 |
| 35000 | 444.04 | 431.01 | 420.06 | 410.81 | 402.93 | 396.19 | 390.39 | 385.39 | 368.63 | 360.02 | 355.45 | 352.98 |
| 36000 | 456.72 | 443.32 | 432.07 | 422.55 | 414.44 | 407.51 | 401.54 | 396.40 | 379.17 | 370.31 | 365.60 | 363.06 |
| 37000 | 469.41 | 455.63 | 444.07 | 434.28 | 425.95 | 418.83 | 412.70 | 407.41 | 389.70 | 380.59 | 375.76 | 373.15 |
| 38000 | 482.10 | 467.95 | 456.07 | 446.02 | 437.47 | 430.15 | 423.85 | 418.42 | 400.23 | 390.88 | 385.91 | 383.23 |
| 39000 | 494.78 | 480.26 | 468.07 | 457.76 | 448.98 | 441.47 | 435.01 | 429.43 | 410.76 | 401.16 | 396.07 | 393.32 |
| 40000 | 507.47 | 492.58 | 480.07 | 469.50 | 460.49 | 452.79 | 446.16 | 440.44 | 421.29 | 411.45 | 406.22 | 403.40 |
| 41000 | 520.16 | 504.89 | 492.07 | 481.23 | 472.00 | 464.10 | 457.31 | 451.45 | 431.83 | 421.74 | 416.38 | 413.49 |
| 42000 | 532.84 | 517.21 | 504.08 | 492.97 | 483.52 | 475.42 | 468.47 | 462.46 | 442.36 | 432.02 | 426.54 | 423.57 |
| 43000 | 545.53 | 529.52 | 516.08 | 504.71 | 495.03 | 486.74 | 479.62 | 473.47 | 452.89 | 442.31 | 436.69 | 433.66 |
| 44000 | 558.22 | 541.83 | 528.08 | 516.44 | 506.54 | 498.06 | 490.77 | 484.48 | 463.42 | 452.59 | 446.85 | 443.74 |
| 45000 | 570.90 | 554.15 | 540.08 | 528.18 | 518.05 | 509.38 | 501.93 | 495.49 | 473.96 | 462.88 | 457.00 | 453.83 |
| 46000 | 583.59 | 566.46 | 552.08 | 539.92 | 529.56 | 520.70 | 513.08 | 506.50 | 484.49 | 473.17 | 467.16 | 463.91 |
| 47000 | 596.28 | 578.78 | 564.08 | 551.66 | 541.08 | 532.02 | 524.24 | 517.52 | 495.02 | 483.45 | 477.31 | 474.00 |
| 48000 | 608.96 | 591.09 | 576.09 | 563.39 | 552.59 | 543.34 | 535.39 | 528.53 | 505.55 | 493.74 | 487.47 | 484.08 |
| 49000 | 621.65 | 603.41 | 588.09 | 575.13 | 564.10 | 554.66 | 546.54 | 539.54 | 516.08 | 504.03 | 497.62 | 494.17 |
| 50000 | 634.34 | 615.72 | 600.09 | 586.87 | 575.61 | 565.98 | 557.70 | 550.55 | 526.62 | 514.31 | 507.78 | 504.25 |
| 55000 | 697.77 | 677.29 | 660.10 | 645.55 | 633.17 | 622.58 | 613.47 | 605.60 | 579.28 | 565.74 | 558.56 | 554.68 |
| 60000 | 761.20 | 738.86 | 720.11 | 704.24 | 690.73 | 679.18 | 669.24 | 660.66 | 631.94 | 617.17 | 609.33 | 605.10 |
| 65000 | 824.64 | 800.43 | 780.11 | 762.93 | 748.30 | 735.77 | 725.01 | 715.71 | 684.60 | 668.60 | 660.11 | 655.53 |
| 70000 | 888.07 | 862.01 | 840.12 | 821.61 | 805.86 | 792.37 | 780.77 | 770.77 | 737.26 | 720.03 | 710.89 | 705.95 |
| 75000 | 951.50 | 923.58 | 900.13 | 880.30 | 863.42 | 848.97 | 836.54 | 825.82 | 789.92 | 771.46 | 761.67 | 756.38 |
| 80000 | 1014.94 | 985.15 | 960.14 | 938.99 | 920.98 | 905.57 | 892.31 | 880.87 | 842.58 | 822.90 | 812.44 | 806.80 |
| 85000 | 1078.37 | 1046.72 | 1020.15 | 997.67 | 978.54 | 962.16 | 948.08 | 935.93 | 895.25 | 874.33 | 863.22 | 857.23 |
| 90000 | 1141.80 | 1108.29 | 1080.16 | 1056.36 | 1036.10 | 1018.76 | 1003.85 | 990.98 | 947.91 | 925.76 | 914.00 | 907.65 |
| 95000 | 1205.24 | 1169.86 | 1140.16 | 1115.04 | 1093.66 | 1075.36 | 1059.62 | 1046.04 | 1000.57 | 977.19 | 964.78 | 958.08 |
| 100000 | 1268.67 | 1231.43 | 1200.17 | 1173.73 | 1151.22 | 1131.96 | 1115.39 | 1101.09 | 1053.23 | 1028.62 | 1015.55 | 1008.50 |

# 12.50%

# MONTHLY

## PAYMENT REQUIRED TO AMORTIZE A LOAN

| TERM AMOUNT | 1 year | 2 years | 3 years | 4 years | 5 years | 6 years | 7 years | 8 years | 9 years | 10 years | 11 years | 12 years |
|---|---|---|---|---|---|---|---|---|---|---|---|---|
| 50 | 4.46 | 2.37 | 1.68 | 1.33 | 1.13 | 1.00 | .90 | .83 | .78 | .74 | .70 | .68 |
| 100 | 8.91 | 4.74 | 3.35 | 2.66 | 2.25 | 1.99 | 1.80 | 1.66 | 1.55 | 1.47 | 1.40 | 1.35 |
| 200 | 17.82 | 9.47 | 6.70 | 5.32 | 4.50 | 3.97 | 3.59 | 3.31 | 3.10 | 2.93 | 2.80 | 2.69 |
| 300 | 26.73 | 14.20 | 10.04 | 7.98 | 6.75 | 5.95 | 5.38 | 4.96 | 4.65 | 4.40 | 4.20 | 4.04 |
| 400 | 35.64 | 18.93 | 13.39 | 10.64 | 9.00 | 7.93 | 7.17 | 6.62 | 6.19 | 5.86 | 5.60 | 5.38 |
| 500 | 44.55 | 23.66 | 16.73 | 13.29 | 11.25 | 9.91 | 8.97 | 8.27 | 7.74 | 7.32 | 6.99 | 6.72 |
| 600 | 53.45 | 28.39 | 20.08 | 15.95 | 13.50 | 11.89 | 10.76 | 9.92 | 9.29 | 8.79 | 8.39 | 8.07 |
| 700 | 62.36 | 33.12 | 23.42 | 18.61 | 15.75 | 13.87 | 12.55 | 11.58 | 10.83 | 10.25 | 9.79 | 9.41 |
| 800 | 71.27 | 37.85 | 26.77 | 21.27 | 18.00 | 15.85 | 14.34 | 13.23 | 12.38 | 11.72 | 11.19 | 10.76 |
| 900 | 80.18 | 42.58 | 30.11 | 23.93 | 20.25 | 17.84 | 16.13 | 14.88 | 13.93 | 13.18 | 12.58 | 12.10 |
| 1000 | 89.09 | 47.31 | 33.46 | 26.58 | 22.50 | 19.82 | 17.93 | 16.53 | 15.47 | 14.64 | 13.98 | 13.44 |
| 2000 | 178.17 | 94.62 | 66.91 | 53.16 | 45.00 | 39.63 | 35.85 | 33.06 | 30.94 | 29.28 | 27.96 | 26.88 |
| 3000 | 267.25 | 141.93 | 100.37 | 79.74 | 67.50 | 59.44 | 53.77 | 49.59 | 46.41 | 43.92 | 41.93 | 40.32 |
| 4000 | 356.34 | 189.23 | 133.82 | 106.32 | 90.00 | 79.25 | 71.69 | 66.12 | 61.88 | 58.56 | 55.91 | 53.76 |
| 5000 | 445.42 | 236.54 | 167.27 | 132.90 | 112.49 | 99.06 | 89.61 | 82.65 | 77.34 | 73.19 | 69.88 | 67.20 |
| 6000 | 534.50 | 283.85 | 200.73 | 159.48 | 134.99 | 118.87 | 107.53 | 99.18 | 92.81 | 87.83 | 83.86 | 80.64 |
| 7000 | 623.59 | 331.16 | 234.18 | 186.06 | 157.49 | 138.68 | 125.45 | 115.71 | 108.28 | 102.47 | 97.83 | 94.08 |
| 8000 | 712.67 | 378.46 | 267.63 | 212.64 | 179.99 | 158.49 | 143.37 | 132.24 | 123.75 | 117.11 | 111.81 | 107.51 |
| 9000 | 801.75 | 425.77 | 301.09 | 239.22 | 202.49 | 178.31 | 161.30 | 148.76 | 139.21 | 131.74 | 125.78 | 120.95 |
| 10000 | 890.83 | 473.08 | 334.54 | 265.80 | 224.98 | 198.12 | 179.22 | 165.29 | 154.68 | 146.38 | 139.76 | 134.39 |
| 11000 | 979.92 | 520.39 | 367.99 | 292.38 | 247.48 | 217.93 | 197.14 | 181.82 | 170.15 | 161.02 | 153.73 | 147.83 |
| 12000 | 1069.00 | 567.69 | 401.45 | 318.96 | 269.98 | 237.74 | 215.06 | 198.35 | 185.62 | 175.66 | 167.71 | 161.27 |
| 13000 | 1158.08 | 615.00 | 434.90 | 345.54 | 292.48 | 257.55 | 232.98 | 214.88 | 201.08 | 190.29 | 181.69 | 174.71 |
| 14000 | 1247.17 | 662.31 | 468.36 | 372.12 | 314.98 | 277.36 | 250.90 | 231.41 | 216.55 | 204.93 | 195.66 | 188.15 |
| 15000 | 1336.25 | 709.61 | 501.81 | 398.70 | 337.47 | 297.17 | 268.82 | 247.94 | 232.02 | 219.57 | 209.64 | 201.58 |
| 16000 | 1425.33 | 756.92 | 535.26 | 425.28 | 359.97 | 316.98 | 286.74 | 264.47 | 247.49 | 234.21 | 223.61 | 215.02 |
| 17000 | 1514.41 | 804.23 | 568.72 | 451.86 | 382.47 | 336.80 | 304.67 | 280.99 | 262.95 | 248.84 | 237.59 | 228.46 |
| 18000 | 1603.50 | 851.54 | 602.17 | 478.44 | 404.97 | 356.61 | 322.59 | 297.52 | 278.42 | 263.48 | 251.56 | 241.90 |
| 19000 | 1692.58 | 898.84 | 635.62 | 505.02 | 427.47 | 376.42 | 340.51 | 314.05 | 293.89 | 278.12 | 265.54 | 255.34 |
| 20000 | 1781.66 | 946.15 | 669.08 | 531.60 | 449.96 | 396.23 | 358.43 | 330.58 | 309.36 | 292.76 | 279.51 | 268.78 |
| 21000 | 1870.75 | 993.46 | 702.53 | 558.18 | 472.46 | 416.04 | 376.35 | 347.11 | 324.82 | 307.39 | 293.49 | 282.22 |
| 22000 | 1959.83 | 1040.77 | 735.98 | 584.76 | 494.96 | 435.85 | 394.27 | 363.64 | 340.29 | 322.03 | 307.46 | 295.65 |
| 23000 | 2048.91 | 1088.07 | 769.44 | 611.34 | 517.46 | 455.66 | 412.19 | 380.17 | 355.76 | 336.67 | 321.44 | 309.09 |
| 24000 | 2137.99 | 1135.38 | 802.89 | 637.92 | 539.96 | 475.47 | 430.11 | 396.70 | 371.23 | 351.31 | 335.42 | 322.53 |
| 25000 | 2227.08 | 1182.69 | 836.35 | 664.50 | 562.45 | 495.28 | 448.04 | 413.23 | 386.69 | 365.95 | 349.39 | 335.97 |
| 26000 | 2316.16 | 1230.00 | 869.80 | 691.08 | 584.95 | 515.10 | 465.96 | 429.75 | 402.16 | 380.58 | 363.37 | 349.41 |
| 27000 | 2405.24 | 1277.30 | 903.25 | 717.66 | 607.45 | 534.91 | 483.88 | 446.28 | 417.63 | 395.22 | 377.34 | 362.85 |
| 28000 | 2494.33 | 1324.61 | 936.71 | 744.24 | 629.95 | 554.72 | 501.80 | 462.81 | 433.10 | 409.86 | 391.32 | 376.29 |
| 29000 | 2583.41 | 1371.92 | 970.16 | 770.82 | 652.45 | 574.53 | 519.72 | 479.34 | 448.56 | 424.50 | 405.29 | 389.72 |
| 30000 | 2672.49 | 1419.22 | 1003.61 | 797.40 | 674.94 | 594.34 | 537.64 | 495.87 | 464.03 | 439.13 | 419.27 | 403.16 |
| 31000 | 2761.57 | 1466.53 | 1037.07 | 823.98 | 697.44 | 614.15 | 555.56 | 512.40 | 479.50 | 453.77 | 433.24 | 416.60 |
| 32000 | 2850.66 | 1513.84 | 1070.52 | 850.56 | 719.94 | 633.96 | 573.48 | 528.93 | 494.97 | 468.41 | 447.22 | 430.04 |
| 33000 | 2939.74 | 1561.15 | 1103.97 | 877.14 | 742.44 | 653.77 | 591.41 | 545.46 | 510.43 | 483.05 | 461.19 | 443.48 |
| 34000 | 3028.82 | 1608.45 | 1137.43 | 903.72 | 764.93 | 673.59 | 609.33 | 561.98 | 525.90 | 497.68 | 475.17 | 456.92 |
| 35000 | 3117.91 | 1655.76 | 1170.88 | 930.30 | 787.43 | 693.40 | 627.25 | 578.51 | 541.37 | 512.32 | 489.15 | 470.36 |
| 36000 | 3206.99 | 1703.07 | 1204.34 | 956.88 | 809.93 | 713.21 | 645.17 | 595.04 | 556.84 | 526.96 | 503.12 | 483.79 |
| 37000 | 3296.07 | 1750.38 | 1237.79 | 983.46 | 832.43 | 733.02 | 663.09 | 611.57 | 572.30 | 541.60 | 517.10 | 497.23 |
| 38000 | 3385.15 | 1797.68 | 1271.24 | 1010.04 | 854.93 | 752.83 | 681.01 | 628.10 | 587.77 | 556.23 | 531.07 | 510.67 |
| 39000 | 3474.24 | 1844.99 | 1304.70 | 1036.63 | 877.42 | 772.64 | 698.93 | 644.63 | 603.24 | 570.87 | 545.05 | 524.11 |
| 40000 | 3563.32 | 1892.30 | 1338.15 | 1063.20 | 899.92 | 792.45 | 716.85 | 661.16 | 618.71 | 585.51 | 559.02 | 537.55 |
| 41000 | 3652.40 | 1939.60 | 1371.60 | 1089.78 | 922.42 | 812.26 | 734.78 | 677.69 | 634.17 | 600.15 | 573.00 | 550.99 |
| 42000 | 3741.49 | 1986.91 | 1405.06 | 1116.36 | 944.92 | 832.07 | 752.70 | 694.21 | 649.64 | 614.78 | 586.97 | 564.43 |
| 43000 | 3830.57 | 2034.22 | 1438.51 | 1142.94 | 967.42 | 851.89 | 770.62 | 710.74 | 665.11 | 629.42 | 600.95 | 577.86 |
| 44000 | 3919.65 | 2081.53 | 1471.96 | 1169.52 | 989.91 | 871.70 | 788.54 | 727.27 | 680.58 | 644.06 | 614.92 | 591.30 |
| 45000 | 4008.73 | 2128.83 | 1505.42 | 1196.10 | 1012.41 | 891.51 | 806.46 | 743.80 | 696.04 | 658.70 | 628.90 | 604.74 |
| 46000 | 4097.82 | 2176.14 | 1538.87 | 1222.68 | 1034.91 | 911.32 | 824.38 | 760.33 | 711.51 | 673.34 | 642.87 | 618.18 |
| 47000 | 4186.90 | 2223.45 | 1572.33 | 1249.26 | 1057.41 | 931.13 | 842.30 | 776.86 | 726.98 | 687.97 | 656.85 | 631.62 |
| 48000 | 4275.98 | 2270.76 | 1605.78 | 1275.84 | 1079.91 | 950.94 | 860.22 | 793.39 | 742.45 | 702.61 | 670.83 | 645.06 |
| 49000 | 4365.07 | 2318.06 | 1639.23 | 1302.42 | 1102.40 | 970.75 | 878.15 | 809.92 | 757.91 | 717.25 | 684.80 | 658.50 |
| 50000 | 4454.15 | 2365.37 | 1672.69 | 1329.00 | 1124.90 | 990.56 | 896.07 | 826.45 | 773.38 | 731.89 | 698.78 | 671.93 |
| 55000 | 4899.56 | 2601.91 | 1839.95 | 1461.90 | 1237.39 | 1089.62 | 985.67 | 909.09 | 850.72 | 805.07 | 768.65 | 739.13 |
| 60000 | 5344.98 | 2838.44 | 2007.22 | 1594.80 | 1349.88 | 1188.68 | 1075.28 | 991.73 | 928.06 | 878.26 | 838.53 | 806.32 |
| 65000 | 5790.39 | 3074.98 | 2174.49 | 1727.70 | 1462.37 | 1287.73 | 1164.89 | 1074.38 | 1005.40 | 951.45 | 908.41 | 873.51 |
| 70000 | 6235.81 | 3311.52 | 2341.76 | 1860.60 | 1574.86 | 1386.79 | 1254.49 | 1157.02 | 1082.73 | 1024.64 | 978.29 | 940.71 |
| 75000 | 6681.22 | 3548.05 | 2509.03 | 1993.50 | 1687.35 | 1485.84 | 1344.10 | 1239.67 | 1160.07 | 1097.83 | 1048.16 | 1007.90 |
| 80000 | 7126.63 | 3784.59 | 2676.30 | 2126.40 | 1799.84 | 1584.90 | 1433.70 | 1322.31 | 1237.41 | 1171.01 | 1118.04 | 1075.09 |
| 85000 | 7572.05 | 4021.13 | 2843.56 | 2259.30 | 1912.33 | 1683.96 | 1523.31 | 1404.95 | 1314.75 | 1244.20 | 1187.92 | 1142.28 |
| 90000 | 8017.46 | 4257.66 | 3010.83 | 2392.20 | 2024.82 | 1783.01 | 1612.92 | 1487.60 | 1392.08 | 1317.39 | 1257.79 | 1209.48 |
| 95000 | 8462.88 | 4494.20 | 3178.10 | 2525.10 | 2137.31 | 1882.07 | 1702.52 | 1570.24 | 1469.42 | 1390.58 | 1327.67 | 1276.67 |
| 100000 | 8908.29 | 4730.74 | 3345.37 | 2658.00 | 2249.80 | 1981.12 | 1792.13 | 1652.89 | 1546.76 | 1463.77 | 1397.55 | 1343.86 |

# MONTHLY 12.50%

## PAYMENT REQUIRED TO AMORTIZE A LOAN

| TERM<br>AMOUNT | 13<br>year | 14<br>years | 15<br>years | 16<br>years | 17<br>years | 18<br>years | 19<br>years | 20<br>years | 25<br>years | 30<br>years | 35<br>years | 40<br>years |
|---|---|---|---|---|---|---|---|---|---|---|---|---|
| 50 | .65 | .64 | .62 | .61 | .60 | .59 | .58 | .57 | .55 | .54 | .53 | .53 |
| 100 | 1.30 | 1.27 | 1.24 | 1.21 | 1.19 | 1.17 | 1.15 | 1.14 | 1.10 | 1.07 | 1.06 | 1.05 |
| 200 | 2.60 | 2.53 | 2.47 | 2.42 | 2.37 | 2.34 | 2.30 | 2.28 | 2.19 | 2.14 | 2.12 | 2.10 |
| 300 | 3.90 | 3.79 | 3.70 | 3.63 | 3.56 | 3.50 | 3.45 | 3.41 | 3.28 | 3.21 | 3.17 | 3.15 |
| 400 | 5.20 | 5.06 | 4.94 | 4.83 | 4.74 | 4.67 | 4.60 | 4.55 | 4.37 | 4.27 | 4.23 | 4.20 |
| 500 | 6.50 | 6.32 | 6.17 | 6.04 | 5.93 | 5.84 | 5.75 | 5.69 | 5.46 | 5.34 | 5.28 | 5.25 |
| 600 | 7.80 | 7.58 | 7.40 | 7.25 | 7.11 | 7.00 | 6.90 | 6.82 | 6.55 | 6.41 | 6.34 | 6.30 |
| 700 | 9.10 | 8.85 | 8.63 | 8.45 | 8.30 | 8.17 | 8.05 | 7.96 | 7.64 | 7.48 | 7.39 | 7.35 |
| 800 | 10.40 | 10.11 | 9.87 | 9.66 | 9.48 | 9.33 | 9.20 | 9.09 | 8.73 | 8.54 | 8.45 | 8.40 |
| 900 | 11.70 | 11.37 | 11.10 | 10.87 | 10.67 | 10.50 | 10.35 | 10.23 | 9.82 | 9.61 | 9.50 | 9.45 |
| 1000 | 13.00 | 12.64 | 12.33 | 12.07 | 11.85 | 11.67 | 11.50 | 11.37 | 10.91 | 10.68 | 10.56 | 10.49 |
| 2000 | 26.00 | 25.27 | 24.66 | 24.14 | 23.70 | 23.33 | 23.00 | 22.73 | 21.81 | 21.35 | 21.11 | 20.98 |
| 3000 | 39.00 | 37.90 | 36.98 | 36.21 | 35.55 | 34.99 | 34.50 | 34.09 | 32.72 | 32.02 | 31.66 | 31.47 |
| 4000 | 52.00 | 50.53 | 49.31 | 48.27 | 47.39 | 46.65 | 46.00 | 45.45 | 43.62 | 42.70 | 42.22 | 41.96 |
| 5000 | 64.99 | 63.16 | 61.63 | 60.34 | 59.24 | 58.31 | 57.50 | 56.81 | 54.52 | 53.37 | 52.77 | 52.45 |
| 6000 | 77.99 | 75.80 | 73.96 | 72.41 | 71.09 | 69.97 | 69.00 | 68.17 | 65.43 | 64.04 | 63.32 | 62.94 |
| 7000 | 90.99 | 88.43 | 86.28 | 84.47 | 82.94 | 81.63 | 80.50 | 79.53 | 76.33 | 74.71 | 73.87 | 73.43 |
| 8000 | 103.99 | 101.06 | 98.61 | 96.54 | 94.78 | 93.29 | 92.00 | 90.90 | 87.23 | 85.39 | 84.43 | 83.92 |
| 9000 | 116.98 | 113.69 | 110.93 | 108.61 | 106.63 | 104.95 | 103.50 | 102.26 | 98.14 | 96.06 | 94.98 | 94.41 |
| 10000 | 129.98 | 126.32 | 123.26 | 120.67 | 118.48 | 116.61 | 115.00 | 113.62 | 109.04 | 106.73 | 105.53 | 104.90 |
| 11000 | 142.98 | 138.95 | 135.58 | 132.74 | 130.32 | 128.27 | 126.50 | 124.98 | 119.94 | 117.40 | 116.08 | 115.39 |
| 12000 | 155.98 | 151.59 | 147.91 | 144.81 | 142.17 | 139.93 | 138.00 | 136.34 | 130.85 | 128.08 | 126.64 | 125.88 |
| 13000 | 168.97 | 164.22 | 160.23 | 156.87 | 154.02 | 151.59 | 149.50 | 147.70 | 141.75 | 138.75 | 137.19 | 136.36 |
| 14000 | 181.97 | 176.85 | 172.56 | 168.94 | 165.87 | 163.25 | 161.00 | 159.06 | 152.65 | 149.42 | 147.74 | 146.85 |
| 15000 | 194.97 | 189.48 | 184.88 | 181.01 | 177.71 | 174.91 | 172.50 | 170.43 | 163.56 | 160.09 | 158.29 | 157.34 |
| 16000 | 207.97 | 202.11 | 197.21 | 193.07 | 189.56 | 186.57 | 184.00 | 181.79 | 174.46 | 170.77 | 168.85 | 167.83 |
| 17000 | 220.97 | 214.74 | 209.53 | 205.14 | 201.41 | 198.23 | 195.50 | 193.15 | 185.37 | 181.44 | 179.40 | 178.32 |
| 18000 | 233.96 | 227.38 | 221.86 | 217.21 | 213.26 | 209.89 | 207.00 | 204.51 | 196.27 | 192.11 | 189.95 | 188.81 |
| 19000 | 246.96 | 240.01 | 234.18 | 229.27 | 225.10 | 221.55 | 218.50 | 215.87 | 207.17 | 202.78 | 200.50 | 199.30 |
| 20000 | 259.96 | 252.64 | 246.51 | 241.34 | 236.95 | 233.21 | 230.00 | 227.23 | 218.08 | 213.46 | 211.06 | 209.79 |
| 21000 | 272.96 | 265.27 | 258.83 | 253.41 | 248.80 | 244.87 | 241.49 | 238.59 | 228.98 | 224.13 | 221.61 | 220.28 |
| 22000 | 285.95 | 277.90 | 271.16 | 265.47 | 260.64 | 256.53 | 252.99 | 249.96 | 239.88 | 234.80 | 232.16 | 230.77 |
| 23000 | 298.95 | 290.53 | 283.49 | 277.54 | 272.49 | 268.19 | 264.49 | 261.32 | 250.79 | 245.47 | 242.71 | 241.26 |
| 24000 | 311.95 | 303.17 | 295.81 | 289.61 | 284.34 | 279.85 | 275.99 | 272.68 | 261.69 | 256.15 | 253.27 | 251.75 |
| 25000 | 324.95 | 315.80 | 308.14 | 301.67 | 296.19 | 291.51 | 287.49 | 284.04 | 272.59 | 266.82 | 263.82 | 262.23 |
| 26000 | 337.94 | 328.43 | 320.46 | 313.74 | 308.03 | 303.17 | 298.99 | 295.40 | 283.50 | 277.49 | 274.37 | 272.72 |
| 27000 | 350.94 | 341.06 | 332.79 | 325.81 | 319.88 | 314.83 | 310.49 | 306.76 | 294.40 | 288.16 | 284.92 | 283.21 |
| 28000 | 363.94 | 353.69 | 345.11 | 337.87 | 331.73 | 326.49 | 321.99 | 318.12 | 305.30 | 298.84 | 295.48 | 293.70 |
| 29000 | 376.94 | 366.32 | 357.44 | 349.94 | 343.58 | 338.15 | 333.49 | 329.49 | 316.21 | 309.51 | 306.03 | 304.19 |
| 30000 | 389.93 | 378.96 | 369.76 | 362.01 | 355.42 | 349.81 | 344.99 | 340.85 | 327.11 | 320.18 | 316.58 | 314.68 |
| 31000 | 402.93 | 391.59 | 382.09 | 374.07 | 367.27 | 361.47 | 356.49 | 352.21 | 338.01 | 330.85 | 327.13 | 325.17 |
| 32000 | 415.93 | 404.22 | 394.41 | 386.14 | 379.12 | 373.13 | 367.99 | 363.57 | 348.92 | 341.53 | 337.69 | 335.66 |
| 33000 | 428.93 | 416.85 | 406.74 | 398.21 | 390.96 | 384.79 | 379.49 | 374.93 | 359.82 | 352.20 | 348.24 | 346.15 |
| 34000 | 441.93 | 429.48 | 419.06 | 410.27 | 402.81 | 396.45 | 390.99 | 386.29 | 370.73 | 362.87 | 358.79 | 356.64 |
| 35000 | 454.92 | 442.11 | 431.39 | 422.34 | 414.66 | 408.11 | 402.49 | 397.65 | 381.63 | 373.55 | 369.34 | 367.13 |
| 36000 | 467.92 | 454.75 | 443.71 | 434.41 | 426.51 | 419.77 | 413.99 | 409.02 | 392.53 | 384.22 | 379.90 | 377.62 |
| 37000 | 480.92 | 467.38 | 456.04 | 446.47 | 438.35 | 431.43 | 425.49 | 420.38 | 403.44 | 394.89 | 390.45 | 388.11 |
| 38000 | 493.92 | 480.01 | 468.36 | 458.54 | 450.20 | 443.09 | 436.99 | 431.74 | 414.34 | 405.56 | 401.00 | 398.59 |
| 39000 | 506.91 | 492.64 | 480.69 | 470.61 | 462.05 | 454.75 | 448.49 | 443.10 | 425.24 | 416.24 | 411.55 | 409.08 |
| 40000 | 519.91 | 505.27 | 493.01 | 482.67 | 473.90 | 466.41 | 459.99 | 454.46 | 436.15 | 426.91 | 422.11 | 419.57 |
| 41000 | 532.91 | 517.90 | 505.34 | 494.74 | 485.74 | 478.07 | 471.48 | 465.82 | 447.05 | 437.58 | 432.66 | 430.06 |
| 42000 | 545.91 | 530.54 | 517.66 | 506.81 | 497.59 | 489.73 | 482.98 | 477.18 | 457.95 | 448.25 | 443.21 | 440.55 |
| 43000 | 558.90 | 543.17 | 529.99 | 518.87 | 509.44 | 501.39 | 494.48 | 488.55 | 468.86 | 458.93 | 453.76 | 451.04 |
| 44000 | 571.90 | 555.80 | 542.31 | 530.94 | 521.28 | 513.05 | 505.98 | 499.91 | 479.76 | 469.60 | 464.32 | 461.53 |
| 45000 | 584.90 | 568.43 | 554.64 | 543.01 | 533.13 | 524.71 | 517.48 | 511.27 | 490.66 | 480.27 | 474.87 | 472.02 |
| 46000 | 597.90 | 581.06 | 566.97 | 555.07 | 544.98 | 536.37 | 528.98 | 522.63 | 501.57 | 490.94 | 485.42 | 482.51 |
| 47000 | 610.90 | 593.69 | 579.29 | 567.14 | 556.83 | 548.03 | 540.48 | 533.99 | 512.47 | 501.62 | 495.97 | 493.00 |
| 48000 | 623.89 | 606.33 | 591.62 | 579.21 | 568.67 | 559.69 | 551.98 | 545.35 | 523.37 | 512.29 | 506.53 | 503.49 |
| 49000 | 636.89 | 618.96 | 603.94 | 591.27 | 580.52 | 571.35 | 563.48 | 556.71 | 534.28 | 522.96 | 517.08 | 513.98 |
| 50000 | 649.89 | 631.59 | 616.27 | 603.34 | 592.37 | 583.01 | 574.98 | 568.08 | 545.18 | 533.63 | 527.63 | 524.46 |
| 55000 | 714.88 | 694.75 | 677.89 | 663.67 | 651.60 | 641.31 | 632.48 | 624.88 | 599.70 | 587.00 | 580.39 | 576.91 |
| 60000 | 779.86 | 757.91 | 739.52 | 724.01 | 710.84 | 699.61 | 689.98 | 681.69 | 654.22 | 640.36 | 633.16 | 629.36 |
| 65000 | 844.85 | 821.06 | 801.14 | 784.34 | 770.08 | 757.91 | 747.47 | 738.50 | 708.74 | 693.72 | 685.92 | 681.80 |
| 70000 | 909.84 | 884.22 | 862.77 | 844.67 | 829.31 | 816.21 | 804.97 | 795.30 | 763.25 | 747.09 | 738.68 | 734.25 |
| 75000 | 974.83 | 947.38 | 924.40 | 905.01 | 888.55 | 874.51 | 862.47 | 852.11 | 817.77 | 800.45 | 791.45 | 786.69 |
| 80000 | 1039.82 | 1010.54 | 986.02 | 965.34 | 947.79 | 932.81 | 919.97 | 908.92 | 872.29 | 853.81 | 844.21 | 839.14 |
| 85000 | 1104.81 | 1073.70 | 1047.65 | 1025.67 | 1007.02 | 991.11 | 977.46 | 965.72 | 926.81 | 907.17 | 896.97 | 891.59 |
| 90000 | 1169.79 | 1136.86 | 1109.27 | 1086.01 | 1066.26 | 1049.41 | 1034.96 | 1022.53 | 981.32 | 960.54 | 949.73 | 944.03 |
| 95000 | 1234.78 | 1200.01 | 1170.90 | 1146.34 | 1125.49 | 1107.71 | 1092.46 | 1079.34 | 1035.84 | 1013.90 | 1002.50 | 996.48 |
| 100000 | 1299.77 | 1263.17 | 1232.53 | 1206.67 | 1184.73 | 1166.01 | 1149.96 | 1136.15 | 1090.36 | 1067.26 | 1055.26 | 1048.92 |

# 13.00%
# MONTHLY
### PAYMENT REQUIRED TO AMORTIZE A LOAN

| TERM<br>AMOUNT | 1<br>year | 2<br>years | 3<br>years | 4<br>years | 5<br>years | 6<br>years | 7<br>years | 8<br>years | 9<br>years | 10<br>years | 11<br>years | 12<br>years |
|---|---|---|---|---|---|---|---|---|---|---|---|---|
| 50 | 4.47 | 2.38 | 1.69 | 1.35 | 1.14 | 1.01 | .91 | .85 | .79 | .75 | .72 | .69 |
| 100 | 8.94 | 4.76 | 3.37 | 2.69 | 2.28 | 2.01 | 1.82 | 1.69 | 1.58 | 1.50 | 1.43 | 1.38 |
| 200 | 17.87 | 9.51 | 6.74 | 5.37 | 4.56 | 4.02 | 3.64 | 3.37 | 3.16 | 2.99 | 2.86 | 2.75 |
| 300 | 26.80 | 14.27 | 10.11 | 8.05 | 6.83 | 6.03 | 5.46 | 5.05 | 4.73 | 4.48 | 4.29 | 4.13 |
| 400 | 35.73 | 19.02 | 13.48 | 10.74 | 9.11 | 8.03 | 7.28 | 6.73 | 6.31 | 5.98 | 5.72 | 5.50 |
| 500 | 44.66 | 23.78 | 16.85 | 13.42 | 11.38 | 10.04 | 9.10 | 8.41 | 7.88 | 7.47 | 7.14 | 6.88 |
| 600 | 53.60 | 28.53 | 20.22 | 16.10 | 13.66 | 12.05 | 10.92 | 10.09 | 9.46 | 8.96 | 8.57 | 8.25 |
| 700 | 62.53 | 33.28 | 23.59 | 18.78 | 15.93 | 14.06 | 12.74 | 11.77 | 11.03 | 10.46 | 10.00 | 9.63 |
| 800 | 71.46 | 38.04 | 26.96 | 21.47 | 18.21 | 16.06 | 14.56 | 13.45 | 12.61 | 11.95 | 11.43 | 11.00 |
| 900 | 80.39 | 42.79 | 30.33 | 24.15 | 20.48 | 18.07 | 16.38 | 15.13 | 14.18 | 13.44 | 12.85 | 12.38 |
| 1000 | 89.32 | 47.55 | 33.70 | 26.83 | 22.76 | 20.08 | 18.20 | 16.81 | 15.76 | 14.94 | 14.28 | 13.75 |
| 2000 | 178.64 | 95.09 | 67.39 | 53.66 | 45.51 | 40.15 | 36.39 | 33.62 | 31.51 | 29.87 | 28.56 | 27.50 |
| 3000 | 267.96 | 142.63 | 101.09 | 80.49 | 68.26 | 60.23 | 54.58 | 50.43 | 47.27 | 44.80 | 42.83 | 41.24 |
| 4000 | 357.27 | 190.17 | 134.78 | 107.31 | 91.02 | 80.30 | 72.77 | 67.23 | 63.02 | 59.73 | 57.11 | 54.99 |
| 5000 | 446.59 | 237.71 | 168.47 | 134.14 | 113.77 | 100.38 | 90.96 | 84.04 | 78.77 | 74.66 | 71.39 | 68.74 |
| 6000 | 535.91 | 285.26 | 202.17 | 160.97 | 136.52 | 120.45 | 109.16 | 100.85 | 94.53 | 89.59 | 85.66 | 82.48 |
| 7000 | 625.23 | 332.80 | 235.86 | 187.80 | 159.28 | 140.52 | 127.35 | 117.66 | 110.28 | 104.52 | 99.94 | 96.23 |
| 8000 | 714.54 | 380.34 | 269.56 | 214.62 | 182.03 | 160.60 | 145.54 | 134.46 | 126.03 | 119.45 | 114.21 | 109.98 |
| 9000 | 803.86 | 427.88 | 303.25 | 241.45 | 204.78 | 180.67 | 163.73 | 151.27 | 141.79 | 134.38 | 128.49 | 123.72 |
| 10000 | 893.18 | 475.42 | 336.94 | 268.28 | 227.54 | 200.75 | 181.92 | 168.08 | 157.54 | 149.32 | 142.77 | 137.47 |
| 11000 | 982.50 | 522.97 | 370.64 | 295.11 | 250.29 | 220.82 | 200.12 | 184.88 | 173.29 | 164.25 | 157.04 | 151.21 |
| 12000 | 1071.81 | 570.51 | 404.33 | 321.93 | 273.04 | 240.89 | 218.31 | 201.69 | 189.05 | 179.18 | 171.32 | 164.96 |
| 13000 | 1161.13 | 618.05 | 438.03 | 348.76 | 295.79 | 260.97 | 236.50 | 218.50 | 204.80 | 194.11 | 185.59 | 178.71 |
| 14000 | 1250.45 | 665.59 | 471.72 | 375.59 | 318.55 | 281.04 | 254.69 | 235.31 | 220.56 | 209.04 | 199.87 | 192.45 |
| 15000 | 1339.76 | 713.13 | 505.41 | 402.42 | 341.30 | 301.12 | 272.88 | 252.11 | 236.31 | 223.97 | 214.15 | 206.20 |
| 16000 | 1429.08 | 760.67 | 539.11 | 429.24 | 364.05 | 321.19 | 291.08 | 268.92 | 252.06 | 238.90 | 228.42 | 219.95 |
| 17000 | 1518.40 | 808.22 | 572.80 | 456.07 | 386.81 | 341.26 | 309.27 | 285.73 | 267.82 | 253.83 | 242.70 | 233.69 |
| 18000 | 1607.72 | 855.76 | 606.50 | 482.90 | 409.56 | 361.34 | 327.46 | 302.54 | 283.57 | 268.76 | 256.97 | 247.44 |
| 19000 | 1697.03 | 903.30 | 640.19 | 509.73 | 432.31 | 381.41 | 345.65 | 319.34 | 299.32 | 283.70 | 271.25 | 261.18 |
| 20000 | 1786.35 | 950.84 | 673.88 | 536.55 | 455.07 | 401.49 | 363.84 | 336.15 | 315.08 | 298.63 | 285.53 | 274.93 |
| 21000 | 1875.67 | 998.38 | 707.58 | 563.38 | 477.82 | 421.56 | 382.04 | 352.96 | 330.83 | 313.56 | 299.80 | 288.68 |
| 22000 | 1964.99 | 1045.93 | 741.27 | 590.21 | 500.57 | 441.64 | 400.23 | 369.76 | 346.58 | 328.49 | 314.08 | 302.42 |
| 23000 | 2054.30 | 1093.47 | 774.97 | 617.04 | 523.33 | 461.71 | 418.42 | 386.57 | 362.34 | 343.42 | 328.36 | 316.17 |
| 24000 | 2143.62 | 1141.01 | 808.66 | 643.86 | 546.08 | 481.78 | 436.61 | 403.38 | 378.09 | 358.35 | 342.63 | 329.92 |
| 25000 | 2232.94 | 1188.55 | 842.35 | 670.69 | 568.83 | 501.86 | 454.80 | 420.19 | 393.84 | 373.28 | 356.91 | 343.66 |
| 26000 | 2322.25 | 1236.09 | 876.05 | 697.52 | 591.58 | 521.93 | 473.00 | 436.99 | 409.60 | 388.21 | 371.18 | 357.41 |
| 27000 | 2411.57 | 1283.63 | 909.74 | 724.35 | 614.34 | 542.01 | 491.19 | 453.80 | 425.35 | 403.14 | 385.46 | 371.15 |
| 28000 | 2500.89 | 1331.18 | 943.44 | 751.17 | 637.09 | 562.08 | 509.38 | 470.61 | 441.11 | 418.08 | 399.74 | 384.90 |
| 29000 | 2590.21 | 1378.72 | 977.13 | 778.00 | 659.84 | 582.15 | 527.57 | 487.42 | 456.86 | 433.01 | 414.01 | 398.65 |
| 30000 | 2679.52 | 1426.26 | 1010.82 | 804.83 | 682.60 | 602.23 | 545.76 | 504.22 | 472.61 | 447.94 | 428.29 | 412.39 |
| 31000 | 2768.84 | 1473.80 | 1044.52 | 831.66 | 705.35 | 622.30 | 563.96 | 521.03 | 488.37 | 462.87 | 442.56 | 426.14 |
| 32000 | 2858.16 | 1521.34 | 1078.21 | 858.48 | 728.10 | 642.38 | 582.15 | 537.84 | 504.12 | 477.80 | 456.84 | 439.89 |
| 33000 | 2947.48 | 1568.89 | 1111.91 | 885.31 | 750.86 | 662.45 | 600.34 | 554.64 | 519.87 | 492.73 | 471.12 | 453.63 |
| 34000 | 3036.79 | 1616.43 | 1145.60 | 912.14 | 773.61 | 682.52 | 618.53 | 571.45 | 535.63 | 507.66 | 485.39 | 467.38 |
| 35000 | 3126.11 | 1663.97 | 1179.29 | 938.97 | 796.36 | 702.60 | 636.72 | 588.26 | 551.38 | 522.59 | 499.67 | 481.12 |
| 36000 | 3215.43 | 1711.51 | 1212.99 | 965.79 | 819.12 | 722.67 | 654.92 | 605.07 | 567.13 | 537.52 | 513.94 | 494.87 |
| 37000 | 3304.74 | 1759.05 | 1246.68 | 992.62 | 841.87 | 742.75 | 673.11 | 621.87 | 582.89 | 552.45 | 528.22 | 508.62 |
| 38000 | 3394.06 | 1806.59 | 1280.38 | 1019.45 | 864.62 | 762.82 | 691.30 | 638.68 | 598.64 | 567.39 | 542.50 | 522.36 |
| 39000 | 3483.38 | 1854.14 | 1314.07 | 1046.28 | 887.37 | 782.90 | 709.49 | 655.49 | 614.39 | 582.32 | 556.77 | 536.11 |
| 40000 | 3572.70 | 1901.68 | 1347.76 | 1073.10 | 910.13 | 802.97 | 727.68 | 672.30 | 630.15 | 597.25 | 571.05 | 549.86 |
| 41000 | 3662.01 | 1949.22 | 1381.46 | 1099.93 | 932.88 | 823.04 | 745.88 | 689.10 | 645.90 | 612.18 | 585.33 | 563.60 |
| 42000 | 3751.33 | 1996.76 | 1415.15 | 1126.76 | 955.63 | 843.12 | 764.07 | 705.91 | 661.66 | 627.11 | 599.60 | 577.35 |
| 43000 | 3840.65 | 2044.30 | 1448.84 | 1153.59 | 978.39 | 863.19 | 782.26 | 722.72 | 677.41 | 642.04 | 613.88 | 591.09 |
| 44000 | 3929.97 | 2091.85 | 1482.54 | 1180.41 | 1001.14 | 883.27 | 800.45 | 739.52 | 693.16 | 656.97 | 628.15 | 604.84 |
| 45000 | 4019.28 | 2139.39 | 1516.23 | 1207.24 | 1023.89 | 903.34 | 818.64 | 756.33 | 708.92 | 671.90 | 642.43 | 618.59 |
| 46000 | 4108.60 | 2186.93 | 1549.93 | 1234.07 | 1046.65 | 923.41 | 836.84 | 773.14 | 724.67 | 686.83 | 656.71 | 632.33 |
| 47000 | 4197.92 | 2234.47 | 1583.62 | 1260.90 | 1069.40 | 943.49 | 855.03 | 789.95 | 740.42 | 701.77 | 670.98 | 646.08 |
| 48000 | 4287.23 | 2282.01 | 1617.31 | 1287.72 | 1092.15 | 963.56 | 873.22 | 806.76 | 756.18 | 716.70 | 685.26 | 659.83 |
| 49000 | 4376.55 | 2329.55 | 1651.01 | 1314.55 | 1114.91 | 983.64 | 891.41 | 823.56 | 771.93 | 731.63 | 699.53 | 673.57 |
| 50000 | 4465.87 | 2377.10 | 1684.70 | 1341.38 | 1137.66 | 1003.71 | 909.60 | 840.37 | 787.68 | 746.56 | 713.81 | 687.32 |
| 55000 | 4912.46 | 2614.81 | 1853.17 | 1475.52 | 1251.42 | 1104.08 | 1000.56 | 924.40 | 866.45 | 821.21 | 785.19 | 756.05 |
| 60000 | 5359.04 | 2852.51 | 2021.64 | 1609.65 | 1365.19 | 1204.45 | 1091.52 | 1008.44 | 945.22 | 895.87 | 856.57 | 824.78 |
| 65000 | 5805.63 | 3090.22 | 2190.11 | 1743.79 | 1478.95 | 1304.82 | 1182.48 | 1092.48 | 1023.99 | 970.52 | 927.95 | 893.51 |
| 70000 | 6252.21 | 3327.93 | 2358.58 | 1877.93 | 1592.72 | 1405.19 | 1273.44 | 1176.51 | 1102.76 | 1045.18 | 999.33 | 962.24 |
| 75000 | 6698.80 | 3565.64 | 2527.05 | 2012.07 | 1706.49 | 1505.56 | 1364.40 | 1260.55 | 1181.52 | 1119.84 | 1070.71 | 1030.97 |
| 80000 | 7145.39 | 3803.35 | 2695.52 | 2146.20 | 1820.25 | 1605.93 | 1455.36 | 1344.59 | 1260.29 | 1194.49 | 1142.09 | 1099.71 |
| 85000 | 7591.97 | 4041.06 | 2863.99 | 2280.34 | 1934.02 | 1706.30 | 1546.32 | 1428.62 | 1339.06 | 1269.15 | 1213.47 | 1168.44 |
| 90000 | 8038.56 | 4278.77 | 3032.46 | 2414.48 | 2047.78 | 1806.67 | 1637.28 | 1512.66 | 1417.83 | 1343.80 | 1284.85 | 1237.17 |
| 95000 | 8485.15 | 4516.48 | 3200.93 | 2548.62 | 2161.55 | 1907.05 | 1728.24 | 1596.69 | 1496.60 | 1418.46 | 1356.24 | 1305.90 |
| 100000 | 8931.73 | 4754.19 | 3369.40 | 2682.75 | 2275.31 | 2007.42 | 1819.20 | 1680.73 | 1575.36 | 1493.11 | 1427.62 | 1374.63 |

# MONLY

### PAYMENT REQUIRED TO AMORTIZE A LOAN

| TERM AMOUNT | 13 year | 14 years | 15 years | 16 years | 17 years | 18 years | 19 years | 20 years | 25 years | 30 years | 35 years | 40 years |
|---|---|---|---|---|---|---|---|---|---|---|---|---|
| 50 | .67 | .65 | .64 | .62 | .61 | .61 | .60 | .59 | .57 | .56 | .55 | .55 |
| 100 | 1.34 | 1.30 | 1.27 | 1.24 | 1.22 | 1.21 | 1.19 | 1.18 | 1.13 | 1.11 | 1.10 | 1.09 |
| 200 | 2.67 | 2.60 | 2.54 | 2.48 | 2.44 | 2.41 | 2.37 | 2.35 | 2.26 | 2.22 | 2.20 | 2.18 |
| 300 | 4.00 | 3.89 | 3.80 | 3.72 | 3.66 | 3.61 | 3.56 | 3.52 | 3.39 | 3.32 | 3.29 | 3.27 |
| 400 | 5.33 | 5.19 | 5.07 | 4.96 | 4.88 | 4.81 | 4.74 | 4.69 | 4.52 | 4.43 | 4.39 | 4.36 |
| 500 | 6.66 | 6.48 | 6.33 | 6.20 | 6.10 | 6.01 | 5.93 | 5.86 | 5.64 | 5.54 | 5.48 | 5.45 |
| 600 | 7.99 | 7.78 | 7.60 | 7.44 | 7.32 | 7.21 | 7.11 | 7.03 | 6.77 | 6.64 | 6.58 | 6.54 |
| 700 | 9.32 | 9.07 | 8.86 | 8.68 | 8.54 | 8.41 | 8.30 | 8.21 | 7.90 | 7.75 | 7.67 | 7.63 |
| 800 | 10.65 | 10.37 | 10.13 | 9.92 | 9.75 | 9.61 | 9.48 | 9.38 | 9.03 | 8.85 | 8.77 | 8.72 |
| 900 | 11.99 | 11.66 | 11.39 | 11.16 | 10.97 | 10.81 | 10.67 | 10.55 | 10.16 | 9.96 | 9.86 | 9.81 |
| 1000 | 13.32 | 12.96 | 12.66 | 12.40 | 12.19 | 12.01 | 11.85 | 11.72 | 11.28 | 11.07 | 10.96 | 10.90 |
| 2000 | 26.63 | 25.91 | 25.31 | 24.80 | 24.38 | 24.01 | 23.70 | 23.44 | 22.56 | 22.13 | 21.91 | 21.80 |
| 3000 | 39.94 | 38.86 | 37.96 | 37.20 | 36.56 | 36.02 | 35.55 | 35.15 | 33.84 | 33.19 | 32.86 | 32.69 |
| 4000 | 53.25 | 51.82 | 50.61 | 49.60 | 48.75 | 48.02 | 47.40 | 46.87 | 45.12 | 44.25 | 43.81 | 43.59 |
| 5000 | 66.57 | 64.77 | 63.27 | 62.00 | 60.94 | 60.03 | 59.25 | 58.58 | 56.40 | 55.31 | 54.76 | 54.48 |
| 6000 | 79.88 | 77.72 | 75.92 | 74.40 | 73.12 | 72.03 | 71.10 | 70.30 | 67.68 | 66.38 | 65.72 | 65.38 |
| 7000 | 93.19 | 90.67 | 88.57 | 86.80 | 85.31 | 84.04 | 82.95 | 82.02 | 78.95 | 77.44 | 76.67 | 76.27 |
| 8000 | 106.50 | 103.63 | 101.22 | 99.20 | 97.49 | 96.04 | 94.80 | 93.73 | 90.23 | 88.50 | 87.62 | 87.17 |
| 9000 | 119.81 | 116.58 | 113.88 | 111.60 | 109.68 | 108.04 | 106.65 | 105.45 | 101.51 | 99.56 | 98.57 | 98.06 |
| 10000 | 133.13 | 129.53 | 126.53 | 124.00 | 121.87 | 120.05 | 118.49 | 117.16 | 112.79 | 110.62 | 109.52 | 108.96 |
| 11000 | 146.44 | 142.48 | 139.18 | 136.40 | 134.05 | 132.05 | 130.34 | 128.88 | 124.07 | 121.69 | 120.48 | 119.85 |
| 12000 | 159.75 | 155.44 | 151.83 | 148.80 | 146.24 | 144.06 | 142.19 | 140.59 | 135.35 | 132.75 | 131.43 | 130.75 |
| 13000 | 173.06 | 168.39 | 164.49 | 161.20 | 158.42 | 156.06 | 154.04 | 152.31 | 146.62 | 143.81 | 142.38 | 141.64 |
| 14000 | 186.37 | 181.34 | 177.14 | 173.60 | 170.61 | 168.07 | 165.89 | 164.03 | 157.90 | 154.87 | 153.33 | 152.54 |
| 15000 | 199.69 | 194.29 | 189.79 | 186.00 | 182.80 | 180.07 | 177.74 | 175.74 | 169.18 | 165.93 | 164.28 | 163.43 |
| 16000 | 213.00 | 207.25 | 202.44 | 198.40 | 194.98 | 192.07 | 189.59 | 187.46 | 180.46 | 177.00 | 175.24 | 174.33 |
| 17000 | 226.31 | 220.20 | 215.10 | 210.80 | 207.17 | 204.08 | 201.44 | 199.17 | 191.74 | 188.06 | 186.19 | 185.22 |
| 18000 | 239.62 | 233.15 | 227.75 | 223.20 | 219.36 | 216.08 | 213.29 | 210.89 | 203.02 | 199.12 | 197.14 | 196.12 |
| 19000 | 252.93 | 246.11 | 240.40 | 235.60 | 231.54 | 228.09 | 225.14 | 222.60 | 214.29 | 210.18 | 208.09 | 207.01 |
| 20000 | 266.25 | 259.06 | 253.05 | 248.00 | 243.73 | 240.09 | 236.98 | 234.32 | 225.57 | 221.24 | 219.04 | 217.91 |
| 21000 | 279.56 | 272.01 | 265.71 | 260.40 | 255.91 | 252.10 | 248.83 | 246.04 | 236.85 | 232.31 | 230.00 | 228.80 |
| 22000 | 292.87 | 284.96 | 278.36 | 272.80 | 268.10 | 264.10 | 260.68 | 257.75 | 248.13 | 243.37 | 240.95 | 239.70 |
| 23000 | 306.18 | 297.92 | 291.01 | 285.20 | 280.29 | 276.10 | 272.53 | 269.47 | 259.41 | 254.43 | 251.90 | 250.59 |
| 24000 | 319.50 | 310.87 | 303.66 | 297.60 | 292.47 | 288.11 | 284.38 | 281.18 | 270.69 | 265.49 | 262.85 | 261.49 |
| 25000 | 332.81 | 323.82 | 316.32 | 310.00 | 304.66 | 300.11 | 296.23 | 292.90 | 281.96 | 276.55 | 273.80 | 272.38 |
| 26000 | 346.12 | 336.77 | 328.97 | 322.40 | 316.84 | 312.12 | 308.08 | 304.61 | 293.24 | 287.62 | 284.76 | 283.28 |
| 27000 | 359.43 | 349.73 | 341.62 | 334.80 | 329.03 | 324.12 | 319.93 | 316.33 | 304.52 | 298.68 | 295.71 | 294.17 |
| 28000 | 372.74 | 362.68 | 354.27 | 347.20 | 341.22 | 336.13 | 331.78 | 328.05 | 315.80 | 309.74 | 306.66 | 305.07 |
| 29000 | 386.06 | 375.63 | 366.93 | 359.60 | 353.40 | 348.13 | 343.63 | 339.76 | 327.08 | 320.80 | 317.61 | 315.96 |
| 30000 | 399.37 | 388.58 | 379.58 | 372.00 | 365.59 | 360.13 | 355.47 | 351.48 | 338.36 | 331.86 | 328.56 | 326.86 |
| 31000 | 412.68 | 401.54 | 392.23 | 384.40 | 377.78 | 372.14 | 367.32 | 363.19 | 349.63 | 342.93 | 339.51 | 337.75 |
| 32000 | 425.99 | 414.49 | 404.88 | 396.80 | 389.96 | 384.14 | 379.17 | 374.91 | 360.91 | 353.99 | 350.47 | 348.65 |
| 33000 | 439.30 | 427.44 | 417.53 | 409.20 | 402.15 | 396.15 | 391.02 | 386.62 | 372.19 | 365.05 | 361.42 | 359.54 |
| 34000 | 452.62 | 440.39 | 430.19 | 421.60 | 414.33 | 408.15 | 402.87 | 398.34 | 383.47 | 376.11 | 372.37 | 370.44 |
| 35000 | 465.93 | 453.35 | 442.84 | 434.00 | 426.52 | 420.16 | 414.72 | 410.06 | 394.75 | 387.17 | 383.32 | 381.33 |
| 36000 | 479.24 | 466.30 | 455.49 | 446.40 | 438.71 | 432.16 | 426.57 | 421.77 | 406.03 | 398.24 | 394.27 | 392.23 |
| 37000 | 492.55 | 479.25 | 468.14 | 458.80 | 450.89 | 444.17 | 438.42 | 433.49 | 417.30 | 409.30 | 405.23 | 403.13 |
| 38000 | 505.86 | 492.21 | 480.80 | 471.20 | 463.08 | 456.17 | 450.27 | 445.20 | 428.58 | 420.36 | 416.18 | 414.02 |
| 39000 | 519.18 | 505.16 | 493.45 | 483.60 | 475.26 | 468.17 | 462.12 | 456.92 | 439.86 | 431.42 | 427.13 | 424.92 |
| 40000 | 532.49 | 518.11 | 506.10 | 496.00 | 487.45 | 480.18 | 473.96 | 468.64 | 451.14 | 442.48 | 438.08 | 435.81 |
| 41000 | 545.80 | 531.06 | 518.75 | 508.40 | 499.64 | 492.18 | 485.81 | 480.35 | 462.42 | 453.55 | 449.03 | 446.71 |
| 42000 | 559.11 | 544.02 | 531.41 | 520.80 | 511.82 | 504.19 | 497.66 | 492.07 | 473.70 | 464.61 | 459.99 | 457.60 |
| 43000 | 572.43 | 556.97 | 544.06 | 533.20 | 524.01 | 516.19 | 509.51 | 503.78 | 484.97 | 475.67 | 470.94 | 468.50 |
| 44000 | 585.74 | 569.92 | 556.71 | 545.60 | 536.20 | 528.20 | 521.36 | 515.50 | 496.25 | 486.73 | 481.89 | 479.39 |
| 45000 | 599.05 | 582.87 | 569.36 | 558.00 | 548.38 | 540.20 | 533.21 | 527.21 | 507.53 | 497.79 | 492.84 | 490.29 |
| 46000 | 612.36 | 595.83 | 582.02 | 570.40 | 560.57 | 552.20 | 545.06 | 538.93 | 518.81 | 508.86 | 503.79 | 501.18 |
| 47000 | 625.67 | 608.78 | 594.67 | 582.80 | 572.75 | 564.21 | 556.91 | 550.65 | 530.09 | 519.92 | 514.75 | 512.08 |
| 48000 | 638.99 | 621.73 | 607.32 | 595.20 | 584.94 | 576.21 | 568.76 | 562.36 | 541.37 | 530.98 | 525.70 | 522.97 |
| 49000 | 652.30 | 634.68 | 619.97 | 607.60 | 597.13 | 588.22 | 580.61 | 574.08 | 552.64 | 542.04 | 536.65 | 533.87 |
| 50000 | 665.61 | 647.64 | 632.63 | 620.00 | 609.31 | 600.22 | 592.45 | 585.79 | 563.92 | 553.10 | 547.60 | 544.76 |
| 55000 | 732.17 | 712.40 | 695.89 | 682.00 | 670.24 | 660.24 | 651.70 | 644.37 | 620.31 | 608.41 | 602.36 | 599.24 |
| 60000 | 798.73 | 777.16 | 759.15 | 744.00 | 731.17 | 720.26 | 710.94 | 702.95 | 676.71 | 663.72 | 657.12 | 653.71 |
| 65000 | 865.29 | 841.93 | 822.41 | 806.00 | 792.10 | 780.29 | 770.19 | 761.53 | 733.10 | 719.03 | 711.88 | 708.19 |
| 70000 | 931.85 | 906.69 | 885.67 | 868.00 | 853.04 | 840.31 | 829.43 | 820.11 | 789.49 | 774.34 | 766.64 | 762.66 |
| 75000 | 998.41 | 971.45 | 948.94 | 930.00 | 913.97 | 900.33 | 888.68 | 878.69 | 845.88 | 829.65 | 821.40 | 817.14 |
| 80000 | 1064.97 | 1036.22 | 1012.20 | 992.00 | 974.90 | 960.35 | 947.92 | 937.27 | 902.27 | 884.96 | 876.16 | 871.62 |
| 85000 | 1131.53 | 1100.98 | 1075.46 | 1053.99 | 1035.83 | 1020.37 | 1007.17 | 995.84 | 958.67 | 940.27 | 930.92 | 926.09 |
| 90000 | 1198.09 | 1165.74 | 1138.72 | 1115.99 | 1096.76 | 1080.39 | 1066.41 | 1054.42 | 1015.06 | 995.58 | 985.68 | 980.57 |
| 95000 | 1264.65 | 1230.51 | 1201.99 | 1177.99 | 1157.69 | 1140.42 | 1125.66 | 1113.00 | 1071.45 | 1050.89 | 1040.44 | 1035.04 |
| 100000 | 1331.22 | 1295.27 | 1265.25 | 1239.99 | 1218.62 | 1200.44 | 1184.90 | 1171.58 | 1127.84 | 1106.20 | 1095.20 | 1089.52 |

# REAL ESTATE GLOSSARY

□　□　□

## A

ABSOLUTE TITLE—Exclusive claim, right, or interest to a property described in a title.

ABSTRACT—A short summary which contains the history of the ownership and title to a property, a listing of conveyances and legal proceedings, and a description of the land and conditions of ownership. Referred to sometimes as an *Abstract of Title* or an *Abstractor's Certificate.*

ABUT—To border, adjoin, or touch; adjacent to.

ACCEPT—To receive with approval, satisfaction, or the intention to keep.

ACCEPTANCE—Voluntarily agreeing to the price and terms of an offer and becoming bound to its terms. For example, a buyer offers to buy and a seller accepts the offer. See also CONTRACT.

---

*Note:* These definitions have been excerpted from *The Real Estate Greenbook* by Marc Stephen Garrison, copyright 1988, published by the National Committee for Real Estate Investment. Complete copies of the *Greenbook* are available by contacting M. S. Garrison and Company at (801) 225-8777, or by writing to P.O. Box 1096, Orem, Utah 84057. The price, including shipping, is $24.95.

---

223

ACCESS—The ability to approach a property. For example, most city lots have access to the street. Access also implies the right to approach. The public is also guaranteed the right of access to public records.

ACCESS RIGHTS—The right of an owner to passage over adjoining property in order to enter and leave his own property.

ACQUISITION—The process of obtaining property and becoming an owner.

ACQUISITION COST—The costs involved in acquiring a property other than the purchase price. Examples would be points, title insurance fees, closing costs, and recording fees.

ACT OF GOD—Damage caused entirely by acts of nature (floods, tornadoes, storms, etc.) rather than caused by man.

ACTUAL POSSESSION—Physically occupying or controlling a property. This is a legal term which compares with the saying "possession is nine tenths of the law." Actual possession is differentiated from constructive possession, which comes about from possession of a title.

ADDENDUM—Something added to a document, letter, contractual agreement, etc. *See also* AMENDMENT.

ADDITION—A part of a building added on after the original structure was built.

ADD-ON INTEREST—The interest that is added to the principal of a loan.

ADDRESS—Also known as street address. This refers to the common description of a property location for mailing purposes. It denotes the street name and number where the property lies, as well as the city, state, and postal zip code.

ADJUSTABLE MORTGAGE LOAN—Established in 1981 by the Federal Home Loan Bank Board to be used by savings and loans. It provides maximum flexibility in term selection. See also ADJUSTABLE RATE MORTGAGE.

ADJUSTABLE RATE MORTGAGE (ARM)—Mortgage wherein the interest rate fluctuates according to different factors. An example of a factor which some ARMS are tied to is the prime interest rate. Care should be taken before taking responsibility for an Adjustable Rate Mortgage to fully understand the factors which can increase your interest rate. You should also check the limits (if any) called for by the ARM on both the annual and loan duration interest rate increases. Many good ARMS limit the yearly increase to 1.5 percent or less and put a ceiling on interest that the loan can charge at 15 percent. See also the Latin expression CAVEAT EMPTOR.

ADJUSTED SALES PRICE—The sale price minus both the costs of "fixing up" and of selling a property.

ADMINISTRATOR'S DEED—The court document that specifies the conveyance of real property when a person dies intestate (without leaving a will).

ADULT—A person old enough to legally act without the consent of a parent or guardian. The legal age of adulthood varies between eighteen and twenty-one from state to state. An adult may enter into a binding contractual relationship, as opposed to a minor, whose contracts are voidable.

AD VALOREM—Taxes based "according to property value." See ASSESSED VALUATION.

ADVANCE FEE—A nonrefundable fee charged by a realtor to a seller to cover the broker's costs of marketing a property. The fee would be credited against commissions upon sale of the property.

ADVERSE TITLE—A property title which is claimed to differ or oppose another title or claim.

AESTHETIC VALUE—The added value placed on a property because of the beauty of the features or surroundings.

AGENCY—A legal relationship in which one person (the agent) acts on behalf of another (the principal) in business or legal affairs with third parties.

AGENT CLAUSE—A clause contained within or added to a listing agreement or a purchase agreement which outlines the terms and conditions of a realtor's listing. Examples of two agent clauses are:

> "In addition to the purchase price, purchaser agrees to pay a commission to _____ in the sum of $_____ to be paid as follows _____ for services rendered with this transaction."

> "Seller agrees to sell the property on the terms and conditions specified herein and further agrees to pay a commission of _____% of the sales price. Total commission not to exceed $_____."

AGREEMENT OF SALE CONTRACT—A contract whereby the purchaser agrees to buy and the seller agrees to sell under specific terms and conditions. Title remains with the seller until all conditions of the contract have been fulfilled. In some states this is synonymous with a purchase agreement. Also called *Conditional Sales Contract, Land Contract,* or *Sales Contract.*

ALIENATION—The process by which title is transferred from one owner to another.

ALL-INCLUSIVE TRUST DEED (AITD, WRAPAROUND MORTGAGE)—A junior mortgage with a face value of both the amount it secures and the balance due under the existing loans. The mortgagee himself—or through a trust company—collects payments on its face value, then pays the payments on the underlying existing loans. The difference between the amount he collects and the amount he pays out in loans serves as his income. It is most effective when the underlying loans have a lower interest rate than the rate which is charged on the "wrap." The use of an all-inclusive trust deed in creative real estate investing has been made popular by Wade B. Cook in his book *How to Build a Real Estate Money Machine*.

AMERICAN INSTITUTE OF REAL ESTATE APPRAISERS (AIREA)—A part of the National Association of Realtors, which publishes reference materials on appraising properties and trains people in this field.

AMERICAN LAND TITLE INSURANCE (ALTA)—A group of title insurance companies which promotes and issues title insurance.

AMERICAN SOCIETY OF APPRAISERS—A professional society of real estate appraisers. Their address is Dulles International Airport, P.O. Box 17265, Washington, D.C., 20041.

AMERICAN SOCIETY OF REAL ESTATE COUNSELORS—An affiliate organization of the National Association of Realtors (NAR) whose members specialize in giving fee-based advice and counsel on real estate matters.

AMORTIZED LOAN—A loan in which the payments are to be made in certain, specified, usually equal payments.

ANNUAL PERCENTAGE RATE (APR)—The "true" percentage rate (stated as a yearly percentage) that a person pays a lender for the use of money. To comply with Federal Regulation Z of the truth-in-lending-law, the APR must be accurately stated.

APPOINTMENTS—Furnishings and features of a building (usually thought of as nonessential decorative features).

APPRAISAL—An estimate of quality, quantity, and value of an asset, as of a specific date, made by a qualified, unbiased, and disinterested person. See APPRAISAL METHODS.

APPRAISAL METHODS—The processes by which the market value of a specific piece of property is determined. There are three basic methods of appraisal:

- Replacement Cost (cost approach): The process of determining the cost for building and improving an identical structure at current market prices.

- Market Comparison: This is the most commonly used of the three methods. This approach involves an analysis of the recent sales prices of comparable properties in similar locations. Three or four comparable properties are usually used as a base for comparison. Adjustments should be made to the prices of these comparable properties to provide an accurate base.

- Capitalization of Income Approach: This method determines the market value of a property in terms of its ability to produce income. Income means net operating income (NOI). Capitalization means to relate future income to its present future net income, before depreciation.

APPRAISAL REPORT—A written report by an appraiser containing his determination of value and his method or reasoning in arriving at value.

APPRAISED VALUE—The appraiser's determination of value or price, given specific conditions of the property at the time of the appraisal.

APPRAISER—A person who, for a fee, estimates property values. Care should be taken to check the appraiser's qualifications, experience, and training.

APPRECIATION—Increase in value of a property, excluding increases due to improvements.

APPURTENANCE—Anything attached to or incident to the land and part of the property, such as an easement to some land or a garage to a house. It is part of the property and passes with it upon sale or transfer of title.

ARREARS—A loan, rental, or lease agreement for which payments have not been made according to the schedule called for in the legal contract.

AS-IS CONDITION—Property that is accepted by either the buyer or tenant to be conveyed or rented in the state existing at the time of the sale or lease. Selling "as is" is not binding in the case of an illegal or unenforceable contract.

ASKING PRICE—The price quoted by a seller as the amount for which he will part with a property. The asking price is usually considered the starting price for negotiations with a seller. Also called upset price.

ASSESSED VALUATION—Value placed upon a property for the purpose of determining property taxes by an assessor.

ASSESSMENT—This is the charge or tax levied against a property by a unit of government.

ASSESSMENT TAX DISTRICT—An area, such as a county or a city, which is used for tax assessment purposes.

ASSESSOR—The government official or appointee whose duty it is to appraise, value, or access property for taxation.

ASSIGNABILITY—Any property which may be transferred by assignment. Some contracts have a clause restricting assignability.

ASSIGNMENT—To transfer an interest in any property, real or personal, or of any estate or right therein.

ASSIGNMENT CLAUSE—A clause contained within or added to a purchase agreement which outlines how agreement may be assigned. Examples of two assignment clauses are:

> Seller reserves the right to transfer his interest herein described or assign his interest under this contract, but such assignment or transfer shall not affect any right or interest of purchase hereunder and shall be made subject to all the terms and provisions of this contract.

> Any attempted assignment or transfer by purchaser in violation of the foregoing provisions may at seller's option be deemed a default by purchaser under this contract, and seller may pursue such remedy as may be available to seller for material breach by purchaser.

ASSUMPTION—Purchase of property with the buyer taking over the existing mortgage and assuming liability for the payments. See ASSUMPTION OF MORTGAGE.

ASSUMPTION CLAUSE—A clause contained within or added to a purchase agreement which outlines the terms and rights of both the buyer and the seller concerning an assumption of the existing loan or loans. Examples of two assumption clauses are:

If there is a conflict in assuming the existing loans, purchasers agree to secure financing to pay the above amount.

Purchaser agrees to assume and pay said mortgage according to its own terms and conditions.

ASSUMPTION FEE—The loan institution's charge for the assumption report and paperwork involved in processing the assumption of a mortgage.

ASSUMPTION OF MORTGAGE—Taking over the payments and terms of a mortgage. Two common ways of assuming a mortgage are:

Simple Assumption: Common in many FHA and VA loans. The loan is taken over without qualification or formal application and approval. The original holder of the note still retains some liability for the loan.

Formal assumption: Taking over a loan through application, credit check, and approval by the lender who holds the note. The original holder of the note is released from all liability of the note.

ATTRACTIVE NUISANCE—Anything on a property which may attract small children and be a hazard to them. Examples of attractive nuisances would be swimming pools, old refrigerators, broken glass. These items should be fenced off, locked up, and, if necessary, cleaned up to prevent injury to children.

AUTOMATIC RENEWAL CLAUSE—A clause contained within a contract that specifies an automatic renewal or rollover unless specific action is taken to stop it.

# B

BACKFILL—Soil and other nondecomposing material used to fill in around a foundation or low area.

BACKUP OFFER—An offer that would be considered second to another offer.

BALLOON PAYMENT—A payment larger than the usual payment which is due at the end of a note's payment schedule.

BALLOON PAYMENT MORTGAGE—A mortgage in which payments are structured in such a way as to require a large lump sum payment at the end of its payment schedule.

BANKRUPTCY—A legal motion on behalf of a person or company unable to pay debts. The person filing bankruptcy is asking the court for protection from creditors. There are several forms of bankruptcy, called "chapters." The subject is much too complex to be treated in a few sentences. For more information on your own state's laws, seek competent local legal advice.

BARTER—To trade or exchange goods for services for something else of equal value. (An example would be negotiating a trade of something other than cash for a down payment on a house.)

BASE AND MERIDIAN LINES—Survey lines used to describe the location of a property.

BASEBOARD—A strip of wood or some other material installed on the wall where it meets the floor.

BASIS—Basis is a way of measuring your investment in property for tax purposes. You must know the basis of your property to calculate depreciation, amortization, depletion, casualty losses, or whether you have a gain or loss on its sale or exchange. The basis of a property is usually its cost. The cost is the amount of cash you pay for it, the fair market value of other property or services you provide in the transaction, and all settlement fees or closing costs. Some special points concerning the determination of basis are:

- Unstated Interest: If you buy property on any time-payment plan that charges little or no interest, the basis of your property is your purchase price, less the amount considered to be interest.

- Real Estate Taxes: If you buy real property and agree to pay taxes that were owed by the seller, the taxes you pay are treated as part of the cost of the property.

- Fair Market Value: There are times when you cannot use cost as a basis. In these cases fair market value may be important. Several examples of these cases are: partial and nontaxable exchanges, property trades, discounted property purchases from employers, or if you receive property for services rendered.

BASIS POINT—One point + 1/100 of 1% (.01).

BEAM/BEAMS—The main horizontal supports of a building.

BEARING WALL—A main supporting wall that helps carry the weight of the structure.

BETTERMENT—A city or state improvement that adds to the value of real estate, such as sidewalks, street lights, sewers, and streets.

BID—The amount offered by the buyer.

BINDER—An agreement to cover part or all of the down payment for buying real estate. See also EARNEST MONEY.

BLENDED RATE—An interest rate applied to a refinanced loan that is higher than the old loan but lower than the existing loan.

BOOK VALUE—The value of a property that is shown in the financial records of an individual or a corporation. This is usually purchase price plus any improvement minus any accrued depreciation.

BOUNDARY—A natural or artificial separation which marks the property line between two adjacent properties.

BREACH OF CONTRACT—Failure to perform a contract without proper legal excuse.

BREACH OF WARRANTY—In real estate, this means the failure to pass clear title as implied in the purchase offer and closing documents.

BROKER—A state-licensed person, who for compensation or expectation of compensation acts as an agent in buying, selling, leasing, renting, and exchanging properties.

BUDGET MORTGAGE—A mortgage that includes monthly payments for taxes, insurance, principal, and interest.

BUFFER ZONE—An area of transition between areas of different land usage. (Home versus freeway, for example.)

BUILDING CODE—The federal, state, and local rules regulating the construction of a building. These codes are adopted and enforced by the local city or county.

BUNDLE OF RIGHTS—The rights that a person has to enjoy, use, and dispose of his real or personal property.

BUY-BACK AGREEMENT—A clause in which the seller agrees to repurchase the property on the occurrence of an event specified. (A time limit or price or both may be specified.)

BUYER—A purchaser; an agent responsible for purchasing something for another party.

BUYER'S MARKET—A housing market in which there is an oversupply of houses for sale. This oversupply drives down the prices of the properties for sale.

# C

CAE (CERTIFIED ASSESSMENT EVALUATOR)—A title earned by examination, experience, and course study given to property assessors by the International Association of Assessing Officers.

CALLED MORTGAGE—A loan that is due and payable at the demand of the lender as a result of an acceleration or due-on-sale clause that has been acted upon.

CANCELLATION CLAUSE—A clause canceling the contract when a specified event(s) or condition(s) is not met.

CAP—A term referring to either the maximum interest rate allowed to be charged on an adjustable rate mortgage or the largest maximum increase in charged interest.

CARPORT—A roof supported by pillars used to shelter cars. Typically there are no supporting or enclosing walls.

CARRYING CHARGES—Costs that are incidental to ownership, such as insurance, taxes, maintenance.

CASH FLOW—A person's spendable income from an investment after operating expenses and loan payments are made.

CASHING OUT—Sale of a property in which the buyer pays the seller for his total equity. An example would be when a person bought a home for $60,000 and assumed the existing loan for $52,000. If the buyer were to cash out the seller, he would pay the entire $8,000 equity in cash at closing.

CAVEAT EMPTOR—A Latin term meaning "Let the buyer beware!" The buyer takes the risk when purchasing a property or an item without the protection of title insurance or warranties.

CELLAR—A room or group of rooms beneath a home under ground level; sometimes called a basement.

CEMENT BLOCK—A hollow block made of cement used in building homes and buildings.

CERTIFICATE OF OCCUPANCY—A certificate issued by the local city or county building inspection department stating that a building is approved for occupancy. Many home insurance policies are null and void in the event of a fire if the certificate of occupancy has never been issued for the insured structure.

CHAIN OF TITLE—A documented history of encumbrances and conveyances affecting the title of a property as far back as records are available.

CHATTEL—Personal property. Any item of property other than real estate.

CHATTEL MORTGAGE—A mortgage on personal property.

CHECKLIST—A list of important things to consider and check when buying and/or closing a home or property.

CIRCUIT BREAKER—An electrical device which limits the flow of electricity on a conductor under abnormal conditions. Circuit breakers are usually found in the outside electrical disconnect and the electrical distribution panel.

CLAUSES—A particular part of a legal document, such as a purchase agreement, clarifying, describing, and outlining a specific plan of action. Clauses in real estate transactions cover such areas as agents, assignment, assumption, closing, closing costs, collateral, deposits, down payments, earnest money, escrow agents, financing, owner financing, personal property, possession, price, subject to, subordination, and title. *For examples of these clauses refer to the specific titles, such as FINANCING CLAUSE.*

CLAIM—A right or title to a property.

CLEAR TITLE—A title not clouded with encumbrances, liens, or other defects.

CLOSED MORTGAGE—A mortgage containing the provision that it cannot be paid off until it matures.

CLOSING—A term used to refer to the final signing of papers to purchase a home or property. A closing usually takes place at a title office, lending institution, or attorney's office.

CLOSING CHECKLIST—A checklist used by a purchaser or closing officer to make sure that everything has been done to ensure the proper sale or transfer of a property.

CLOSING COST CLAUSE—A clause contained within or added to a purchase agreement which refers to the payment or terms of a property's closing. Two examples of closing cost clauses are:

> Buyer and seller to split equally the costs for title insurance, closing fee, and all recording fees.

> Seller shall pay the following costs and expenses of the transaction on close of escrow:_____
> _____

> (Specify charges, such as title insurance, assumption fees, closing fees, transfer tax, legal fees, etc.)

CLOSING COSTS—The fees required to finalize the purchase of a home or property. These fees usually include remainder of down payment, property insurance, property taxes, title insurance, points, assumption fee, mortgage insurance premium, and filing and recording fees.

CLOSING STATEMENT—A final itemized statement of all disbursements. There is a closing statement for the buyer and another for the seller, listing the final financial settlement between them.

CLOUD ON TITLE—A lien, encumbrance, or legal action against the title of a property that comes up during a sale that the purchaser or seller was previously unaware of. The cloud on title usually comes through a recording mistake or invalid claim.

CODE OF ETHICS—The set of standards to which every broker and agent must adhere.

COLLATERAL—Personal property that a person pledges as security for an obligation. In real estate the collateral for a mortgage is usually the mortgaged property.

COLOR OF TITLE—This term is used to refer to a defect in a property's title that is not obvious. See CLOUDED TITLE.

COMMITMENT—A written promise or oral affirmation to act according to an agreed-upon commitment. This commitment is most common with government FHA loans. After applying for a loan and being approved by the FHA, you would then receive a firm commitment for the loan. This firm commitment would require that you close by a certain date, etc.

COMPOUND INTEREST—Paying interest on both the principal and the accumulated interest on a note. An example would be a bank deposit of $100 which earned 10-percent annual interest. After one year the note with interest would be worth $110.

The next year that $110 would earn $11 interest, the extra $1 being the interest paid on interest—the compound interest.

CONDITIONAL COMMITMENT—A loan commitment given on the condition of the mortgagee meeting certain conditions set by the lender.

CONSIDERATION—Something of value given to bind a promise. All contracts, to be legal, must include consideration. In real estate transactions earnest money is given to bind the purchase offer.

CONTINGENCY—An act which is dependent on the prior completion of another act. An example would be a purchase offer which is contingent on the purchaser being able to sell his own home within a certain amount of time (subject-to clause).

CONTRACT—1. An agreement between two parties, oral or written, usually based on one person (the offeree) accepting the offer of another person (the offeror). 2. In real estate, the idea of "selling on contract" or "taking a contract" means that the seller is willing to take monthly payments from the buyer, rather than a lump-sum payment for his equity. See ALL-INCLUSIVE TRUST DEED.

CONTRACT ACCEPTANCE CLAUSE—A clause contained within or added to a purchase agreement which describes terms relating to the acceptance of the contract. Examples of two contract acceptance clauses are:

> Said counteroffer expires on _____ date, at __:_____am/pm.

> Seller reserves the right to accept offers from other buyers. All offers must be accepted junior to this offer. If the following conditions are not met _____
> _____

then this offer will be considered null and void and the offer junior to this one will be considered valid. Time is of the essence.

CONVENTIONAL LOAN—A loan that is insured by real estate and not guaranteed by an agency of the government, such as the Veterans Administration or the Federal Housing Authority.

CO-OWNERSHIP—The ownership of a property by two or more people.

CORRECTION DEED (DEED OF CONFIRMATION OR REFORMATION DEED)—A correction of an error in a deed which is both written and recorded.

COUNTEROFFER—An offer given by the seller in response to a purchase offer by a prospective buyer. An example would be a seller who received a purchase offer on his home for $59,000 with $5,000 down. He might agree with the down payment but feel that the sales price was too low. He might then counter back with a sales price of $62,000 with the same down payment. A counteroffer is *always* a rejection of the original offer, combined with a new offer.

COVENANT—An agreement between two or more people who are legally bound to either perform or not perform a certain act, or that a given state of things does or does not exist.

COVENANTS—In all contracts there are five basic covenants that give full "warranty" to the property. These five basic covenants are:

- The owner has a right to convey the property.

- The owner will "forever" warrant the title.

- The owner will obtain title insurance.

- The property is encumbered only by the liens listed in the purchase offer.

- The owner has the right of quiet enjoyment.

CREATIVE FINANCING—Financing a property using methods other than traditional bank financing. Creative financing usually refers to owner financing. Wade B. Cook, Dr. Albert Lowry, Mark O. Haroldsen, and myself are just four of the authors who have written books which have helped change the direction of real estate investing, away from reliance on the high interest rates associated in the eighties with traditional financing.

CREDIT REPORT—A report on the credit history of an individual. Increasingly today, many sellers are finding it necessary to check the credit record of the people interested in their properties.

CURING THE TITLE—Clearing up or rectifying a defect in a property's title.

# D

DEBT SERVICE—The amount of money required to make the payments on a loan according to the payment schedule.

DEBTOR—A person who owes a debt.

DEED—A written document, properly made out, executed, and under proper seal. Types of commonly used deeds are the administrator's, condominium, corporation, county, executor's, foreclosure, gift, grant, guardian's, mineral, quick claim, reconveyance, referee's, sheriff's, trust, and warranty.

DEED, BARGAIN AND SALE—A simple deed conveying property ownership but not guaranteeing the title, right, or interest. See also QUITCLAIM DEED.

DEED, QUITCLAIM—A simple deed which conveys all claims that a person possesses in a property to another. See also DEED, BARGAIN AND SALE.

DEED IN LIEU OF FORECLOSURE—A property owner in a distressed situation may find it advantageous to deed his property back to the creditor rather than have the creditor complete the foreclosure process at auction. Using a deed like this may save the property owner's credit rating. Seek competent local legal advice for more information on this process.

DEED OF TRUST (TRUST DEED, TRUST DEED MORTGAGE, OR TRUST INDENTURE)—This is a form of deed on a mortgaged property in which a third party (trustee) holds the deed. Upon payment of the note in full, the trustee delivers the deed to the property owner. The use of trust deeds in the United States is fast becoming the rule because of the ease of foreclosure in default situations and the advantages of having a third party holding the deed.

DEFAULT—Failure to perform according to the terms of a note or an obligation.

DEFECTS IN TITLE—Flaws or problems in a property's title. See also CLOUD ON TITLE.

DEFEASANCE—An instrument or clause which defeats or alters a deed, or a mortgage.

DEFERRED INTEREST MORTGAGE—A mortgage where the loan payment is initially lower to begin with than a normal amortization schedule would require. The deficit, or deferred interest, is added on to the principal of the loan. This negative amortization is most commonly seen in the Federal Housing Administration's 245. loan. Benefits include being able to qualify for a higher loan on a home than you would normally. Problems include having your loan actually increase in value every month for the first several years.

DEFERRED PAYMENTS—Payments to be made at a future date.

DEPARTMENT OF REAL ESTATE—Each state and district has a government body that administers and regulates local state real estate laws.

DEPOSIT—Money placed in trust to show good faith; also known as earnest money.

DESCRIPTION—A legal method of giving dimensions to the property. See DEED.

DIRECT REDUCTION MORTGAGE—A loan in which level payments include a set amount to be attributed to principal and interest at an amount which will reduce the loan balance to zero by the end of its payment schedule.

DISCOUNT—To sell a note or home for less than its face or market value.

DISCOUNT POINTS—The percentage of a loan's value that upon closing must be given to the lender to secure the loan. In essence, discount points represent what you have to pay to get a loan at a certain interest rate.

DISCRIMINATION IN REAL ESTATE (CIVIL RIGHTS ACTS OF 1866 AND 1968)—These laws forbid any racial discrimination in the sale, lease, or rental of property. The 1968 civil rights act extended this to include race, color, religion, sex, or national origin.

DISTRESSED PROPERTY—In real estate terms a distressed property refers to a property which is in danger of being foreclosed on by a lender because of nonpayment of a loan.

DOCUMENT—A written instrument. In order for a document to be legally binding it must be properly prepared, witnessed, and recorded. For more information, seek competent local legal counsel.

DOMICILE—A legal term signifying a place which an individual calls his legal residence; a home.

DOWN PAYMENT—The amount of payment (either cash or services) required to secure the purchase of a property.

DOWN PAYMENT CLAUSE—A clause contained within or added to a purchase agreement which refers to the form and amount of a purchaser's down payment. Examples of two down payment clauses would be:

Said down payment of $_____ will be paid in full in the form of personal property described as follows:_____.

_____

The down payment of $_____ will be paid in the following manner. $_____ including earnest money, will be paid on closing. The balance of $_____ to be paid _____ from closing date. Above total down payment of $_____ to be considered a payment of interest in advance toward said property.

DRAINAGE—The flowing of water off a property.

DRY MORTGAGE—A mortgage which places no personal liability on the mortgagor, looking only to the property as collateral for the loan.

DUE-ON-SALE (CLAUSE)—A clause calling for a debt under a deed of trust or a mortgage to be due upon sale or transfer of title of the secured property. Also called an Acceleration or Alienation Clause.

DUTY TO RECONVEY—The responsibility of a party to return property and/or fill out the necessary papers when a note is paid in full.

## E

EARNEST MONEY—A payment made as evidence of a purchaser's good faith to go through with the purchase of real estate. It is given along with an earnest money, or binder, agreement, outlining the terms and conditions of the sale and payment for the property.

EARNEST MONEY CLAUSE—A clause contained within or added to a purchase agreement which refers to the form and terms of a buyer's earnest money. Two examples of earnest money clauses are:

Earnest money and this agreement shall be held by broker or _____ for the benefit of the parties hereto.

The parties agree to refund earnest money in full in the event financing contemplated by the purchaser is not obtainable.

EASEMENT—The right of a person to use someone else's land for a particular purpose, such as access to property. The right of easement is inherent with ownership of certain properties.

EASEMENT APPURTENANT—An easement for the benefit of another property. An example would be an easement which allowed the right to cross a property to get to another property.

EASEMENT BY NECESSITY—The right to cross a property of another person because of a necessity which is apparent.

EASEMENT IN GROSS—An easement granted to a utility company which is not specifically attached to any parcel of land.

EFFECTIVE AGE—The age of property based upon wear and tear. Example: A house is fifteen years old but current remodeling gives an effective age of two years.

EGRESS—The right to exit from your own property by crossing another property.

ELECTRICAL PROBLEMS—Most electrical repairs and problems require a competent state licensed electrician to repair them. If in any doubt at all about how to fix an electrical problem, call in a licensed professional.

ELIGIBLE—Properly qualified; worthy to apply.

ENCROACHMENT—Anything, such as a building overhang, that extends over the property line into another person's property. Encroachment can also refer to building a structure partly or wholly on another's property.

ENCUMBRANCE—Any claim against or attached to a property, such as a judgment, mortgage, lien, or easement.

EQUITABLE TITLE—The interest or share of ownership that a party holds in a property. This equity increase can be attributed to mortgage reduction through amortization of a loan; property improvements; outside factors, such as city street lighting, a new school, paved streets, a general rise in property values, locational value; and goodwill.

ESCALATOR CLAUSE—A clause contained in most adjustable rate mortgages which allows for certain changes in the mortgage in conjunction with specified eventualities, i.e., inflation rate, T Bill rates, etc.

ESCROW—A deed, bond, or something of value held by a third party for delivery to the grantee upon the completion of a prescribed event. A common example of an escrow would be the tax and insurance funds that a mortgage company holds for property owners. Each month a portion of most first mortgage payments includes one twelfth of the yearly anticipated tax assessments and insurance costs. These amounts are held in escrow by the mortgage company and paid yearly.

ESCROW ACCOUNT—Same as a trust account, in which a broker, by law, deposits all monies collected for a client.

ESCROW AGENT—The party or concern who holds the items of value in escrow and administers the escrow transactions.

ESCROW CLAUSE—A clause contained within or added to a purchase agreement which refers to the use of an escrow agent or trustee. Two examples of escrow clauses are:

> Seller agrees to deliver to an escrow agent at closing a warranty deed to be released to buyer, his assigns or heirs upon final payment of all obligations at the time and manner described.

> All costs and fees of the escrow agent shall be split equally between the buyer and the seller.

ESCROW CLOSING—A closing in which an item may be missing. The closing will take place, but the satisfactory items are held in escrow pending receipt of the missing items.

ESTATE—The extent of legal interest a party has in real property.

EXCEPTION TO TITLE—The situation in which a title is found to be clouded or with a defect.

EXCLUSIVE AGENT—A real estate broker who is under written contract with the seller to be the only broker with the right to sell a certain property within a certain time in exchange for an agreed-upon percentage of the sale price.

EXCLUSIVE LISTING—In most listing contracts the broker is granted the "exclusive right to sell the property." This right to sell means that if the seller makes the sale himself, he must pay the broker the regular commission.

EXCULPATORY CLAUSE—A clause contained within a note or mortgage meaning to release the holder from any personal liability in the event of default. An example of an exculpatory clause would be, "The property mentioned herein shall be the sole collateral for this note or mortgage."

EXISTING LIEN—A lien that has not yet been satisfied.

EXISTING MORTGAGE—A mortgage that has not yet been satisfied.

# F

FAILURE OF CONSIDERATION—Giving a bad check as earnest money or not putting any money with it. This would render the earnest money or contract invalid.

FAILURE TO PERFORM—The failure of one of the parties in a contract to perform according to agreement.

FAIR CREDIT REPORTING ACT—A federal law intended to protect the public from having inaccurate information reported by credit agencies concerning their credit ratings. Under this law, an individual has the right to inspect information in his or her files at their local credit bureau and request to amend any incorrect information. This act also requires a lender who refuses credit to an individual to disclose to the individual the credit bureau they based their decision on.

FANNIE MAE—A nickname for the Federal National Mortgage Association. See FEDERAL NATIONAL MORTGAGE ASSOCIATION.

FEDERAL HOME LOAN MORTGAGE CORPORATION—A federally sponsored agency which buys and sells government-backed and conventional mortgages. A common name for this agency is "Freddie Mac."

FEDERAL HOUSING ADMINISTRATION (FHA)—A federal agency that insures private banks, mortgage companies, and savings and loans against loss on real estate loans under the Federal Housing Administration loan programs. In the past this FHA insurance on a loan was paid for by the property buyer in the form of one-half percentage point extra interest charged on the loan. Beginning in 1984, buyers who get new FHA loans are charged one-half point interest in advance, rather than a higher rate over the course of the loan.

FEDERAL NATIONAL MORTGAGE ASSOCIATION (FNMA, FANNIE MAE)—The purpose of the federally sponsored agency which buys mortgages from institutions, such as banks, savings and loans, and insurance companies in order to provide a degree of liquidity in the mortgage market by establishing a secondary market.

FEDERAL SAVINGS AND LOAN ASSOCIATION—A privately or publicly owned savings and loan which is federally chartered.

FEDERAL SAVINGS AND LOAN INSURANCE CORPORATION (FSLIC)—A private corporation which provides insurance (up to $100,000) on accounts deposited in a savings and loan association.

FEE (ABSOLUTE, CONDITIONAL, DETERMINABLE, SIMPLE)—Ownership of real estate free and clear from all mortgages, liens, conditions, or limitations.

FIDUCIARY—A relationship of trust; for example, a real estate broker who has the duty to represent and act in the best interests of the seller.

FILE—To place an original document on public record.

FINANCE CHARGE—The sum of all costs charged directly or indirectly by the creditor and payable either directly or indirectly by the customer as defined by the federal truth-in-lending laws.

FINANCING CLAUSE—A clause contained within or added to a purchase agreement which refers to the terms and conditions of the financing involved in the transaction. Examples of two financing clauses are:

> Buyer to obtain and qualify for a new _____ year _____ loan in the amount of $_____. Seller's costs in obtaining the loan are not to exceed _____.

> Seller is to obtain a new loan against the property for the maximum amount allowable. Buyer is to assume this loan and pay the seller the balance of the purchase price according to the following terms:

> _____
> _____
> _____

FINANCING STATEMENT—A brief statement in the public record for recording and establishing a creditor's interest or lien on a personal property.

FIRM COMMITMENT—A definite commitment by a lender to loan a set amount of money at a set interest rate for a set period of time. Time should be taken to verify that the interest rate has been locked in with the lender.

FIRST MORTGAGE—The senior mortgage attached to a property. It is essentially the lien which has been recorded first against the property, and is not necessarily the largest or longest to amortize.

FIXTURE—Personal property, such as an air conditioner or stove, which has become real estate either because it is attached to the property or because of custom in that area.

FLAT FEE BROKER—A broker who lists and sells a home for a set fee rather than a percentage of sale price.

FORBEARANCE—Not taking legal action in the situation where a mortgage or deed of trust is in arrears. Forbearance is usually only granted in a case where a borrower makes a satisfactory arrangement in which he will make up the late payments by an-agreed upon future date.

FORCE MAJEURE—An unavoidable delay in performing a contract obligation in the specified time.

FORECLOSURE—A legal procedure initiated by a lender because of nonpayment of a debt to take property from the present person, who has it mortgaged. The procedure of foreclosure varies from state to state. For more information on your own area, seek competent legal advice from an attorney.

FOUNDATION WALL—The basic supporting structure of a home or building. In most modern homes this wall is made of concrete or cinderblock. In many older homes it is made out of wood. Care should be taken to inspect the condition of the foundation on older homes to see that, if it is made out of wood, it is free from any dry rot or termite damage.

FREE AND CLEAR TITLE—A title to a real property which is free from any liens, mortgages, defects, clouds, or other encumbrances.

FURTHER ASSURANCE—A warranty that is expressly stated in a deed. This warranty states that the grantor will be liable for, and will cure, any defect that is discovered in a title after the property is sold.

## G

GENERAL LIEN—A lien directed by a court against the entire estate of a debtor.

GIFT LETTER—Most lending institutions require that the borrower show proof of sufficient deposits to cover the proposed down payment on closing. These funds must usually be free and clear and, in the case of FHA loans, not borrowed from another source. In the case of many young home purchasers, their parents lend them the money for the down payment. In this instance, the bank usually requires a letter from the donee (parent) stating that the money given is specifically a gift and not a loan.

GOOD FAITH MONEY—A deposit, such as earnest money, used to bind a contract.

GOOD RECORD TITLE—A title that has been researched and found to have no encumbrances that would adversely affect a sale or transfer.

GOVERNMENT NATIONAL MORTGAGE ASSOCIATION (GNMA, GINNIE MAE)—A federally chartered agency organized in 1968 as a result of a reorganization of the Federal National Mortgage Association, FNMA. GINNIE MAE is a corporation without capital stock which serves to stabilize mortgage lending and residential construction by buying, selling, and servicing residential construction.

GRACE PERIOD—The time period between the due date and the date when a mortgage payment is assessed late charges. An example would be mortgages which are due by the first of each month and which are assessed late charges if the payment is received after the fifteenth of each month.

GRANT DEED—A type of deed which warrants the property being conveyed by the grantor to be free from any defects in title or encumbrances other than those addressed for in the sales contract. The grant deed also conveys all rights to the property that may come to the grantor at any time in the future.

GRANTOR—The seller in a deed or a party conveying property.

GRANTOR'S LIEN—A lien which goes into effect whenever all of the selling price of a property is not paid upon closing or transfer of title. The balance of the seller's equity automatically becomes a grantor's deed.

GROWING EQUITY MORTGAGE (GEM)—A loan in which the payment increases by a predetermined amount yearly. This makes the payoff time shorter.

GUARANTEED MORTGAGE—A mortgage that is guaranteed against default. Examples of guaranteed mortgages are government-insured FHA and VA loans. This guarantee is paid for by the mortgagee in the form of a mortgage insurance premium. Also known as an insured mortgage.

# H

HAND MONEY—A term meaning earnest money. See EARNEST MONEY.

HAZARD INSURANCE—Insurance to cover catastrophic events or acts of God such as tornadoes, floods, earthquakes, fires, wind, or workman injury.

HOMEOWNER POLICY—Property insurance protecting a homeowner against all expected perils such as fire, theft, personal liability, and wind.

HOME WARRANTY INSURANCE—Private insurance that insures a buyer of either a new or used home against defects such as plumbing, heating, and electrical problems in the home purchased.

HOUSING AND URBAN DEVELOPMENT—A branch of the federal government responsible for most major housing programs in the United States.

# I

IMPOUND ACCOUNT—A trust account established to hold funds which may be required at a future time. An example would be the impound accounts set up for FHA loans in which a tax reserve of six months and an insurance reserve of one full year are held by the lender.

IMPROVEMENTS—Additions to a property or building which are more than basic repairs. Examples of improvements would be a new fireplace, a new fence, adding on a garage, etc.

INDENTURE DEED—A deed between a grantor and a grantee guaranteeing that both parties will work together according to agreement.

INDEXED LOAN—A long term loan in which the terms may be adjusted periodically per a specified index as stated in the mortgage contract.

INSPECTION—A visit to a property or building to check and review it. Examples of inspections would be an inspection by the city building inspector to check for safety- or building-code violations. Another type is the inspection of a property by a partner which a purchase agreement was contingent upon.

INSTITUTIONAL LENDERS—A bank, savings and loan, mortgage company, or insurance company which loans money and is regulated by law.

INSTRUMENT—A legal document, such as a deed, lease agreement, contract of sale, or will.

INSURANCE—Protection against loss from a specific hazard or peril. Examples of real estate insurance would be a title insurance policy, liability insurance against theft and vandalism, and hazard insurance protecting against flood, fire, or other hazard.

INTEREST RATE—The annualized percentage rate that is charged for the use of a sum of money, as in a mortgage loan.

INVOLUNTARY LIEN—A lien put against a person's property by a creditor. An example of an involuntary lien would be a mechanic's or tax lien put against a property because of nonpayment.

IRONCLAD AGREEMENT—A contract that cannot be broken by the parties involved.

# J

JOINT NOTE—A note signed by two or more people who are both equally liable for repayment.

JOINT TENANTS (TENANCY)—Property held by two or more parties with each having the legal right to assume full title upon the death of the other. Under joint tenancy probate is avoided. See TENANTS IN COMMON for another form of property ownership by two or more parties.

JUDGMENT LIEN—A court-appointed lien against a property. The property cannot be sold without resolving this judgment.

JUNIOR LIEN—A lien subordinate (junior) to another lien against a property.

JUNIOR MORTGAGE—A mortgage which falls in title claim behind another mortgage. Also known as a secondary mortgage. An example would be a second mortgage whose mortgage rights fall in line after the first mortgagee's rights.

# K

KEY LOT—A lot which has a premium price because of its location.

# L

LAND CERTIFICATE—A document held by a landowner, giving the legal description of the property and the name and address of the current owner.

LAND CONTRACT—An installment contract for the sale of a property in which the seller retains legal title until paid in full. The buyer holds only equitable title on the property during the payment period.

LAND DESCRIPTION—A description of a particular piece of real property; should be a complete legal description.

LAND TRUST—The title held by a trustee. Under this arrangement, the actual landowner is not recorded on public records. Only the name of the trustee (third party) is known.

LATENT DEFECT—1. Titles which appear originally to be sound but are found later to contain a fault. 2. Hidden structural defects resulting from faulty construction materials or inferior craftsmanship.

LEGAL DESCRIPTION—A land description measured in metes (measurements) and bounds (boundaries) recognized by law.

LEGAL RATE OF INTEREST—The maximum rate of interest permitted by law in each local state. Charging of interest above the legal rate is illegal and in violation of state usury laws.

LEGAL TITLE—Any title that would be or has been recognized as valid by a court of law.

LETTER OF INTENT—The expressed desire to enter into a contract without actually doing so.

LEVEL PAYMENT—A payment which is made in equal installments during the full payment period of a loan.

LIABILITY INSURANCE—Insurance to protect a property owner from claims due to injury on the property.

LIEN—The claim one party has on the property of another as the result of a legal judgment, or as security for a debt. Examples of types of liens would be tax liens, mortgage liens, judgment liens, and other specified liens.

LIEN WAIVER—A legal document releasing a lien.

LIQUIDATED DAMAGES—A clause contained within a contract specifying payment in the eventuality of default on a contract. An example of liquidated damages would be where a seller would retain a buyer's earnest money in the event of default.

LOAN APPLICATION—Documents required before a loan commitment is issued. It is an in-depth information sheet.

LOAN BROKERAGE FEE—A charge or premium given to an individual or company for arranging for a loan.

LOAN-TO-VALUE RATIO—The ratio of a property's appraised value to the amount of proposed financing.

LOAN VALUE—1. The current amount needed to pay a loan in full. 2. The current maximum of money that could be borrowed against a property.

## M

MAINTENANCE—Necessary repairs that are made to a property to preserve the property at its present condition.

MARKETABLE TITLE—A title free from any unusual or unreasonable attachment which a court would require a buyer to assume. Also known as merchantable title.

MARKET VALUE (fair market value)—The price at which a property can realistically be sold. The highest price a buyer will pay and the lowest price a seller will take for a property when both are acting free from any compulsion and collusion.

MATURITY—The time at which a loan or note becomes due.

MECHANIC'S LIEN—A lien placed by a contractor against a property as the result of nonpayment for services or materials supplied by the contractor or mechanic to the property owner.

MORTGAGE—A conditional contract in which real estate is given as security for repayment of a loan. In some states the mortgagee holds a lien only, not a legal title.

MORTGAGE BANKER—A private company that finds borrowers for money obtained from the secondary mortgage market or private investors.

MORTGAGE COMMITMENT—A firm commitment by a lending institution stating that it will lend money against a property according to certain conditions.

MORTGAGE GUARANTY INSURANCE CORPORATION (MGIC)—A private organization which serves as a secondary market for conventional mortgages.

MORTGAGE LIEN—The lien which is recorded against a property when a mortgage is owed against it.

# N

NATIONAL ASSOCIATION OF REALTORS—The largest and most prestigious real estate association in the United States. Its membership includes real estate professionals in all fifty states. It serves as an association which promotes modern techniques and education as well as professional standards within its membership. For more information, write the National Association of Realtors, 430 North Michigan, Chicago, Illinois 60611.

NEGATIVE AMORTIZATION—Increase in the outstanding balance of the loan resulting from the failure of periodic debt service. Negative Amortization will occur if the indexed interest rate increases.

NEGOTIATION—When people meet for the purpose of resolving differences so that agreement can be achieved.

NONASSUMPTION CLAUSE—A clause in a mortgage or loan stating that it is due on sale.

NO-RECOURSE CLAUSE—A clause in a purchase offer or a loan stating that the mortgaged property is sole collateral for the loan.

NOTE—A legal instrument which acknowledges a debt and guarantees payment.

# O

OCCUPANCY CODE—A local law enforced by police power designed to establish socially acceptable minimum standards for safety and health in both newly constructed buildings and existing structures.

OFFER—A written document signed by a buyer offering to purchase a specific property at a specific price under a specific set of terms. When a seller signs and accepts the terms of the offer, the written document becomes a contract. See also CONTRACT.

OPEN END MORTGAGE—In an open end mortgage the borrower has the right to pay off the loan at any time without penalty and also to refinance it and receive additional funds prior to its maturity date.

OPINION OF TITLE—The legal opinion which is rendered by a title company or attorney about the condition of a property's title. This opinion is rendered by studying an abstract of title and done to determine whether the title is invalid and defective or good and marketable.

OPTION—An option is the right to purchase a property at a certain price, during a certain period of time, under some set of specified terms. To conform with legal requirements, an option must:

1. Involve some consideration to bind the agreement.

2. Contain a legal description of the property involved.

3. Specify conditions and terms.

4. Specify time period for exercising the option.

5. Be in writing and in many cases witnessed.

ORAL CONTRACT—An agreement that is verbal, not written. These are unenforceable as far as property is concerned.

ORIGINAL COST—The total amount of money, consideration, and sweat equity extended out to purchase a property.

ORIGINATION FEE—A fee charged by a mortgage company for processing the paperwork on a loan. This origination fee is above and beyond the "points" which may be charged.

OVERALL CAP RATE—This term means both the maximum interest rate increase that an adjustable rate mortgage may rise during the life of the loan and also the capitalization formula which is found by dividing net operating income by the market price of a property.

OWNER-FINANCING CLAUSES—A clause contained within or added to a purchase agreement which refers to the form and terms of the owner financing involved in the sale. Two examples of owner financing clauses are:

Seller to carry back a second trust deed in the approximate amount of $_____ bearing _____% interest per annum on the remaining equity in the property. Payments to be made as follows:

Purchasers agree to pay a $_____ late charge if payment is not received within 10 days of due date.

# P

PACKAGE MORTGAGE—A mortgage which covers both real and personal property.

PASSING TITLE—The act of transferring the title of a property to another. A title may be passed by will, gift, or sale.

PERMANENT MORTGAGE—A long-term (more than ten years) mortgage.

PERSONAL PROPERTY—Property which is not designated as real property. Examples of personal property in a home are a stereo, clothing, and lawn equipment. Examples of real property in a home would be a dishwasher, a garbage disposal, or a heater.

PITI—A term meaning Principal, Interest, Taxes, and Insurance. See BUDGET MORTGAGE.

POINT—One percentage point. The typical use of points is in reference to discount points that a lender charges a buyer for the "right to borrow money."

PREPAYMENT CLAUSE/PENALTY—A penalty which a lender may assess a party for paying off a loan before the due date.

PRICE—The amount of money or consideration paid in exchange for a property.

PRICE CLAUSE—A clause contained within or added to a purchase agreement which sets up conditions to the agreement concerning the property's price. Examples of two price clauses are:

Purchase price for the property is _____ dollars ($_____), which shall be paid on delivery of warranty deed and satisfactory evidence of good and marketable title conveyed thereby to the purchaser.

Price to be established by the average of three independent appraisals.

PRIME RATE—The rate charged by lending institutions on short-term loans to their best customers.

PROPERTY CLAUSE—A clause contained within or added to a purchase agreement which refers to the disposition of personal property located on the ground and in the structure being purchased. Examples of two property clauses are:

Buyer accepts the property in its present condition subject only to

_____.

Purchaser agrees to pay for remaining oil in fuel tank provided that, prior to closing, seller obtains a written statement as to the quantity and price thereof from his regular supplier.

PROPERTY LINES—The boundary of a property.

PROPERTY TAX—A tax which is assessed against both real and personal properties by the local governments.

PRORATE—To separate something, such as property taxes or insurance, into the actual amounts that a seller is responsible for at the closing.

PUNCH LIST—A list of items that must be corrected prior to the sale.

PURCHASE MONEY MORTGAGE—A mortgage made by the buyer to make a down payment on a specific property or as part of the purchase price.

## Q

QUALIFYING—The process of determining whether a buyer is financially able to assume the responsibility of ownership of a property and paying the required debt service. This process may include checking credit history, employment, past landlords, and other sources of financial history which may help determine the capability of the buyer.

# R

RATE—The annual percentage rate of a loan. An example would be a thirty-year FHA loan with an annual percentage rate of 12.5% interest.

REAL ESTATE—The land and everything built on it, attached to it with the intention of its becoming a permanent part of the property and passing with it upon sale, or growing on it.

REAL ESTATE BOARD—A local organization whose membership consists primarily of real estate brokers and salesmen.

REAL ESTATE COMMISSION (STATE)—A state agency which regulates and licenses real estate brokers and salespeople. Many state agencies are also responsible for making the local state's real estate rules and regulations.

REAL ESTATE LIEN NOTE—The document which attests to an existing mortgage or lien.

REAL PROPERTY LAWS—The local and federal laws which regulate the real estate market.

RECONVEYANCE—The process of transferring the title of a property back to the original owner.

RECOURSE—The ability for a lender to reclaim money from a borrower who is in default and the property used as collateral as well.

REFINANCING—To obtain a new loan and pay off the existing financing. People usually refinance to get the equity out of their homes.

REGULATION Z—A federal truth-in-lending law which requires that consumers be made aware of the costs of financing.

RELEASE OF LIEN—The removal of a lien, judgment, mortgage, or claim from a certain property.

RESCIND—The right to withdraw from an offer/contract. Regulation Z gives the consumer/buyer three days to change his/her mind.

RESIDENTIAL—Property or land which is zoned to be used for single-family homes or other living quarters.

RIDER—An attached amendment to a contract.

RIGHT-OF-WAY—The easement that a person may have to cross another's property in order to gain access to his own property.

ROOT OF TITLE—The record of initial ownership in a property.


# S

SETTLEMENT AGENT—The party which administers the actual signing of the sales documents of a property transaction.

SIMPLE INTEREST—Interest which is computed on the principal of a loan only. Another type of interest is compound interest, in which interest is charged not only on the remaining principal but also on the accumulated interest.

SPECIAL ASSESSMENT—A special charge placed against property owners to pay for public improvements or repairs.

SREA—Senior Real Estate Appraiser. The highest award given in this field.

STANDBY FEE—The fee required by a lender to provide a commitment. It is nonrefundable if the loan is not closed within a specified period of time.

STANDBY LOAN—A lender's commitment to loan a sum of money for a fixed period of time and a fixed interest. A fee is charged for this, and the borrower retains the option of closing or lapsing the loan commitment.

STATUTE OF FRAUDS—A doctrine of contract law which requires certain contracts, including all real estate contracts, to be in writing to be enforceable.

STATUTORY QUITCLAIM DEED—A quitclaim deed form designated and approved by local state statute.

SUBORDINATE—Making a senior lien junior to another lien. An example would be if you held a first mortgage against a lot, and the owner needed to get a construction loan for it. You would most likely be asked to "subordinate" or move your first position mortgage into second position behind the construction loan. This changing of positions in the line of title is called subordination.

SUBORDINATION CLAUSE—A clause contained within or added to a purchase agreement which refers to the subordination of existing financing. Two examples of subordination clauses are:

Seller agrees to subordinate seller's equity to buyer's new mortgage.

Seller hereby agrees to subordinate said note and trust deed to buyer's new loan; both parties agree that the loan amount of the new deed of trust or mortgage will not be greater than the increase of the value of the property as a result of, but not exclusively from, the new improvements made by buyer from the proceeds of buyer's new loan.

# T

TAX LIEN—A lien placed against a property because of nonpayment of taxes.

TENANCY BY THE ENTIRETY—A type of ownership for married partners wherein they own property as a sole owner if married at the time of receiving the deed.

TENANTS IN COMMON—Two or more parties who own equal shares of a property. If one partner dies, his share goes to his estate. For another form of joint property ownership, see JOINT TENANCY.

TENDER—An offer made in the form of money.

TENURE—The right or act of owning or occupying real estate.

TERM AMORTIZATION—A type of debt service where the entire debt is paid in one final payment at maturity. See also BALLOON PAYMENT.

TERMITE BOND—An insurance policy issued against future termite damage to a property after a satisfactory inspection and treatment by a licensed pest control company.

TERMITE INSPECTION—An inspection of a property by a licensed pest control company in which a written statement is issued stating whether the property is free from termite damage or not.

TIME-IS-OF-THE-ESSENCE CLAUSE—The phrase, when put into a contract, gives specific legally binding commitments and cannot be subordinated by the recalcitrant party. Failure to insert this phrase can cause serious delays.

TITLE—The formal document which establishes legal right to ownership or a lien against a property.

TITLE CLAUSE—A clause contained within or added to a purchase agreement which refers to a property's title. Examples of two title clauses are:

> Purchaser and seller agree that if the title to the above property be defective, ninety (90) days from the date hereof, it shall be given to the seller, or his agent, to perfect same. If said title cannot be perfected within said time limit, the earnest money receipted for herein shall, upon the demand of purchaser, be returned to purchaser in full and the contract cancelled.

> The land contract shall be completed and executed by the parties at the close of escrow. Title to property shall be reserved to seller, his heirs, personal representatives, and assigns, until full payment of the balance is made, as provided in the land contract.

TITLE COMPANY—A private company that prepares real estate title abstracts, helps in property closings, and provides title insurance.

TITLE INSURANCE—Insurance protection sold to the purchaser of a property by an insurance company to cover any loss from undiscovered defects in title.

TITLE REPORT—A record stating the current condition of the title. (For example: easements, liens, defects of title, covenants, etc.)

TITLE SEARCH—An examination of public records showing encumbrances on the real property.

TRUTH-IN-LENDING LAWS—See REGULATION Z.

# U

UNENCUMBERED—Property that is "free and clear." An unencumbered property is said to have no mortgages, liens, claims, or other attachments or limitations of rights placed against it.

UNRECORDED DEED—An instrument that transfers title but is not publicly recorded. This can be *very* dangerous; recording a title protects your interest.

USEFUL LIFE—The time period over which real property may be termed "of use." Useful life for a home is eighteen years under federal depreciation laws. (This is subject to change.)

UTILITY EASEMENT—The use of property, by utility companies, to lay service lines. The easement gives them access to work on these services.

# V

VALID—A document or instrument which has been prepared according to law and is legally binding.

VA LOAN—A loan, of low interest, backed by the government that is given to qualified veterans.

VALUABLE CONSIDERATION—A note that stipulates a promised payment on which the bearer can enforce a claim against the party signing the note. This can be a promise of money, chattel, time, or other consideration for the grantor of the note.

VALUATION—The estimated worth of a property. It should be noted that estimations or valuations are subjective and subject to error.

VARIABLE RATE MORTGAGE (VRM)—A mortgage in which the borrower allows the lender to alter the interest rate and monthly payments under prespecified criteria. Most variable rate mortgages contain "caps" which limit both the annual interest rate increase and the total interest rate increase which a loan may jump over its lifetime.

VARIANCE—An exception to a zoning ordinance.

VENDEE—The buyer of real estate under a purchase agreement. Often referred to as the purchaser or the party of the first part.

VENDEE'S LIEN—A lien brought against property by a contract of sale, to secure the deposit paid by the purchaser. This keeps the seller from selling to someone else.

VETERANS ADMINISTRATION—A government agency that administers benefits to qualified veterans.

VOID—A contract that is not legally enforceable.

VOLUNTARY LIEN—A debt against the property that the owner agrees to have recorded.

# W

WAIVER—The voluntary surrender or abandonment of a right, claim, or privilege.

WARRANT—To promise; to certify.

WARRANTY DEED—A legal document which contains guarantees that the grantor is the legal owner and has the right to sell a property.

WARRANTY OF HABITABILITY—A deed which warrants that a property is habitable.

WEASEL CLAUSE—A clause contained within or added to a purchase agreement which makes the offer subject to the performance of an act or some other event. Subject-to clauses are also known as weasel clauses. Examples of two subject-to clauses are:

> Offer subject to partners approval.

> Subject to buyer's approval of appraisal.

WITHOUT RECOURSE—Usually written in endorsing a note/contract denoting that the holder cannot go to the debtor personally if payment of note/contract is not fulfilled. The creditor has recourse only to the property.

WRAPAROUND MORTGAGE—See ALL-INCLUSIVE TRUST DEED.

# Z

ZONING (BOARD/COMMISSION/ORDINANCES)—Rules pertaining to the usage of real estate imposed by the local city or county government. See VARIANCE.

ZONING MAP—A map showing where the zones lie within an area. It will show C (commercial), R (residential), and I (industrial) areas within a city.

# INDEX

□   □   □

## ABOUT THE AUTHOR

□   □   □

**A**t the age of twenty-two, Marc Stephen Garrison began investing part-time in real estate to pay for a college education. His success as an investor paid for several undergraduate degrees and an M.B.A. Since then, he has achieved complete financial freedom through his real estate investments and has dedicated himself to teaching others how to achieve the same level of financial freedom.

He is the author of several books on real estate investing, financial planning, and time management, including Financially Free, and, most recently, How to Buy Your Own Home in 90 Days. Marc is on the National Institute for Financial Planning's board of advisers, writes monthly articles in several national magazines and newsletters, and lectures at investment workshops and conventions across the country.

He lives near the Sundance ski resort in the Wasatch Range of the Rocky Mountains with his wife DeAnn and their four children—Ryan, Kelly, Hunter, and Matthew—and golden retriever Jodi. Sarah "Rose" Frisby is his favorite neighbor.

□   □   □